Intangible Heritage Embodied

D. Fairchild Ruggles · Helaine Silverman
Editors

Intangible Heritage Embodied

Editors
D. Fairchild Ruggles
Department of Landscape
 Architecture
University of Illinois
 at Urbana-Champaign
611 Taft Drive
Champaign IL 61820
USA
dfr1@illinois.edu

Helaine Silverman
Department of Anthropology
University of Illinois
 at Urbana-Champaign
607 S. Mathews Street
Urbana, IL 61801
USA
helaine@illinois.edu

ISBN 978-1-4419-0071-5   e-ISBN 978-1-4419-0072-2
DOI 10.1007/978-1-4419-0072-2
Springer Dordrecht Heidelberg London New York

Library of Congress Control Number: 2009926984

© Springer Science+Business Media, LLC 2009
All rights reserved. This work may not be translated or copied in whole or in part without the written permission of the publisher (Springer Science+Business Media, LLC, 233 Spring Street, New York, NY 10013, USA), except for brief excerpts in connection with reviews or scholarly analysis. Use in connection with any form of information storage and retrieval, electronic adaptation, computer software, or by similar or dissimilar methodology now known or hereafter developed is forbidden. The use in this publication of trade names, trademarks, service marks, and similar terms, even if they are not identified as such, is not to be taken as an expression of opinion as to whether or not they are subject to proprietary rights.

Printed on acid-free paper

Springer is part of Springer Science+Business Media (www.springer.com)

Preface

This volume examines international cases where heritage is complicated by issues of ephemerality, reiterative performance, and local, regional, and national interests. The essays herein were first presented in spring 2007 at a conference organized by the Collaborative for Cultural Heritage and Museum Practices (CHAMP) at the University of Illinois at Urbana-Champaign. Funding was generously provided by the Office of the Dean of the College of Fine and Applied Arts, the Department of Landscape Architecture, the Department of Anthropology, and the Center for Global Studies. We would like to express our gratitude to these sponsors and to our editor at Springer, Teresa Krauss. Teresa has enabled this second volume in our series on cultural heritage which began with *Cultural Heritage and Human Rights* (2007).

The introductory essay (Ruggles and Silverman) in this volume provides a history of the expansion of heritage discourse from an object-centered practice to one that includes the intangible dimension of lived human experience. Its bibliography is followed by an appendix that contains a list of the conventions and documents pertinent to the evolution of the UNESCO Intangible Heritage Convention of 2003. The subsequent essays address the themes of voice and performance (Sather-Wagstaff, Wong, and Gandhi and Gandhi), landscape and space (Conan, Fennell, Keller, and Ruggles and Sinha), and memory (Fennell, Keller, Sather-Wagstaff, Gandhi and Gandhi, and Salomon and Peters). The volume concludes with explorations of new technologies and media (Graham and Sather-Wagstaff).

Champaign, IL D. Fairchild Ruggles
Urbana, IL Helaine Silverman

Contents

1 From Tangible to Intangible Heritage 1
   D. Fairchild Ruggles and Helaine Silverman

2 The Heritage of *Kunqu*: Preserving Music and Theater
   Traditions in China.. 15
   Isabel K. F. Wong

3 Partition Memories: The Hidden Healer 37
   Rajmohan Gandhi and Usha Gandhi

4 Gardens and Landscapes: At the Hinge of Tangible
   and Intangible Heritage 53
   Michel Conan

5 Preserving the Cultural Landscape Heritage of
   Champaner-Pavagadh, Gujarat, India 79
   D. Fairchild Ruggles and Amita Sinha

6 Governance and Conservation of the Rapaz *Khipu* Patrimony 101
   Frank Salomon and Renata Peters

7 Geographies of Memory and Identity in Oceania................ 127
   Janet Dixon Keller

8 Combating Attempts of Elision: African American
   Accomplishments at New Philadelphia, Illinois 147
   Christopher Fennell

9 Folk Epigraphy at the World Trade Center, Oklahoma
   City, and Beyond 169
   Joy Sather-Wagstaff

10 Problematizing of Technologies for Documenting Intangible Culture: Some Positive and Negative Consequences.................... 185
Laura R. Graham

Index 201

Contributors

Michel Conan Landscape Studies, Dumbarton Oaks, Washington, DC 20007, USA, michel.conan@gmail.com

Christopher Fennell Department of Anthropology, University of Illinois at Urbana-Champaign, Urbana, IL 61801, USA, cfennell@illinois.edu

Rajmohan Gandhi Center for South Asian and Middle Eastern Studies, University of Illinois at Urbana-Champaign, Champaign, IL 61820, USA, rgandhi@illinois.edu

Usha Gandhi International Programs and Studies, University of Illinois at Urbana-Champaign, Champaign, IL 61820, USA, ugandhi@illinois.edu

Laura R. Graham Department of Anthropology, University of Iowa, Iowa City, IA 52242, USA, laura-graham@viowa.edu

Janet Dixon Keller Department of Anthropology, University of Illinois at Urbana-Champaign, Urbana, IL 61801, USA, jdkeller@illinois.edu

Renata Peters Institute of Archaeology, University College, London WC1H 0PY, UK, m-peters@ucl.ac.uk

D. Fairchild Ruggles Department of Landscape Architecture, University of Illinois at Urbana-Champaign, Champaign, IL 61820, USA, dfr1@illinois.edu

Frank Salomon Department of Anthropology, University of Wisconsin, Madison, WI 53706, USA, fsalomon@wisc.edu

Joy Sather-Wagstaff Department of Sociology, Anthropology and Emergency Management, North Dakota State University, Fargo, ND 58108, USA, joy.sather-wagstaff@ndsu.edu

Helaine Silverman Department of Anthropology, University of Illinois at Urbana-Champaign, Urbana, IL 61801, USA, helaine@illinois.edu

Amita Sinha Department of Landscape Architecture, University of Illinois of Urbana-Champaign, Champaign, IL 61820, USA, sinha2@illinois.edu

Isabel K.F. Wong School of Music, and International Programs and Studies, University of Illinois at Urbana-Champaign, Champaign, IL 61820, USA, ikfwong@illinois.edu

Chapter 1
From Tangible to Intangible Heritage

D. Fairchild Ruggles and Helaine Silverman

Two popular television programs on the air in Fall 2007—the Travel Channel's "No Reservations" with Anthony Bourdain and National Geographic Channel's "Taboo"—play to the public's fascination with exotic peoples. National Geographic's website (www9.nationalgeographic.com/channel/taboo/) specifically uses exoticism as an enticement, urging the audience: "Test your boundaries. Push beyond your comfort zone. Understand seemingly bizarre and shocking practices from around the world." The audience is comprised of comfortably insular U.S. Americans, and the source of their enjoyment is the intangible cultural heritage of others—what used to be known among earlier generations of anthropologists as "primitive customs and traditions." Whereas National Geographic's intent is simply to startle an increasingly unflappable public, Anthony Bourdain attempts to more respectfully involve the viewer in the larger cultural world of the distant peoples he visits. In both cases the audience observes practices that recently have come under the protective lens of UNESCO through its 2003 Convention for the Safeguarding of the Intangible Cultural Heritage (hereafter, Intangible Heritage Convention; see Appendix).

What is intangible cultural heritage? William Logan (2007) defines it succinctly as "heritage that is embodied in people rather than in inanimate objects," and hence the title of this volume as *Intangible Heritage Embodied*. But beyond this characterization, the question of the meanings and values of intangible heritage becomes vastly complex. Indeed, whether because the convention is still very new, or because of its inherent complexity, most publications on the topic address themselves primarily to questions of definition. UNESCO devotes many pages of its website to explanation and discussion of the convention, defining intangibility as "the practices, representations, expressions, as well as the knowledge and skills, that communities, groups and, in some cases, individuals recognize as part of their cultural heritage" (Intangible Heritage

---

D.F. Ruggles (✉)
Department of Landscape Architecture, University of Illinois at Urbana-Champaign, Champaign, IL 61820, USA
e-mail: dfr1@illinois.edu

Convention). But intangible cultural heritage may best be understood by examples. UNESCO specifically identifies the following categories of intangible culture:

- Oral traditions and expressions including language
- Performing arts (such as traditional music, dance, and theater)
- Social practices, rituals, and festive events
- Knowledge and practices concerning nature and the universe
- Traditional craftsmanship

Furthermore, the Intangible Heritage Convention describes intangible culture as a living force that is "transmitted from generation to generation" and "constantly recreated by communities and groups" in response to their social and physical environment. Intangible heritage is an essential aspect of community identity and "promotes respect for cultural diversity and human creativity."

Finally, the Intangible Heritage Convention states that intangible heritage is "compatible with international human rights instruments." This last statement is a particularly important and potentially contentious assertion that will surely be tested in practice. Indeed, Logan (2007) predicts problems in this area and sees "the notion of human rights as a way of limiting the proposed Intangible List." For instance, there is the question of the human body itself, a site for the assertion of personal autonomy, yet also a site in which social identity and political attitudes are expressed. With respect to human rights, permanent body mutilation (e.g., female genital circumcision, foot binding) and permanent body-deforming adornment (e.g., tattoos, the neck rings of the Karen hill tribes of Thailand) are subjected to scrutiny. There are also social practices such as the Muslim *chador* or *burqa* that, to foreign eyes, may seem burdensome and oppressive, but may be embraced by the wearer variously as signs of faith and a rejection of western modes. Conversely, there is the abandonment of social practices, as when the children of a tradition-bearing group prefer to move to the city, rather than remain in the countryside as objects of intangible heritage. In the latter, the community may lose not only its traditional ways, but also its tourism revenues. Could a government take measures to perpetuate their culture by restricting their assimilation, keeping them ethnographically "pure"? Finally, there are some practices that, although traditional, are now widely accepted as abhorrent and have been officially outlawed, such as ritual *sati* (widow burning) in South Asia.

In this introductory chapter we consider the history and relevance of the concept of "intangible cultural heritage," asking why the concept emerged when it did, and examining the important role that such cultural behaviors and values play in the well-being of societies. The charters and documents discussed are listed chronologically at the end of this chapter.

The Development of Intangibility as a Concept

There are dozens of official documents (variously known as proclamations, recommendations, conventions, charters, and codes) of UNESCO, ICOMOS, and regional, national, and multinational organizations that deal with cultural heritage, but they overwhelmingly focus on its tangible, monumental form. The earliest such proclamations did not conceive of the issue in terms of heritage per se—as is the prevalent view today—but specifically as a problem of architectural conservation. The urgency and need for conservation has changed according to the pressures of each age, at times couched as the need to save ancient buildings from abandonment and ruin; at other times, a need to restore buildings damaged by war; and in still other moments, a need to save a particular vernacular or obsolete type from disappearance.

When an international congress of architects was held in 1904 in Madrid, the members recommended minimal intervention in dealing with ruined structures and argued that restoration ought to operate on the principle of unity of style, according to a single stylistic expression. Interestingly, this conference suggested that a functional use for historic buildings was important if they were still serving the purposes for which they were originally intended. As such, the architects argued, these "living monuments ought to be restored so that they may continue to be of use, for in architecture utility is one of the bases of beauty." The architects specifically addressed the issue of "dead monuments, that is, those belonging to a past civilization or serving obsolete purposes" and which "should be preserved only by such strengthening as is indispensable in order to prevent their falling into ruin; for the importance of such a monument consists in its historical and technical value, which disappears with the monument itself." The value placed on human usage here was a small but significant acknowledgment of the interrelationship of built form and human society.

The 1932 Athens Charter for the Restoration of Historic Monuments (adopted at the First International Congress of Architects and Technicians of Historic Monuments) reprised the Madrid theme, recommending that "the occupation of buildings, which ensures the continuity of their life, should be maintained but that they should be used for a purpose which respects their historic or artistic character." Indeed, they could observe creative examples of such adaptation in the spirit of rehabilitation. For example, the Spanish government's national chain of paradores, beginning in 1928, converted semi-derelict palaces and convents into high-style hotels with the specific goal of enticing more tourism among Spaniards. The restorations may have focused a great deal more on providing modern plumbing than on preservation and site interpretation; however, by inviting the public to experience historic monuments personally by actually inhabiting them, even if only temporarily, they offered an experience that was quite different from the didactic and often chilly encounters with cultural heritage in the museum environment. The paradores fostered a new kind of tourism in Spain among both nationals and foreigners.

At subsequent congresses throughout the twentieth century, other criteria and values in historic preservation were articulated. There were changes in the way that preservation was to be achieved, the nature of the monuments that were to be restored and safeguarded, and finally, a major change in the understanding of the purpose served by historic preservation. All of these have relevance for intangible heritage.

Beginning with the 1904 Madrid Conference and the 1932 Athens Charter for the Restoration of Historic Monuments, the earliest declarations articulated the need for common cause in the preservation of architectural and material fabric. In these and later statements, one can observe a shift in preservation techniques. While the Athens Charter admits the utility of reinforced concrete in stabilizing shaky structures, it advocates that the new material be concealed in order to preserve the historic character of the monument. But later charters, most notably the 1964 ICOMOS International Charter for the Conservation and Restoration of Monuments and Sites, called the Venice Charter, insisted that the difference between original fabric and the new additions be clearly marked through the use of a contrasting material so that "restoration does not falsify the artistic or historic evidence." Although the preservation goals differed, both attitudes assumed a monument made of permanent materials in which the line between original material and restoration could be clearly drawn (or conversely, obscured).

Permanence was especially valued in the aftermath of the two World Wars, when the distressing sight of destroyed monuments provoked international agencies to take measures to protect them. Some of these preserved monuments became emblematic of much more than architectural history: from places of worship the French cathedrals became symbols of nationhood to the people of France and Francophiles around the world, expanding upon their earlier appropriation as historical artifacts by the state in the nineteenth century (Emery 2009). The notion that cultural monuments deserve stewardship is also indicated in the pan-American 1935 Washington Pact (also known as the Roerich Pact), which argued for the neutrality of historic buildings in times of war. In this, it anticipated the 1954 Hague Convention (Convention for the Protection of Cultural Property in the Event of Armed Conflict). The Hague Convention directly responded to the unprecedented scale of destruction during World War II and addressed the need for preservation of cultural property in times of war. With the aim of providing as much protection as possible, it offered a very broad definition of cultural property: "[M]ovable or immovable property of great importance to the cultural heritage of every people, such as monuments of architecture, art or history, whether religious or secular; archaeological sites; groups of buildings which, as a whole, are of historical or artistic interest; works of art; manuscripts, books and other objects of artistic, historical or archaeological interest; as well as scientific collections and important collections of books or archives or of reproductions of the property defined above."

Agreements promulgated in each subsequent decade added further clauses to protect the built environment. In 1964 and again in 1970, portable cultural property was specifically targeted by UNESCO's "Recommendation on the Means of Prohibiting and Preventing the Illicit Import, Export and Transfer of Ownership of Cultural Property" and the formal convention of the same name. The convention was particularly important in its attempt to hinder the trade in illegally excavated antiquities. While the emphasis was on the object, value was also placed on the group, collection, and archive, which highlighted a regard for qualities that lay not in the material of the building or object but in its relation to other such things.

However, it was only in 1972 that the full-blown concept of "world heritage" took prominence on the global stage with UNESCO's "Convention Concerning the Protection of World Cultural and Natural Heritage" (called the World Heritage Convention). Herein it was explicitly stated that the loss of any specific cultural or natural heritage "constitutes a harmful impoverishment of the heritage of all nations of the world." Moreover, because it was a binding convention—an international instrument of law—rather than a policy agreed upon by non-governmental institutions and architects, or by a mere consortium of national bodies, it had a more powerful effect than the previous charters and pacts.

From 1964 onward, the Venice Charter was the most influential of the aforementioned charters because it laid out the theoretical framework for preservation and restoration. But it was not without detractors who pointed out that its definition of heritage was based on western models that privileged permanence and narrowly defined the categories of authenticity. These definitions were gently but firmly criticized in the ICOMOS 1994 Nara Document on Authenticity. The Nara Document advocated stabilization, yet it permitted an array of restoration approaches that would vary according to their suitability for the kind of object being preserved and the values toward preservation and heritage in the context of its own culture. Article 11 stated:

> All judgements about values attributed to cultural properties as well as the credibility of related information sources may differ from culture to culture, and even within the same culture. It is thus not possible to base judgements of values and authenticity within fixed criteria. On the contrary, the respect due to all cultures requires that heritage properties must [be] considered and judged *within the cultural contexts to which they belong*. (emphasis added)

The Nara Document was a declaration, not a universally adopted ICOMOS charter or UNESCO convention, but it had a resounding impact nonetheless. In the ICOMOS and UNESCO framework, founded on the principle that permanence and authenticity are inseparable, the Nara Document asserted the existence of different heritage values and criteria. By stating that "truthfulness" could be culturally contextualized, it admitted a criterion by which an annually renewed mud structure or a ritually rebuilt wooden temple could be designated as both historic and authentic. Ephemerality thus took its place alongside permanence as a legitimate characteristic of some kinds of historic structures. The Nara Document also permitted authenticity to be judged not simply in terms of an original, from which later states were understood to be mere copies (and thus inauthentic), but measured instead by the meaning attributed to an object or monument.

The acknowledgment of impermanence and renewal had an impact that far exceeded that of monument preservation because it admitted the human being as integral to the construction of meaning and the ongoing creation of material culture. If a building or a work of art is to be ritually renewed, then the actors who effect the renewal become essential elements in the preservation process. In this period, a shift was occurring from the exclusive emphasis on material culture to a definition that included performed culture—or rather, the complex interdependence of them had been highlighted.

In fact, however, the door to alternative forms of heritage preservation had been opened prior to the Nara Document. On a smaller, national scale, there had been other instruments that insisted on an understanding of the historic monument in terms that were different from those of UNESCO. For example, as early as 1950, Japan had defined its national patrimony to include human beings themselves, identified as "living treasures" (Kurin 2004). But there was a disconnect between, on one side, the international bodies of UNESCO (a branch of the United Nations) and ICOMOS (a non-governmental organization with advisory capacity), and on the other, individual nations. The process by which intangible heritage shifted from a local concern to an internationally recognized value was reached slowly and incrementally.

The 1972 World Heritage Convention had provided a *static* definition of cultural heritage (monuments, groups of monuments, and sites) and natural heritage (geological or biological formations striking for their beauty or scientific value). It was followed in 1982 by the ICOMOS Florence Charter which specifically emphasized the *living* nature of historic sites. Article 2 of the Florence Charter underscored that gardens and landscapes themselves are alive and thus in a constant state of balance between renewal and decay. It also included water and the surrounding environment in the materials of the site, thus introducing the question of scale and interdependence. It acknowledged that landscapes are never self-contained, depending as they do upon external water sources (whether from springs, streams, or rain), insects for pollination, and birds and animals for reseeding. But having admitted time into its framework for preservation, it then added that a garden reflects "the desire of the artist and craftsman to keep it permanently unchanged."

The Florence Charter was full of such contradictions and was undermined by its oddly romantic assumption that all gardens shared meaning as "the cosmic significance of an idealized image of the world, a 'paradise'." This attribution necessarily excludes landscapes that commemorate places of pain and shame— such as the WWII cemetery at Normandy or Wounded Knee in the United

States. With such inherent conflicts and assumptions, it is a deeply flawed charter; yet it admitted a different kind of monument into the preservation portfolio that by its very nature (the double meaning is deliberate) required new preservation values and required the participation of landscape architects (Ruggles n.d.).

The focus of heritage preservation had changed by the 1980s to include cultural values that differed from those of UNESCO's primarily western nations, and it had also begun to recognize issues of time and scale. The third major thread that developed continuously was the recognition that monuments, objects, and performances were endowed with meaning by virtue of their relation to the present. From the very beginning, preservationists understood that the purpose of historic preservation is not to make fossils of the past or past ways of life but to integrate safely into the present those parts of the past that continue to have meaning for the current age and may predictably resonate with meaning for future generations. In the simplest sense this meant ensuring the continued usage of old buildings or finding new uses for them. With this idea evidently in mind, Article 5 of the Venice Charter had stated that reusing old buildings for new purposes aided conservation and was permissible. But in a more profound sense, one of the goals of heritage preservation was to maintain the relationship of a resident community to its patrimony so as to prevent the historic building or precinct from becoming a mere fossil. As early as 1931, the Athens Conference had concluded that "the best guarantee in the matter of the preservation of monuments and works of art derives from the respect and attachment of the peoples themselves." The Declaration of Amsterdam (1975) stipulated that architectural conservation become an integral part of urban and regional planning, and it called for consideration of social factors and cooperation between local authorities and the populace.

With the gradually increasing emphasis on audience reception, the regard for tourism also shifted. Whereas conservators might once have viewed the tourist as a regrettable necessity, sometimes ridiculed for culturally inappropriate behavior and ignorance, they began to recognize in tourism an opportunity for cultural education and even the public's right to access to historic monuments and works of art. In 1976, ICOMOS drafted a Cultural Tourism Statement that called for a change in "the attitude of the public at large towards the phenomena resulting from the massive development of touristic needs ... from school age onwards children and adolescents be educated to understand and respect the monuments, the sites and the cultural heritage and ... information media should express to the public the elements of the problem thereby efficaciously contributing to effective universal understanding." What these and other documents share in common is recognition of the need for community participation in monument preservation, be it a pyramid mound or entire historic district. This developed into a mandate for an interpretive framework that addressed the question of meaning for living societies, culminating in the 1999 ICOMOS International Cultural Tourism Charter that declared the importance of making "the significance of that heritage accessible to the host community and visitors."

The meaning of heritage to living people cannot be underestimated. There has been an increasing recognition of the potential significance of "dead" and "living" monuments for contemporary populations as venues of intangible performances. The attachment that communities feel for places, monuments, and objects—expressed through pilgrimage, religious devotion, story-telling, and tourism—can be a vital means of constructing group identity. The attachment can be so strong that even with the disappearance of a beloved monument, value is not erased. One can reflect upon the Jewish people's multimillennial longing for an almost physically extinct temple in Jerusalem; the highly charged and vacant site of the demolished Babri Masjid in Ayodhya, or more recently, the enormous significance of the ground where the World Trade Center's twin towers formerly stood in New York City. These are powerful "lieux de mémoire" (sites of memory) as Pierre Nora (1989) conceived the idea, and memory is vital to intangible heritage.

As we have seen, during the twentieth century concepts of permanence/impermanence, fixed/living, and audience reception came to the fore in heritage discourse. The next important shift occurred in the admission of non-material entities into the purview of heritage preservation.

Although the Florence Charter and Nara Document had introduced the human actor, and the ICOMOS Cultural Tourism Statement had located meaning as emerging from the mind of the observing audience, the primary object of preservation in all of these remained a tangible, physical thing. This changed in 1989 when UNESCO enunciated a "Recommendation on the Safeguarding of Traditional Culture and Folklore." It was the first document specifically targeted at intangible cultural heritage and its preservation, and it was promulgated because of awareness of the impact of industrialization and mass media on traditional patterns of culture. The document called for United Nations countries to develop a series of conservation strategies that included documentation of traditions, establishment of archives, creation of folklore museums, and support for transmitters of traditions. The document also recommended scientific research complemented by development of educational programs about folklore. The 1989 document explained the value of traditional culture:

> **Considering** that folklore forms part of the universal heritage of humanity and that it is a powerful means of bringing together different peoples and social groups and of asserting their cultural identity,
> **Noting** its social, economic, cultural and political importance, its role in the history of the people, and its place in contemporary culture,
> **Underlining** the specific nature and importance of folklore as an integral part of cultural heritage and living culture,
> **Recognizing** the extreme fragility of the traditional forms of folklore, particularly those aspects relating to oral tradition and the risk that they might be lost...

However, as Richard Kurin (2003:21) commented, the document was "ill-defined, 'top-down,' and 'soft'," and a decade later it had not made a discernible impact as an international instrument. Hence, in 1999 UNESCO instituted a program called "Proclamation of Masterpieces of the Oral and Intangible Heritage" (adopted unanimously in 2001). Equally important was UNESCO's 2001 Universal Declaration on Cultural Diversity. That document states that cultural diversity should be understood as contributing to economic growth, and is "a means to achieve a more satisfactory intellectual, emotional, moral and spiritual existence" and that "cultural diversity is as necessary for humankind as biodiversity is for nature." It states, moreover, that "culture is at the heart of contemporary debates about identity, social cohesion, and the development of a knowledge-based economy" and that while globalization may threaten cultural diversity, it also may foster cultural awareness and interchange. The Universal Declaration on Cultural Diversity is particularly important to a discussion of the Intangible Cultural Heritage Convention because it reflects the idea of world heritage that figured eponymously in the 1972 World Heritage Convention dealing with cultural and natural sites. Implicit in the Intangible Heritage Convention is the idea, expressed in the diversity declaration, that each tradition is an equally valuable element of the whole of humankind's intangible cultural heritage.

In the 2003 Intangible Heritage Convention, the term "intangible cultural heritage" replaces the older terms "traditional culture," "oral tradition," and "folklore." The convention had gained greater urgency in the intervening decade and a half because of the widespread loss of traditional cultures, languages, and performance as a result of modernization and global mass culture. Moreover, as Kurin (2003) again observed, at least some of the States Parties signing the convention were aware that their national cultural heritage had prestige value. Some intangible cultural heritage can be a key attraction for tourism and its revenue.

The new convention is not without problems. Three powerful members of the United Nations—the United States, Canada, and the United Kingdom—abstained from the vote, although none of the 190 member states voted specifically against it. Some countries were fearful that practices that they regard as cultural heritage will be regarded as an abrogation of human rights in the west and therefore censured. Since implicit in the concept of intangible cultural heritage is the notion of "inalienable" heritage, UNESCO is in an awkward position of not wanting to promote practices that contravene its (largely western) understanding of human rights as it evaluates the applications of countries seeking to have their customs registered as intangible cultural heritage (Silverman and Ruggles 2007). Kurin (2003) warns that UNESCO must be careful, for instance, that an epic performance tradition denigrating a particular vanquished group not violate the "respect" clause of the convention. Logan (2007:43) has addressed this question by noting that "the right to protect cultural diversity and cultural heritage is a cultural right, part of the panoply of human rights," that is to say, it is a subset of the larger realm of human rights. He concludes by asserting that the mandate for human rights supercedes individual or regional claims to cultural tradition.

The new convention is politically very sensitive for, as Kirshenblatt-Gimblett (2006) has observed, world heritage implies global policy. But whose world is setting the policy? Amareswar Galla notes that there is a "globalising tendency of World Heritage inscriptions" in which "'European' (including North American) paradigms and their colonial and post-colonial manifestations" are present, although unacknowledged (Galla 2008:10, 18). UNESCO, as the organization that sets and supervises policy, is unlikely to be the most effective critic of this paradigm. Instead, individual cases in real-world settings with real-world outcomes, as documented by heritage managers and scholars, test UNESCO's criteria at both the local and the national scale. Indeed, the interactions between communities at the local and the national scale, as well as between majority and minority populations, have illuminated one of UNESCO's most serious shortcomings: its inability to negotiate with any bodies other than nation-states.

The convention has the potential to pit minority enclaves with "certifiable" intangible cultural heritage against the dominant majority in their countries, or to empower those majorities to control traditional cultural expressions. Logan (2007) gives the example of the Myanmar junta's conservation of Buddhist religious monuments to legitimize the cultural history of the Buddhist majority and thus promote the assimilation of non-Buddhist minorities who sacrifice their distinct heritage in the process. The Myanmar example occurs as a deliberate strategy of oppression. However, the same result can occur as an indirect result of modernization and economic inequalities. For example, in this volume, Janet Keller's discussion of the Oceanic people of Vanuatu addresses the minority question from a different perspective, showing that assimilation has caused a loss of cultural identity for embattled minority groups. Michael Brown (2004) turns the situation the other way around, and with respect to the U.S. Park Service's stewardship of parks containing native sites, asks "How can a federal government which is legally prohibited from privileging religious activities of any one group, manage to make a site accessible to Native Americans, without privileging their religious activities over the legitimate activities of other types of patrons?" Instances such as Champaner-Pavagadh in India (discussed by Ruggles and Sinha in this volume), where a site has been historically shared by communities of different faiths, are rare, and the success may lie in the fact that until the site was nominated for UNESCO World Heritage status, it was relatively ignored by the national government of India. India struggles with diversity issues, and it remains to be seen how the complex character of Champaner-Pavagadh will be accommodated in future protective legislation.

Kurin (2003) raises another important concern. The convention urges states to preserve their traditional cultures by "all necessary means," which has a possible potential for the legitimization of oppressive measures. He asks (as we hypothesized earlier in this essay), could a state force the children of weavers to pursue the family profession rather than becoming lawyers or anthropologists? And he concludes, "The means have to be more 'appropriate' than 'necessary' when understood in the context of national and international laws and human rights accords" (Kurin 2003:22). Fear of governmental abuse is a topic which Albro and Chernela (2006) develop in their consideration of cultural rights and human rights from the perspective of policy-making. With respect to the definition of cultural rights, they recognize that it is too easy to "blur 'rights' and 'regulatory' goals." They conclude that "Governments and institutions are increasingly moved to adopt the terminology of 'culture' and 'cultural diversity' as a way to advance state goals and interests. Meanwhile, local activists leverage tools of cultural identity to affirm more immediate, local and indigenous meanings and concerns" (Albro and Chernela 2006:45). The well-intentioned Intangible Heritage Convention is subject to these contradictory forces.

Because the Intangible Heritage Convention was adopted only a few years ago, intangible heritage is a relatively new topic for discussion among scholars and professionals. Intangibility as a heritage criterion was implicitly present in the papers contributed to *Cultural Heritage and Human Rights* (Silverman and Ruggles 2007). Intangibility also was the subject of a May 2006 seminar at Cambridge University called "Re-visioning the Nation. Cultural Heritage and the Politics of Disaster." It is the topic of a double issue of *Museum International* (2004), and is the central theme of the new *International Journal of Intangible Heritage*, begun in 2006. Much of the literature to date focuses either on the history of the convention (summarized above) or on studies drawn from specific cases. To some extent this is due to the structure of heritage organizations themselves, the largest of which—UNESCO—is organized entirely along national lines. But it is also because heritage preservation and heritage studies are often based on actual experience and thus respond to individual circumstances. Learning is not, in this sense, top down but rather based on comparison of specific case studies and actual practice. For this reason, practitioners and scholars in the different fields of music, theater, anthropology, landscape architecture, and history were asked to brainstorm together in a workshop at the University of Illinois in March 2007. From their efforts have come the chapters for this volume.

The field of intangible heritage studies is growing rapidly, and will have an impact on a wide range of arts and human practices. At first glance, the problems faced in theater history (as in Wong's contribution to this volume) differ markedly from those encountered in the preservation of sites such as New Philadelphia (Fennell, this volume) or Champaner-Pavagadh (Sinha and Ruggles, this volume), but place and performance are bound together through the human body. This is an aspect of the Intangible Heritage Convention that preservationists will have to deal with constantly (and in many cases already have had to confront), but whose full conceptual ramifications are rarely recognized. The dramatic shift in values implied in the Intangible Heritage Convention is not simply the inclusion of new forms of cultural heritage or a shift from permanence to impermanence. It represents a radical paradigm shift from the objective nature of material culture to the subjective experience of the human being. In this sense, it reflects the philosophy of the postmodern world.

Charters, Conventions, and Declarations Cited (Listed by Short and Full Name, Date, Promulgating Organization, Website)

Madrid Charter (1904)
www.getty.edu/conservation/research_resources/charters/charter01.html

Athens Charter for the Restoration of Historic Monuments (1932)
First International Congress of Architects and Technicians of Historic Monuments
http://www.icomos.org/docs/athens_charter.html

Washington Pact (also known as the *Roerich Pact*) (1935)
Seventh International Conference of American States
www.roerich.org/nr_RPact.html
www.icrc.org/ihl.nsf/INTRO/325?OpenDocument

Hague Convention (Convention for the Protection of Cultural Property in the Event of Armed Conflict) (1954)
UNESCO
www.icomos.org/hague/
www.unesdoc.unesco.org/images/0012/001268/126857eb.pdf

Venice Charter (International Charter for the Conservation and Restoration of Monuments and Sites) (1964)
ICOMOS
www.icomos.org/venice_charter.html

World Heritage Convention (Convention Concerning the Protection of the World Cultural and Natural Heritage) (1972)
UNESCO
whc.unesco.org/en/conventiontext/
whc.unesco.org/archive/convention-en.pdf

Declaration of Amsterdam (1975)
Congress on the European Architectural Heritage
http://www.icomos.org/docs/amsterdam.html

Cultural Tourism Statement (1976)
ICOMOS International Seminar on Contemporary Tourism and Humanism
www.international.icomos.org/e_touris.htm

Florence Charter (1982)
ICOMOS-IFLA International Committee for Historic Gardens
www.icomos.org/docs/florence_charter.html

Burra Charter (Australia ICOMOS 1981; rewritten 1999)
ICOMOS Australia
www.icomos.org/australia/burra.html (Note: since the revised 1999 version superceded the 1981 version, ICOMOS has tried to remove all traces of the earlier document. It is no longer available on-line at the ICOMOS website.)

Washington Charter (Charter for the Conservation of Historic Towns and Urban Areas) (1987)
ICOMOS
www.international.icomos.org/charters/towns_e.htm

Recommendation on the Safeguarding of Traditional Culture and Folklore (1989)
UNESCO
http://portal.unesco.org/en/ev.php-URL_ID=13141&URL_DO=DO_TOPIC&URL_SECTION=201.html

Charter for the Protection and Management of the Archaeological Heritage (1990)
ICOMOS
www.international.icomos.org/charters/arch_e.htm

Preservation Brief 36 (1994)
United States National Park Service
www.nps.gov/history/hps/tps/briefs/brief36.htm

Nara Document on Authenticity (1994)
ICOMOS, Nara Conference on Authenticity in Relation to the World Heritage Convention, Nara, Japan
www.international.icomos.org/charters/nara_e.htm

International Charter on Cultural Tourism (1999)
ICOMOS, Managing Tourism at Places of Heritage Significance
www.international.icomos.org/charters/tourism_e.htm

Charter on the Built Vernacular Heritage (1999)
ICOMOS
www.international.icomos.org/charters/vernacular_e.htm

Universal Declaration on Cultural Diversity (2001)
UNESCO
www.unesdoc.unesco.org/images/0012/001271/127160m.pdf

Convention for the Safeguarding of the Intangible Heritage (2003)
UNESCO
www.unesdoc.unesco.org/images/0013/001325/132540e.pdf

References

Albro, Robert and Janet Chernela
    2006 Problems of Cultural Rights, Policy and Agency. *Anthropology News*, September, p. 45.
Brown, Michael F.
    2004 Interview with Michael F. Brown, by Marren Sanders. www.law.suffolk.edu/highlights/stuorgs/jhtl/book_reviews/2003_2004/sanders.pdf (accessed 20 November 2007)
Emery, Elizabeth
    2009 The Martyred Cathedral: American Attitudes toward Notre-Dame de Reims during the First World War. In *Medieval Art and Architecture after the Middle Ages*, edited by Janet T. Marquardt and Alyce A. Jordan, pp. 323–350. Cambridge Scholars Publishing, Newcastle upon Tyne.
Galla, Amareswar
    2008 The First Voice in Heritage Conservation. *International Journal of Intangible Heritage* 3: 10–25 (accessed 25 December 2008)
Kirshenblatt-Gimblett, Barbara

2006 World Heritage and Cultural Economics. In *Museum Frictions*, edited by Ivan Karp, Corinne Kratz, Lynn Szwaja, and Tomás Ybarra-Frausto, pp. 161–202. Duke University Press, Durham.

Kurin, Richard
2003 UNESCO Votes New Intangible Cultural Heritage Convention. *Anthropology News*, December, pp. 21–22. 2004 Safeguarding Intangible Cultural Heritage in the 2003 UNESCO Convention: A Critical Appraisal. *Museum* 56:1–2.

Logan, William
2007 Closing Pandora's Box: Human Rights Conundrums in Cultural Heritage Protection. In *Cultural Heritage and Human Rights*, edited by Helaine Silverman and D. Fairchild Ruggles, pp. 33–52. Springer, New York.

Museum International
2004 Special issue devoted to intangible heritage: Volume 56, Nos. 1–2.

Nora, Pierre
1989 Between Memory and History: Les Lieux de Mémoire. *Representations* 26: 7–25.

Ruggles, D. Fairchild N.d. A Critical View on Landscape Preservation and the Role of Landscape Architects. *Preservation Education Research* 1(2) [forthcoming in 2009].

Silverman, Helaine, and D. Fairchild Ruggles [editors]
2007 *Cultural Heritage and Human Rights*. Springer, New York.

Smithsonian Center for Folklife and Cultural Heritage
2005 *Theorizing Cultural Heritage*, http://www.folklife.si.edu/join_us/rockefeller.aspx (accessed 20 December 2005)

Chapter 2
The Heritage of *Kunqu*: Preserving Music and Theater Traditions in China

Isabel K. F. Wong

Kunqu (pronounced kwun-chü) is a form of Chinese musical theater. The first syllable of the name is derived from the name of its birthplace Kunshan, a small city in the Lower Yangzi region, situated between Shanghai and Suzhou. The second syllable, "*qu*," denotes either aria lyrics, a vocal style, an aria repertory, or a type of musical theater, depending on contexts. As musical theater, *kunqu* rose to a dominant position on the national stage around the mid-sixteenth century when the Ming dynasty (1368–1644) was at the height of its glory. The Ming had remarkable achievements in culture and the arts, and Ming skills in printing and the manufacture of porcelain and silk reached high technical achievements. Flourishing commerce in the Ming period created a new level of prosperity and supported a sophisticated urban life in which *kunqu* formed an important component. The Ming were succeeded by the Manchu, who subsequently established the Qing dynasty (1644–1911). The Manchu realized that in order to rule China as a minority, they must uphold China's traditional beliefs, cultural values and social structure, and thus *kunqu*, as an important cultural component, managed to survive the Manchu rule well into the nineteenth century. By the middle part of that century, however, rapid social changes and widespread rebellions severely challenged the Manchu rule and destroyed *kunqu*'s patronage bases in the Lower Yangzi region, and *kunqu* suffered a steep decline. Around the same period, a new popular musical theater evolved in the northern capital Beijing and gradually eclipsed *kunqu*'s national dominance because it was patronized first by the common people and later by the Qing court. This new theater is known as *Jingju* in China, or as Peking Opera in the West.

In spite of various challenges, nevertheless, *kunqu* has never become totally extinct. Particularly in its old patronage base in the Lower Yangzi region around Kunshan, Suzhou, Shanghai, and Hangzhou, it continues to be practiced and enjoyed today, albeit in much reduced circumstances compared to its

I.K.F. Wong (✉)
School of Music, and International Programs and Studies, University of Illinois at Urbana-Champaign, Champaign, IL 61820, USA
e-mail: ikfwong@illinois.edu

Fig. 2.1 A scene from the *kunqu* play *Pipa Ji (The Lute)*. The Shanghai Kunqu Company prima donna, Liang Guying, plays the heroine Zhao Wuniang, who is writing a letter about the death of her beloved father-in-law to her absent husband. This performance took place in Suzhou as part of a UNESCO conference on cultural heritage in 2006

heyday (Fig. 2.1). Since the establishment of the People's Republic of China in 1949, the government has assumed the role of patron and teacher of the arts, *kunqu* included. The government-sponsored *kunqu* training institutes for actors and performing troupes until the eve of the Cultural Revolution (1966–1976) when the radical elements in Chinese politics, led by Mao Zedong (1893–1976) and his wife Jiang Qing (1914–1991)—who advocated continuous revolution and class struggle—decreed the closing of all Party and educational institutions and censored all traditional theaters, literature, and the arts because they were regarded as feudal and poisonous. After the Cultural Revolution, a new leadership reestablished all institutions that were closed, revived traditional arts, and adopted some measures of economic reform that encouraged investments from Hong Kong, Taiwan, and the West. This open-door policy allowed some elements of Western popular culture to slip into China. The younger generation who grew up after the Cultural Revolution found Western popular culture irresistible, and *kunqu*, together with other traditional theaters, was ignored by the young audience.

In 1999, China, represented by its Ministry of Culture, was among the first group of nations to submit a proposal to UNESCO to designate *kunqu*, China's most enduring living musical and dramatic heritage, as a "Masterpiece of the Oral and Intangible Heritage of Humanity." In its proposal, the Chinese Ministry of Culture guaranteed that the heritage would be protected and perpetuated. Based on international experts' judgment, UNESCO proclaimed *kunqu* in 2001 as such a heritage. In its proposal to UNESCO, the Chinese Ministry of Culture emphasized the preservation of the oral performance heritage of *kunqu* on stage. Similarly, in many Chinese or Western writings on *kunqu*, the development of *kunqu* as theater was emphasized. In this chapter, I wish to present a more complete picture of the totality of the *kunqu* heritage, particularly the role it played in the lives of Chinese cultural elites and their contributions to the scholarship of *kunqu* during the Ming and Qing periods. I will also point out the ramifications of the UNESCO award in *kunqu* based on my fieldwork in several cities in China (Suzhou, Shanghai, and Beijing) since the UNESCO award.

Kunqu as Vocal Art

Kunshan, the birthplace of *Kunqu*, has long been noted for its excellent vocal traditions (Wu et al. 2002:4–5). *Kunqu* first appeared around the early sixteenth century as an intricate and technically demanding vocal style designed mainly for a form of aria—with or without instrumental accompaniment—that involved no staging, makeup, costumes, or action or movement. If instruments were used, they would probably be a *dizi* (bamboo transverse flute) for melodic accompaniment, and a *ban* (wooden clapper) and a *huai gu* (small flat drum) for beats and rhythm. This form of singing is known as *qing chang* (pure singing), and its aria repertory actually came from a preexisting repertory of a south Chinese popular musical theater known as *nanxi* (Southern Theater). Because it catered to the common people, the vocal style adopted by professional actors of *nanxi* was considered crude and unattractive by the elites. The inventors of *kunqu* aimed to create a vocal style that was more sophisticated and would therefore be more appealing to discerning listeners and singers.

In the early sixteenth century, Wei Liangfu, an herbal doctor by profession and a singing master by avocation, is credited with having codified the *kunqu* vocal style. While others in his circle, including other singing masters and literary men living in Kunshan, had also contributed to the long process of experiments and invention (Hu 1989:49–62), Wei was given credit as the codifier of *kunqu* because he was the author of the earliest manuscript on *kunqu*, entitled *Nan Ci Yin Zheng* (The Correct Way of Singing Southern Arias), with a preface dated 1547 (Wong 1978:116, n. 3). It contains 20 short paragraphs on the rules of singing, written in not very polished vernacular prose. Apparently not long after 1547, singers in the Kunshan and Suzhou areas had already adopted this new form of singing. A 1552 record shows that a famous singer gave an *al fresco* performance to many appreciative listeners in the new *kunqu* vocal style in Hu Qiu (Tiger Hill), a scenic spot near Suzhou, where for centuries singers and listeners gathered on the evening of the Harvest Moon Festival (the 15th day of the eighth month of the Lunar calendar) to celebrate with singing (Qiang 1998:27). In 1616, 69 years after the appearance of Wei Liangfu's singing instructions, another version of his work appeared in print, entitled *Wei Liangfu Qu Lu* (Rules of Singing According to Wei Liangfu). Unlike Wei's manuscript in vernacular prose, this later work was written in a very polished literary language, probably by a literary man who had revised and shortened Wei's version into 18 paragraphs of instruction (Wong 1978:116, n. 3). The appearance of his 1616 work leads one to speculate that *kunqu* vocal style had by then been adopted by the educated class shortly after Wei's codification. In subsequent ages, until the early twentieth century, this literary version of Wei's rules was further expanded, annotated, and reprinted by various literary men no fewer than 16 times (Wong 1978:197).

As a pure singing art, *kunqu* singing is governed by precise prescriptions concerning word articulation and vocalization.[1] Of equal importance is the application of ornaments, the principles of which had long been systematized and transmitted orally. In 1953, the foremost *kunqu* actor, Yu Zhengfei (1902–1993) published a treatise explaining the intricacies of the *kunqu* vocal technique, as he had learned from his father Yu Sulu (1847–1930), the foremost *qing chang* (pure singing) master of the late nineteenth and twentieth centuries (Yu Zhengfei 1953; Wong 1978:112–113, 127, n. 59); this work was reprinted in 1982 (Yu 1982:1–33).

The involvement by members of the elite classes—known as *wen ren* (literary men)—with *kunqu* had a long tradition. They not only participated in *qing chang* as their favorite pastime but also wrote many theoretical treatises discussing articulation and vocalization in *qing chang* singing. Many literary men were also involved with creating new verses for aria lyrics, and they compiled dictionaries for rhyming of words to be used in these aria lyrics as well as anthologies of verse exemplars. There are many volumes of this kind of work, and their existence testifies to their importance in the scholarly lives of literary men (Ye 1999:3–8; Wu 2002:877–887; 895–897; 911–913).

The *qing chang* lineage in *kunqu* has been maintained unbroken from Wei Liangfu's time to the twentieth century. In the eighteenth century a great singer by the name of Ye Tang (1722–1792), who was coincidentally also an herbal doctor like Wei Liangfu, had revitalized the *qing chang* tradition with new innovations (Wu 2002:416). He compiled the *Na Shu Ying Qupu* (Aria Anthology from the Na Shu Ying Library) in which he provided details of what he had learned from the Wei Liangfu school of *qing chang* plus his own innovation (Wu 2002:899; Wong 1978:108–110). Ye Tang taught many students, some of whom are known to us. One student was called Niu Feishi (1760–1827) (Wu 2002:416); himself a famous singing master, Niu taught Han Huaqing (ca. late nineteenth century); Han, in turn, was the teacher of the foremost *qing chang* master of the nineteenth and twentieth centuries, Yu Sulu, father and teacher of the foremost *kunqu* actor Yu Zhengfei (Wu 2002:418–419), who was responsible for transplanting the *qing chang* tradition to the stage (for more on the Yu father and son, see below). Today, many famous professional actors who were students of Yu Zhengfei are still active on the *kunqu* stage.

Kunqu's Association with Theater

Around the late 1570s, a literary man by the name of Liang Shengyu (1519–1551), who lived in Kunshan and was a *kunqu* connoisseur, pioneered in creating a libretto specifically designed for stage adaptation of the *kunqu* vocal art with makeup, costumes, and stage actions. Liang's new libretto was written in the form of the *chuanqi* drama, itself a recent Ming literary adaptation of the older and cruder Southern Theater, *nanxi*. Liang's libretto was based on a historical romance, entitled *Huan Sha Ji* (Cleaning the Silk Garment), and he personally coached a group of Kunshan actors to perform his play at the home of his wealthy friends (Wu 2002:457). The association of the *kunqu* vocal style with the stage convention of the *chuanqi* drama quickly became the vogue, and many literary men followed Liang's example in creating new libretti for the *kunqu* stage, primarily for the acting troupes of their own families. Professional actors then adopted these new *chuanqi* plays for the professional stage.

Public theaters did not appear in China until the middle of nineteenth century. Prior to that, theatrical troupes were itinerants journeying from one town to the next performing either for hire in private homes, in village squares, or in temple courtyards (Wu 2002:215–219). As Suzhou professional actors dominated the stage during Ming and Qing periods, their adaptation of the *kunqu* stage had inspired followers from other regions (Lu 1980:133–155).

Wealthy families of the southern Yangzi region had a long tradition of keeping private troupes at home for their own and their friends' enjoyment, and *kunqu* theater became the sole style of theater being staged. Private family troupes were generally made up of 12 young boys or girls purchased from poor families, and singing masters or retired professional actors were hired to teach them how to sing and act. Family troupes usually performed libretti written by private patrons who might also engage in directing the stage actions and singing for their own plays (Lu 1980:116–132; Wu 2002:201–213). Although many libretti have been lost, quite a few have survived. According to a twentieth century estimate, no fewer than 1500 *chuanqi* libretti written between the sixteenth and eighteenth centuries are still extant; most of them are in libraries in China, but a few can be found elsewhere.

The process of creating a *chuanqi* libretto and then having it performed on stage was not a simple task. The playwright provided a plot in many scenes, each of which was made up of many arias (from three to maybe a dozen or more) whose lyrics were written in rhymed verses of unequal lengths; dialogues were interspersed between arias, and some type of action was indicated. As most playwrights were literary men who were not knowledgeable about music, they had to collaborate with singing masters or professional actors who could help to set the lyrics to the melodies of preexisting arias through the process of *pu qu* (tune accommodation). This collaboration between literary playwrights, who generally came from a higher stratum of society, and professional singers/actors, who came from a lower stratum of society, was a common phenomenon in the *kunqu* world.

The term *chuanqi*, literally meaning "tales of the marvelous," first appeared in the Tang dynasty (618–907) and was a genre of stories written in literary language whose subject matters included fictional biographies of historical persons, heroic adventures, Buddhist and Daoist morality tales, and mildly erotic romances and supernatural tales. Many later *chuanqi* plays for the *kunqu* stage in the Ming and Qing periods inherited not only the name but also some of the plots of the older stories, as well as their predilection for supernatural, romantic, and erotic elements (Hanan 1981). A *chuanqi* libretto for the *kunqu* stage is usually quite long, containing 30 to 50 scenes to be laid out in a four-part framework. The basic ingredients for each scene are a series of arias to be sung in the *kunqu* vocal style which are interspersed with spoken passages in prose or in literary language to be recited either in heightened speech (by characters who belonged to the higher stratum of society) or in everyday speech (by characters of a lower stratum); other ingredients are prescribed movements and gestures.

A *chuanqi* libretto customarily features a large cast of actors, each specializing in a particular stock character. Each role is defined by speaking and vocal qualities, costumes, makeup, and movements that serve as markers of gender, deportment, and social status. An actor, who has to go through years of strenuous training, is expected to be a good singer and to be able to master many modes of speech, ranging from recitation and heightened speech to appropriate delivery of everyday language. In addition, convention demands that the actor must master complex gestures and choreographic movements involving elaborate manipulation of the head, eyes, hands, and feet, as well as controlling complicated sleeve movements.

Professional actors learned their crafts personally from teachers, many of whom were professional actors themselves. The oral transmission from one generation to the next was reliable when unbroken by interruptions such as warfare or natural disaster. Luckily, much of this knowledge still survives today in oral tradition and in writing. There is an important body of work, written by literary men or by literate actors themselves, which contains detailed records of *kunqu* stage practices and dramaturgy and other complementing information. This oral tradition, together with written works, represents the most systematic and comprehensive information on *kunqu* theatrical convention; together they cover acting techniques, stage craft and practice, use of costumes, makeup, theatrical devices, etc. (Wu 2002:501–503). This knowledge has become the foundation for many later forms of theater, including the Peking Opera.

Because *chuanqi* libretti are usually very long, not all were performed in their entirety. Toward the eighteenth century it became customary to stage only a handful of scenes in one presentation. A separate scene is called *zhe zi xi* (highlight scene). In the 1980s when the professional actors who were trained in the 1920s before the establishment of the PRC (the so-called *Chuan* actors about whom more will be said later) were still living, they collectively carried the performance tradition of some 700 highlight scenes (containing altogether thousands of arias), but today's professional actors, trained after the 1950s, carry only one-fourth of that repertory. Much has been lost.

On stage, *kunqu* arias could be sung as solos, duos, or ensemble numbers, with instrumental accompaniment. There has never been a standard, but in general, the ensemble usually consists of both melodic and percussion sections with a flute, fiddle, lutes, mouth organ, drums, cymbals, and clappers. Sometimes a long trumpet may be used for festive scenes.

Patron, Garden, and *Kunqu*

The custom of wealthy families keeping private *kunqu* troupes for dramatic presentations during banquets was widespread all through the Ming and early Qing periods, in Suzhou and other areas as well. In a genre of informal literature known as *biji* (anecdotal notebook) that was much favored by literary men in the Ming and Qing periods and that contained a mixture of personal diaries, reminiscences, and miscellaneous historical anecdotes, the subject of banquets with dramatic presentations—mostly *kunqu*-staged presentations—filled the pages. They give the impression that a large part of these authors' social lives consisted of daily comings and goings to view *kunqu* dramatic presentations.

In 1724, the Qing emperor Yong Zheng (r. 1723–1735), who was noted for his fiscal conservatism, considered the custom of entertaining friends at home with family troupes a huge drain on resources, so he issued an imperial edict to forbid it (Wang 1981:31–32). As a result, family actors who were let go by their patrons had to join the ranks of itinerant public troupes. Eventually public theaters began to spring up during the eighteenth century to accommodate the demand for performance (Lu 1980:202–232). But it was in private homes of knowledgeable patrons that *kunqu* had been nurtured and developed. Since information on private patrons is very little known outside China, I will provide some contextual information of this nurturing environment in the following, concentrating on Suzhou.

Kunshan, the birthplace of *kunqu*, was a small suburb adjacent to the ancient city of Suzhou and had evolved around it culturally and economically for a long time. Since the thirteenth century, Suzhou had been noted for its cultural and economic preeminence. With wealth to support an excellent educational system, Suzhou produced more than its share of well-known scholars, officials, poets, painters, playwrights, and fiction writers. Suzhou's wealthy families developed a life style of leisure, luxury, and cultural pursuits which was widely emulated. They built exquisite gardens as dwelling places and a private sphere in which to enjoy music and poetry and to entertain friends in refined conversation.

In the sixteenth century, as soon as the vocal art of *kunqu* was codified by Wei Liangfu, the elites of Suzhou appropriated it and became ardent patrons. Because of Suzhou's high prestige, *kunqu* soon gained regional and national reputations, and *kunqu* actors were in great demand to perform all over the country. For enthusiasts of Suzhou, the garden was an ideal venue for the enjoyment of the art of *kunqu*. Indeed, in the anecdotal notebooks of Ming and Qing times, *kunqu* and gardens were identified as complementary pleasures. For example, in the celebrated reminiscence by the poet Yu Huai (1616–1696) entitled "*Ji chang yuan wen ge ji*" (On Listening to [*Kunqu*] Singing at the Ji Chang Garden), the author lovingly described an *al fresco* gathering attended by half a dozen literary men at the famous Ji Chang Garden in Wuxi, not far from Suzhou. The *qing chang* singers were in the service of a young and wealthy patron by the name of Qin Liuxian who was in the habit of providing music among beautiful scenic spots and various famous gardens. The occasion was described by Yu Huai as follows:

> ...the patron Qin Liuxian brought six or seven singers with him who carried their instruments on board a private boat which crossed the waves and arrived at the Ji Chang Garden for the gathering. The time was late autumn but not quite winter yet, a few leaves still hanging on the branches- an ideal time to listen to music sitting on the balustrade of the zigzag covered walkway or on the rocks while gazing at the tranquil water on the lake. The singers, wearing long blue silk gowns and fine silk shoes, had the deportment of scholars and were as graceful as young ladies. They sat on the rocks along the lake tuning their instruments first, and soon emitting their beautiful voices, first softly, then gathering in strength. [Each musical note] dropped like pearls [on a plate], and soon soared up to the sky and lingered with the clouds. All was hushed.... Afterward, they introduced themselves; sitting modestly with brows downcast, they told us who were their teachers. All of us were totally captivated by them... (translated by Isabel K. F. Wong, as quoted in Zhang Qiao 1985:67)

Suzhou is still famous for its many beautiful garden estates that used to belong to private families. A Suzhou garden estate gives the illusion of nature on a grand scale within a relatively confined urban space. It functioned as a hermitage in the city which could serve as a central arena for staging a life of esthetic sensitivity. A Suzhou garden typically constituted several individual physical objects, chief among them lakes and creeks; various types of fantastic rocks, individual or in cluster; plants such as shrubs, trees, and flowers; dwellings and pavilions in various shapes and sizes; bridges, zigzag-covered walkways, and pebble-paved paths linking the various objects and buildings to enhance viewing enjoyment. Intellectually, a Suzhou garden is a three-dimensional expression of traditional aesthetic ideals and ethical values based on Confucius, Daoist, and literary ideas embraced by educated men. These ideas were expressed either in the name of a garden or of its various parts and in the many decorative objects with the inscription of poems. All of the elements were placed strategically so as to create a sense of beauty in harmony with nature.[2]

Kunqu lyrics are full of references to various elements and objects in a garden, and many scenes take place in a garden. One of the perennial favorites on the *kunqu* stage is scene 23, "*xiao yan*" (An informal feast in the garden) from the famous *Chang sheng Dian* (The Palace of Eternal Youth) by the playwright Hung Sheng (1645–1704) (Sheng 1980:120–121). In this scene, the lovers—the Emperor and his favorite concubine—are enjoying a small feast in the garden, and their arias depict the scenery in the garden on an early autumn day:

> Emperor:
> Clouds drift across the pale blue sky, and wild geese
> Fly past in rows while autumn paints the garden
> With many colors: willow leaves turn yellow,
> The duckweed grows less green, and the red lotus
> Sheds all its petals; but there by the carved railings
> The cassia flowers in bloom give a sweet scent.
>
> Emperor and Lady Yang:
> Hand in hand we wander among the flowers,
> Past the cool pavilion, and past the wind-blown lotus
> Which trembles on the lake. I love the calm
> Of these planes which form such deep green avenues.
> While the duck and drake sleep in the silver pond.

It will be useful at this juncture to provide a portrait of an actual family—the Zhangs of Suzhou—who had for several generations helped to develop and cultivate *kunqu*. A memoir written by one of their descendants was published recently in Suzhou, with help and encouragement of the staff of the Suzhou *Kunqu* Museum, as a recognition of *kunqu* receiving UNESCO designation (Zhang 2004). The Zhang family was also the former owner of one of the most exquisite gardens in Suzhou called Zhuo Zheng Garden (popularly translated as "The Humble Administrator's Garden" in tourist guidebooks on Suzhou), which was named a world cultural heritage site by UNESCO in 1997. The Zhang family rebuilt part of this garden for use as an arena to enjoy *kunqu* in their daily lives.

The Humble Administrator's Garden was built in 1509 by an official of the Ming court. This first owner left a sketch and written description of the garden, which came into the possession of the Zhang family in the nineteenth century. Prior to that, the garden had changed hands several times and had been divided into three parts, each with a different owner. The garden fell into disrepair until 1877 when a scion of a local Zhang family by the name of Zhang Liqiang (1838–1915) bought the crumbling Western part and renovated it based on the sketches and description of the original garden, modestly renaming it Bu Yuan (The Patched up Garden). After the death of his son in 1951, the Zhangs decided to donate it to the Suzhou government. Thereupon the government reconnected and renovated the three parts of the original estate, renamed it The Humble Administrator's Garden, and opened it to the public. In 1997 it was named a World Heritage Site by UNESCO (Zhang 2004:9–11).

Typical of many wealthy families of Suzhou, the Zhang family earned their wealth from land and commerce and lived a life of leisure that included collecting antiques, paintings, calligraphy, and rare books, as well as the enjoyment and practice of *kunqu* (Zhang 2004:12–15). Zhang Liqiang himself was a literary man who had successfully passed the highest level of the civil service examination and became an official. When he retired back home to Suzhou, he proceeded to build his garden with the help of a few painter friends and his good friend Yu Sulu, a renowned *qing chang* master of *kunqu* who traced his *kunqu* lineage to Ye Tang of the eighteenth century, who in turn traced his lineage to Wei Liangfu of the sixteenth century (Zhang 2004:15–20; Wu 2002:418).

Zhang Liqiang was tutored by Yu Sulu in *kunqu* singing, as were his son and daughter. Yu Sulu was paid a very substantial monthly wage and was invited to live inside the Patched Up Garden until his death. After Zhang Liqiang's death in 1915, Yu continued his service to Liqiang's son and heir, Zhang Zidong, who became an excellent singer himself and, in his later life, played a pivotal role in rescuing *kunqu* from oblivion (Zhang 2004:97–98; Wu 2002:427).

Yu Sulu was not only a great singer but also a connoisseur of antique bronze, which his patron avidly collected. Yu Sulu also copied, in his excellent calligraphy, *kunqu* aria lyrics into miniature folded hand scrolls, known as *shou zhe* (hand scrolls), to be used by his patron for *kunqu* singing practice (Zhang 2004:175–178).[3]

Yu Sulu and his patron, Zhang Liqiang shared an artistic conception of making the Patched Up Garden a venue for the enjoyment of *kunqu*. One of the most famous results of this collaboration was the creation of the celebrated pavilion designed for *kunqu* singing known as *San-shi-liu yuan yang guan* (Thirty-six Mandarin Ducks Hall). This is a large rectangular hall having a series of glass windows opening front and back to an elongated lake where 36 mandarin ducks were (and still are) kept. The hall is spacious with a high, wooden domed ceiling designed to amplify music since it was used as a recital hall and as a classroom for daily *kunqu* teaching sessions presided by over by Yu Sulu. Because of his reputation as a singing master, Yu Sulu's students included not only persons related to the Zhangs but also their friends in Suzhou as well as their children. So for a couple of generations while Yu Sulu was alive, the Patched Up Garden became an important incubator where the authentic *kunqu qing chang* tradition was nurtured and from where it was transmitted and perpetuated (Gu 2004:1–2). As *kunqu* suffered a serious decline at the beginning of the twentieth century, many of Yu's former pupils, together with Zhang Zidong, tried to sustain *kunqu* (Sang 2000:11–12, 43–44; Gu 2004:3–4; Zhang 2004:96,104–108). In particular, Yu Sulu's son, Yu Zhengfei, who received his formal education with the Zhang's children developed into the foremost *kunqu* actor and teacher of the twentieth century (Zhang 2004:99–103; Wu 2002:379–380).

The Taiping Uprising and the Modern *Kunqu* Actors School

Until the mid-nineteenth century, the Qing rulers had imposed effective controls over foreign residents, but events soon brought an end to this control which had indirectly and adversely affected not only China but *kunqu* as well.

The Opium War—China's attempt to resist the British import and distribution of opium—resulted in Britain's defeat of the weak Qing navy. Then Britain imposed a treaty on China in 1842 that allowed foreign residents to live and trade in the five coastal cities of Shanghai, Tianjin, Fuzhou, Hankou, and Guangzhou. The anti-foreigner resentment that this provoked among the Chinese people later stimulated China's development of modern nationalism. The new foreign presence in China coincided with and contributed to new waves of domestic turbulence and uprising against the Qing government. From the 1840s four major rebellions erupted: of these, the Taiping in particular almost dealt a death blow to *kunqu*.

The Taiping was based on fundamentalist Christian and egalitarian principles that cut at the heart of Confucian and imperial values. Erupting in the poor rural area of southeastern China, the Taiping movement (1850–1864) quickly attracted a huge number of followers, taking Suzhou in 1860 and setting up a local administrative office in the Western part of the Humble Administrator's Garden (the part that later became part of the Patched Up Garden). By the time the Taiping was finally quashed in 1864, it had decimated Suzhou, and with it, the patronage base for *kunqu*. Many of the *kunqu* patrons and actors fled or were killed. After the Taiping, some former Suzhou residents returned to a ruined city and struggled to rebuild. Some professional actors tried to regroup and continue to perform, but *kunqu* had lost its vitality. This was the time that popular regional theaters emerged, chief among which was the Peking Opera which eventually conquered the *kunqu* stronghold of Suzhou and other cities in the Lower Yangzi region (Hu 1989:511–532, 567–583, 609–633).

China became a modern republic in 1911, yet *kunqu*'s steep decline continued, and many professional troupes folded. Toward the turn of the twentieth century, only one professional *kunqu* troupe in Suzhou managed to give regular performances, but most of the actors were old, and quite a few were opium addicts. After a few years this troupe had also disbanded.

Under this circumstance many *kunqu* practitioners and enthusiasts in Suzhou and Shanghai, worrying that the venerable art was in danger of total extinction, decided to do something to save it. Led by the respected singing master Yu Sulu and joined by the wealthy Shanghai industrialist Mo Ouchu (1876–1943) (Wu 2002:423), a Society for the Preservation of *Kunqu* was established to heighten public awareness. As a result, many *kunqu* practitioners in Suzhou, Shanghai, and other Lower Yangzi cities got together to form local singing clubs, called *qu hui* (singing gatherings), as venues to meet regularly to practice the art of *kunqu* acting and singing, tutored by professional singing masters or retired actors. These singing clubs became an important modern institution where the art of *kunqu* was transmitted and perpetuated among amateur practitioners in the twentieth century (Wu 2002:269–313).

Spurred by the rapid depletion of the ranks of professional *kunqu* actors at the beginning of the twentieth century, Zhang Zidong, then owner of the Patched Up Garden, and a few of his close friends, including Mo Ouchu, Yu

Sulu, and his son Yu Zhengfei, decided to establish a training school for professional actors. In 1921 with donations, they succeeded in establishing the *Kunqu Chuan Xi Suo* (School for the Perpetuation of *Kunqu*) on the outskirts of Suzhou. An Advisory Board of 12 respected citizens of Suzhou was formed (Wu 2002:437; Sang 2000:11), and retired actors were hired as teachers with regular monthly salary. The school adopted a 5-year curriculum which included intensive training on all aspects of *kunqu* acting and singing, plus basic reading in Chinese and simple arithmetic. Tuition and room and board were free. Thirty boys, aged 9–14, from poor families or orphanages, were accepted for the first class. Their life was strictly disciplined, and training was vigorous, starting at 6 a.m. and ending at 8 p.m. They learned basic *kunqu* body movements and gestures, basic martial arts skills, and *kunqu* arias in the traditional method, the most proficient of them gaining a repertory of about 200 highlight scenes and nearly a 1000 arias. Students were trained for particular role types and sat around a table with the teacher who would sing a phrase while beating on the table with a ruler; the students would then repeat the phrase, emulating the teacher while tapping the beat on the table with their palms. In *kunqu* terminology, this is known as "*pai qu*" (literally, "keeping the beat of the aria"). Next they were taught the appropriate accompanying movements and gestures, known as "*da xi*" (literally "walk the part"). By the end of the first year the students had learned to sing at least 200 arias and were able to perform a dozen highlight scenes. In addition to singing and acting, every student was required to learn to play an instrument, the rationale being if a student could no longer sing after his voice changed, he could earn a living as an instrumentalist in a troupe (Sang 2000:8–29).

In 1927, the first class of students graduated, but in 1928, the school had to close down due to lack of funds. In its 7 years of existence, the school had trained 90 students, of which 44 completed the program and went on to become professional actors (Sang 2000:29–30).

In accordance with traditional theatrical convention, the graduates of the "The School for the Perpetuation of *Kunqu*" adopted professional stage names. They retained their family names but adopted a new given name with the word "*chuan*" (meaning "perpetuation"). Since then, this group has been known collectively as the *Chuan Zi Bei* (the *chuan* actors). As it turned out, the *Chuan* actors were to be the last to be trained in *kunqu* for the next 30 years (Sang 2000:31–32; Wu 2002:355–69). In 1927, they formed a professional company called *Xin Yue Fu* (The New Musical Theater) but disbanded by 1931 because they could not compete with the Peking Opera companies which had swept through Shanghai and the Lower Yangzi. A smaller company, called *Xian Ni She* (The Fairy Rainbow Company), was formed and struggled to survive. But in 1937, Japanese forces attacked China and in 1941 the United States declared war on Japan. In the 20 years between 1921 and 1941, the *Chuan* actors who had remained active professionally—despite the political upheavals—continued learning arias and scenes from knowledgeable amateurs whenever they had the chance, and by 1941 they had collectively accumulated 700 highlight scenes in their repertory, 500 more than when they first graduated. This was the total extent of *kunqu* performing heritage that was preserved at that time (Sang 2000:33–43).

During the war years from 1937 to 1945, the *Chuan* actors scattered all over the country, many dying, while others became destitute: one committed suicide; the clown actor, Zhou Chuan Chang (1911–1990), told me that he became a wandering fortune teller; and a few earned a meager living by giving private *kunqu* singing lessons to students. A handful joined theatrical troupes of Peking Opera or other genres, applying and integrating their *kunqu* skills to other kinds of theaters. In 1943, two of the *Chuan* actors joined a small theatrical troupe called *Guo Feng,* which combined *kunqu* and a popular Suzhou theatrical genre called *suju*. The two were thus able to maintain their professional skills by occasionally inserting into the performance a few *kunqu* highlight scenes (Sang 2000:122–176). By the end of the war in 1945, 21 *Chuan* actors survived. Ten of them lived in Shanghai in semi-retirement, and a few joined the *Guo Feng* Company, which had moved to Hangzhou in Zhejiang province (south of Shanghai), and continued to perform until the establishment of the People's Republic of China in 1949 (Sang 2000: 122–176).

Kunqu Under Communism

Kunqu actors passed down their art orally through an apprentice system, and like all actors in the old society, their primary role was to entertain and thereby to get needed support from patrons of a higher stratum of society. But this ran counter to the new ideology of the Chinese Communist Party. In Yan'an, the Party was developing a "Cultural Army" that would play a role in the larger struggle for control in China after the war. A new ideological guideline for theaters had been formulated, based on Mao Zedong's 1942 "Talks at the Yan'an Forum on Literature and Art" (hereafter the "Talks") (Mao 1980), which was rooted in Lenin's view of the role of art as a weapon of propaganda in a socialist state. All culture was seen as reflecting the particular political outlook of the class that it served. Since traditional theaters were products of the feudal classes and served that interest, they were regarded as weapons of control against the proletariat. In a new Communist China, theater and art were to serve the Party of the proletariat, and popularization was the key artistic criterion. New works and new modes of presentation were to be created and new theoretical approaches followed in order to convince the proletariat of the inevitability of success of the socialist revolution. As a result of this utilitarian view of art, the status of actors was suddenly lifted from that of lowly entertainers to members of the Party's cultural army.

Initially, from 1949 to 1955, the Party's attempts to employ the techniques and guidelines developed in the Talks met with considerable resistance from traditionalists, partly due to the actors' resistance to the new mode of presentation and ideology, and partly due to the fact that traditional theaters were still flourishing and attracting large audiences. In the sphere of *kunqu*, the Party appeared to have taken the role of promoter. In 1949, the Ministry of Culture presented a gala performance of a famous *kunqu* play in Beijing, featuring the two most prestigious actors of the Chinese stage, the foremost *kunqu sheng* (young male) actor Yu Zhengfei, and the premier Peking Opera female impersonator of the *dan* role (young female) Mei Lanfang (1894–1961), who was also rooted in the theatrical tradition of *kunqu*. This gala performance sent a signal that the Party was to foster the art of *kunqu*. In Shanghai in the same year, the Shanghai Bureau of Culture invited the 10 *Chuan* actors residing in Shanghai to appear on stage together to give a performance of some 60 famous highlight scenes from the *kunqu* repertory. The series of performances lasted 2 months and was a success: young audiences were introduced to *kunqu*, and the old *kunqu* fans were ecstatic. By 1950, the 10 *Chuan* actors in Shanghai were offered full-time faculty positions in the newly established East China Academy of Dramatic Arts to teach *kunqu* choreography and movements to students in many kinds of traditional theaters (Sang 2000:122–176).

After 1950, the Party tried again to push forward the implementation of the new ideology in the theatrical world. At a national conference in Beijing, the Party gathered representatives of traditional theaters, modern playwrights, stage directors, Party cadres, and institutional personnel at a conference where reform of the theaters was advocated by employing modern Western and Russian techniques and organization. The Party, however, had underestimated the resistance and resiliency of traditional theaters; so in 1952, it adopted a more tolerant policy known as "walk with both legs." On the one hand, the Party allowed some highly popular repertories of traditional theaters to be performed, while on the other hand it pressed the traditional theatrical world to create new plays glorifying the proletariat. The same year, the first list was drawn up of "feudal and poisonous" plays to be banned. The Party also began to reorganize theater into state-owned theater schools and troupes. In the sphere of *kunqu*, in 1953 the Shanghai Bureau of Culture established the Shanghai School of Theatrical Arts which included training for *kunqu* actors, a program of 8 years with free tuition and board. Yu Zhengfei assumed the headship, and the 10 *Chuan* actors in Shanghai were transferred to become full-time faculty members for the *kunqu* department. To Yu Zhengfei and the *Chuan* actors who had lived through a period when *kunqu* seemed destined for extinction, this new opportunity was beyond their wildest dreams. The status of professional actors had been elevated by the Party, and applicants came from many areas of the Lower Yangzi region. Out of 2,000 applicants, the department accepted 60 students (34 boys and 26 girls), all aged 12. The curriculum was quite similar to that of the former School for the Perpetuation of *Kunqu*, including intensive training in singing and acting, plus a regular academic program including Chinese and other subjects. The first class of students graduated in 1961 and was ready to embark on a professional life. For the first time since their own graduation, the *Chuan* actors were able to fulfill their responsibilities to "perpetuate" the art of *kunqu* (Wu 2002:249–250; Ye 2005:15–80).

In Hangzhou, the privately owned *Guo Feng Kunqu* and *Suju* Company was reorganized into a state-owned company in 1956, as the *Kunqu* and *Suju* Company of Zhejiang Province. About half a dozen *Chuan* actors had also joined this company. In 1956, the company staged a revived *kunqu* play called *Shi wu guang* (Fifteen Strings of Cash), based on a well-known detective story involving burglary and homicide in the Ming dynasty. In order to attract an audience with little knowledge of *kunqu*, the play employed lots of mime, physical movements, and dialogue to convey the story, as well as using percussion punctuation to propel the plot. The instant success of this play motivated the company to take the performance on the road. In Beijing the performance was attended by Mao Zedong and Zhou Enlai (1898–1976), and afterward an editorial in the Party's mouthpiece praised the performance: "A single play has saved the life of a theatrical genre [i.e., *kunqu*]." This was a clear signal that the government had whole-heartedly promoted *kunqu*, albeit in its reformed and simplified mode (Sang 2000:124–128, 165–69; Wu 2002:245–247).

Stimulated by this success, two more *kunqu* companies and actors training programs were established in 1956, one in *kunqu*'s cradle Suzhou, and another in Beijing. Retired professional *kunqu* actors, singing masters, accomplished amateurs, and occasionally the *Chuan* actors from Shanghai and Hangzhou, were hired to train the actors in both places (Wu 2002:247–249).

Also in 1956, in a national conference held in Beijing to review all plays in the repertory and attended by the same representatives who had attended the previous conference, many were critical of the earlier high-handedness in pressuring for theater reform, and it was suggested that the role of the Party authorities in setting artistic standards should be reduced. In a 1957 speech, Mao Zedong launched the Hundred Flowers Movement, lifting all restrictions for the theaters. This relaxation of control lasted until 1958, when he launched the Great Leap Forward campaign in which the conciliatory posture was abandoned. The Party once again treated theater as a means of propaganda and forced the theatrical world to produce new plays reflecting the socialist revolution. In 1961, thinking that they were obeying this stricture, the Beijing-*Kunqu* Company staged a new play called "Lady Li" but was surprised when the Propaganda chief rejected it as feudal and poisonous. A year later, the teachers of the Beijing school were dismissed, and no more performances by the company were allowed (Wu 2002:248–249), a disaster not only for the *kunqu* world at large, but particularly for the newly graduated Shanghai *kunqu* students (Ye 1999:61–70).

It later became clear that a radical political storm was gathering. Mao Zedong's wife was Jiang Qing, a former starlet on the Shanghai stage in the 1930s. As the country's spokesperson on culture, Jiang Qing dismissed all traditional theaters and created a modern revolutionary theater based on Mao's "Talks". Throughout 1963 and 1964, Mao and Jiang made speeches criticizing the feudal outlook of the artistic and theatrical worlds and their failure to reflect a socialist revolutionary struggle. In 1964, they held a meeting in Beijing in which 35 plays, including 4 modern revolutionary plays under the personal supervision of Jiang Qing, were presented. Ultimately, on the eve of the Cultural Revolution (1966–76), Mao Zedong and Jiang Qing ordered the closing of all theater schools and companies, and both teachers and actors (including the *Chuan* actors) were humiliated or sent to the countryside to be reeducated (Witke 1977). The Cultural Revolution produced a widespread chaos that greatly affected the theatrical world: only eight so-called Modern Revolutionary Model Plays, supervised by Jiang Qing, were performed in that period.

Shortly after Mao's death in 1976, Jiang Qing was arrested, and in the following year, the close of the Cultural Revolution was officially declared. Under the leadership of Deng Xiaoping, the government revived the former policy of conditionally fostering traditional theaters. Actors were called back from the countryside, and academies and troupes were reestablished. By that time, only 16 *Chuan* actors were still alive and their students had now reached middle age.

In 1981, the Ministry of Culture, and the Bureaus of Culture of Jiangsu province, of Suzhou city, and of Shanghai city co-sponsored 7 days of *kunqu* performances in Suzhou to commemorate the 60th anniversary of the establishment of the School for the Perpetuation of *Kunqu*. Nine *Chuan* actors, now in their seventies and eighties, were still able to perform a few scenes onstage together, though their movements were somewhat feeble. One of the main purposes for this performance was for the *Chuan* actors to demonstrate to their former students and other younger actors, the art of *kunqu* as transmitted to them by their teachers. The younger actors were encouraged to take lessons from the *Chuan* actors while in Suzhou.[4]

In the following year another performance was sponsored in Suzhou, this time so that the former students of the *Chuan* actors and other younger actors could show their teachers what they had learned in the past year. Only four *Chuan* actors attended the occasion, and a couple of them still tried to give a performance. I attended the gala, and that was the first and last time I saw the *Chuan* actors perform. Later that year I visited the living *Chuan* actors, but they were reluctant to talk to someone from outside of China so soon after the Cultural Revolution.

The world of traditional theaters now faced another severe challenge. Because the Cultural Revolution had silenced the traditional theatrical world, a generation of youth had grown up who had never seen traditional theater. At the same time, since the Chinese government adopted economic reform and an open-door policy, popular music from Hong Kong, Taiwan, and the United States was let in and it greatly attracted Chinese young people. Despite the government effort in maintaining traditional theaters, audience taste had changed.

Kunqu After UNESCO

Since the end of the Cultural Revolution, *kunqu* companies had been supported by local governments in Suzhou, Shanghai, and Hangzhou, and by the Ministry of Culture in Beijing. Under local government support, amateur clubs in these cities also resumed weekly singing activities known as *qu hui*. The UNESCO award had stimulated interest among those who had not heard of *kunqu* before, particularly among university students. After UNESCO, an official slogan—"*kunqu* goes to the globe"—was inaugurated and widely interpreted by the theatrical world as an official encouragement to give *kunqu* a globalized veneer. New and lavish stage productions were produced with simple stories or little singing, but with lots of action, to attract foreign audiences in China and abroad. On cultural programs broadcasted by the Chinese Central Television (CCTV), *kunqu* performance is now occasionally included, but in bizarre contexts, such as with a hip hop performance as background accompaniment, something I saw on the CCTV9 program "Cultural Express."

From 2002 to 2007, I have had numerous opportunities for fieldwork in Suzhou, Shanghai, and Beijing to assess the impact of the UNESCO award in *kunqu*. I have interviewed cultural officials and critics as well as professional actors and amateur practitioners. Although there is still one surviving *Chuan* actor in Shanghai, I was told that he was too weak to grant interviews. Through my investigation, I have seen that the UNESCO award has both a positive and a negative impact on the *kunqu* world, varying according to local history, conditions, and the personnel involved.

Beijing, the current capital of the PRC and the birthplace of the Peking Opera, cannot be more different from compact and homogeneous Suzhou in terms of topography, demography, and historical, political, economic, and cultural environments. Prior to *kunqu*'s appearance in Beijing in the eighteenth century, Beijing already had its own theatrical tradition collectively known as *yiyang* theater. This began as a crude, outdoor theater of the north whose aria repertory derived from local folk songs accompanied by loud percussion. When the Qing Emperor Qian Long (r. 1736–96) brought a large group of Suzhou *kunqu* actors to the imperial court in the eighteenth century, the court already was a stronghold of the *yiyang* theater, and in the ensuing decades the *kunqu* and *yiyang* theaters cross-fertilized one another. The resulting amalgam became known as the *kun-yi* theater and it eventually became a public as well as a courtly entertainment. Since 1956, *kun-yi* theater (officially called Northern *Kunqu* Theater) is heavily subsidized by the Ministry of Culture. Even before the Cultural Revolution, this theater could not compete with the popular Peking Opera, and after the Cultural Revolution, it cannot compete with other more trendy entertainments in the capital today. After UNESCO, the Ministry has supported this company and encouraged it to produce lavish historical spectacles to attract a younger audience and international tourists, but the attempt has not been very successful. I saw that the company is really in limbo, and the recent death of a prominent and popular *dan* actress has not helped.

On the positive side, after UNESCO, the Ministry has subsidized the production of some DVDs of classic *kunqu* performances of excellent quality and made them available to the public. Beijing also has a small circle of dedicated *kunqu* amateurs whose lineage can be traced to those same *kunqu* actors recruited to the Qing court from Suzhou. The members of this society, all over 50 (and one man in his nineties), shunned the *kun-yi* tradition and have little interaction with the professional actors. I participated in their *qu hui* several times and gained the impression that by and large the members have ignored the UNESCO proclamation.

Returning to Shanghai, premodern Shanghai and Songjiang (formerly Shanghai's county seat) had a long *kunqu* tradition and Shanghai in particular had very knowledgeable and active *kunqu* amateur groups. In the 1980s when I participated in Shanghai *qu hui* gatherings, most members were in their fifties and older, but by the 1990s I found to my great regret that quite a few had died. Since 2000, amateur activities in Shanghai, though still existing, have not been very active. Today *kunqu* activities are carried on mainly by actors of the Shanghai *Kunqu* Company which has many excellent actors who were trained by Yu Zhengfei and the *Chuan* actors.[5] The company maintains a repertory of some 40 traditional highlight scenes in the *Chuan* actors and Yu Zhengfei tradition (as many actors were students of the *Chuan* actors, they perform these 40 highlight scenes extremely well). As a company existing in multicultural Shanghai, which has many types of national and international entertainments, however, Shanghai *kunqu* actors have never shied from innovation and experiments, notably a *kunqu* play based on Shakespeare's Macbeth ("*xue shou yin*" or "The Blood Stained Hands"). The director was a Chinese Shakespearean scholar and stage director, Huang Zuolin (1906–1994), who trained in London's Old Vic in the 1930s and resided in Shanghai. In the late 1980s he took the company to perform at the Edinburgh Drama Festival where they received international acclaim. The company created the new repertory to attract more university students; it has also incorporated many acrobatic fighting displays from the Peking Opera to attract young kids to the theater.

After UNESCO, the Artistic Director of the Shanghai *Kunqu* Company, the famous *sheng* actor Cai Zhengren, who was one of Yu Zhengfei's best disciples, told me that he has formulated a two-pronged policy with the help of officials in the Shanghai Bureau of Culture. On the one hand, the 40 traditional *kunqu* highlight scenes in the Yu and *Chuan* actors' tradition will be vigorously safeguarded and transmitted intact to younger actors in the company. This repertory will be performed for invited connoisseurs and dignitaries, or for officials during national celebrations, in the company's chamber theater. On the other hand, the company will continue to create fusion plays appealing to a younger urban audience. Many plays in this category could best be described as Sinicized Broadway spectacles with a smattering of *kunqu*-like tunes and actions, lavishly staged and using state-of-the-art lighting techniques. *Kunqu* appears to serve only as a point of departure for new creation in these works.

In Suzhou itself, unlike Beijing and Shanghai, *kunqu* amateur activities are flourishing. The Suzhou amateurs, many of whom are descendants of former Suzhou elites, continue to hold *qu hui* gatherings regularly. After UNESCO, some local bureaucrats suggested that the *qu hui* be held Saturday mornings in gardens frequented by tourists to serve as publicity for *kunqu*. The Suzhou local government has also revived the age-old *al fresco kunqu* singing gathering in Suzhou's Tiger Hill on the date of Harvest Moon Festival. According to reports from friends, instead of being an occasion for individual *kunqu* singers to show off their arts and skill to a large, but quiet audience, this contemporary revival has become a mass singing, aimed mainly at tourists, and is sheer cacophony! Thus what was formerly an artistic pursuit in a private space has now emerged as a public spectacle.

One positive result of UNESCO in Suzhou was the establishment of a nongovernmental Institute for the Preservation and Perpetuation of *Kunqu*, sponsored by dues-paying private citizens. Though it is not an official organization, the Institute does receive support from the local government in the form of a site in a furnished, graceful old house. Every Saturday morning members get together to discuss issues relating to the preservation of an authentic *kunqu* tradition, and these discussions can be very lively. At a session in which I participated, some participants heatedly criticized the radical experimentation in Beijing and Shanghai by trying to produce a globalizing facade for *kunqu* in order to attract a younger audience and foreign tourists, and they accused Beijing and Shanghai of being the "executioners" of the authentic *kunqu* tradition. They were in agreement that as the cradle of *kunqu*, Suzhou's responsibility is to safeguard an authentic *kunqu* heritage as charged by UNESCO. Suzhou expresses this goal in a slogan "*yuan zhi yuan wei*" ("authentic source produces authentic taste"), as opposed to the slogan of Beijing's Ministry of Culture "*kunqu* goes to the globe." Another endeavor of the Institute is a monthly newsletter circulated nationally and internationally, that serves as a public forum for discussions, reports on *kunqu* performances elsewhere, book reviews, and news on members. Finally, the Institute also functions as an informal school where *kunqu* singing and acting is taught to school children by professional actors and knowledgeable amateurs.

One of the key supporters of the tradition is 82-year-old Mr Gu Duhuang, a major theorist and historian of *kunqu*, and himself the heir of a beautiful Suzhou garden, the Yi Yuan. The Gu family, like the Zhang family, was also patron of *kunqu*. After UNESCO, Gu was able to solicit funding to support a *kunqu* archive inside the Suzhou *Kunqu* Museum. This archive will collect all written, musical, and theatrical data of Suzhou *kunqu* and will be open to international researchers.

On the professional front, the Suzhou company was able to solicit support from non-governmental sources, including some from Taiwan, Hong Kong, and the United States, to build a new performing arena in the center of the city which has a traditional projection stage. Professional actors give performances here of authentic *kunqu* highlight scenes on a totally bare stage, following the *Chuan* actors tradition. Every Saturday afternoon, actors give lecture demonstrations of *kunqu* to young students, and those who show promise will be presented on stage to perform a scene in full costumes and makeup. Perhaps, *kunqu* will continue to live in Suzhou after all. One can't but hope.

Conclusion

For a great heritage such as *kunqu* which was created in another age, to survive the modern world, change and reinvention are inevitable. However, the results depend very much on local conditions, on participants' understanding of the heritage, and on their motivations, artistic or otherwise. One thing is sure, *kunqu*, which was created by *literati* for their enjoyment in a rarified private sphere such as Suzhou gardens, has lost its traditional habitat forever. It is now in the public domain of a mass audience, and with the Chinese government as its patron. How *kunqu* will evolve from now on depends very much on the whims of a modern mass audience, on policies shaped by the national and local government, and on the quality of local leadership and supporters.

Notes

1. Prescriptive treatises on singing written by literary men who collaborated with singing masters through the ages provide the following information. With regard to articulation, a word is always broken into three basic phonetic components, each of which must be clearly articulated with the correct durational emphasis. These three phonetic components are defined as the "head of the word" (i.e., the initial consonant), the "belly of the word" (i.e., the vowel), and the "tail of a word" (i.e., the ending component). The transition from one phonetic component to the next should be very smooth, as smooth as a surface that has been polished repeatedly by running water, hence the alternate term for *kunqu* vocal style is *shui mo chang* (water polished sound). With regard to vocalization, parts of the mouth cavity must be used precisely to produce the desired vocal effects when a word is articulated. There are the so-called five sounds, in which the throat, the molar teeth, the incisor teeth, the tongue, and the lips all serve specific functions. There are also prescriptions for the appropriate application of stress, prolongation, and dynamic shadings in conjunction with each word according to its linguistic tone.
2. For further reading on the evolution of intellectual ideas of Chinese garden, see Xiaoshan Yang, *Metamorphosis of the Private Sphere: Gardens and Objects in Tang-Song Poetry* (Harvard University Asian Center, 2003). For a detailed description of objects in Suzhou garden from the point of view of Chinese landscape design, with excellent illustrative photographs (in Chinese with English summary), see Kuang Zhengyan et al., eds., *Suzhou Yuanlin* (Suzhou Garden) (China Architecture & Building Press, 1999).
3. Some of the family's excellent bronze vessels are now in the collection of the Shanghai Museum. Yu Sulu's *shou zhe* are now collectors' items; and a few of them are now stored in the rare book room of the Suzhou *Kunqu* Museum.
4. Based on oral reports related to me by some actor friends who had attended this occasion.
5. I have been interacting with the actors in this company since the 1980s, so I can claim some familiarity.

References

Gu, Duhuang
  2004 Xu [Introduction]. In *Bu Yuan Jiu Shi*[Reminiscence on the Patched Up Garden], edited by Zhang Xiuyun, pp. 104. Gu Wu Xian Chuban She, Suzhou.
Hu, Ji
  1989 *Kunqu fazhang shi* [History of the Kun Theater]. Zhongguo Xiju Chuban She, Beijing.
Lu, O-ting
  1980 *Kunqu yanchu shi gao* [History of Performance of the Kun Theater]. Wenyi Chuban She, Shanghai.
Mao, Zedong,
  1980 *Mao Zedong's "Talk on the Yan'an Conference on Literature and Arts."* Trans. Bonnie S. McDougall. University of Michigan Press, Ann Arbor
Qiang, Yin et al.
  1998 *Suzhou Xiqu Zhi* [History of Suzhou Traditional Musical Theaters]. Gu Wu Xian Chuban She, Suzhou.
Sang, Yuxi
  2000 *Kunju Chuan Zi Bei* [The *Chuan* Actors of the Kun Drama]. Wenshi Zhiliao, Jiangsu.
Sheng, Hong
  1980 [1955] *The Palace of Eternal Youth*, translated by Yang, Xianyi and Glady Yang. Foreign Language Press, Beijing.
Wang, Liqi (editor)
  1981 *Yuan Ming Qing San Dai Jin Hui Xiaoshuo Xiqu Shiliao* [Censored and Destroyed Materials on Fictions and Drama During the Yuan Ming and Qing Dynasties]. Guxi Chuban She, Shanghai.
Witke, Roxane
  1977 *Comrade Chiang Ch'ing*. Little, Brown and Company, Boston and Toronto.
Wong, Isabel K.F.
  1978 *The Printed Collections of Kun-Chü*. Chinoperal Papers, no. 8.
Wu, Xinlei et al.
  2002 *Zhongguo Kunju Da Cidina* [Dictionary of Chinese *Kunqu* Opera]. Nanjing University Press, Nanjing.
Yang, Xiaoshan
  2003 *Metamorphosis of the Private Sphere: Gardens and Objects in Tang-Song Poetry*. Harvard University Asian Center, Cambridge, Mass.
Ye, Changhai
  1999 *Qu xue yu xiqu xue* [Treatises on Versification and on Drama]. Xuelin Chuban She, Shanghai. 2005 *Wu Hui Zhui Meng* [Chasing a Dream Without Regret]. Wenhua Chuban She, Shanghai.
Yu, Zhengfei
  1953 *Xi Qu Yao Jie* [How to Practice *Kunqu* Singing]. Hong Kong.
  1982 *Zheng Fei Qi Pu* [Arias Collection of Yu Zhengfei]. Wenyi Chuban She, Shanghai.
Zhang, Qiao
  1985 Preface (1683) to *Yu Chu Xin Zhi*, edited by Baoqun Luan. Renmin Chuban She, Hebei.
Zhang, Xiuyun
  2004 *Bu Yuan Jiu Shi* [Reminiscence on the Patched Up Garden]. Gu Wu Xian Chuban She, Suzhou.
Zhengyan, Kuang et al. (editors)
  1999 *Suzhou Yuanlin* (Suzhou Garden). China Architecture & Building Press.

Chapter 3
Partition Memories: The Hidden Healer

Rajmohan Gandhi and Usha Gandhi

The *Mahabharata*, the great epic known to most Indians, relates how a mighty battle fought at Kurukshetra destroyed almost all the characters portrayed. The town of Kurukshetra ("the field of Kuru") lies near the eastern end of what once was a single Punjab, only 55 miles north of New Delhi. Divided in 1947 into an Indian state and a Pakistani province, the territory of "the Punjab" (as it was known before its division) is watered by the great Indus river and by five others that give Punjab (which means "five rivers" in Urdu and Farsi) its name: Jhelum, Chenab, Ravi, Sutlej, and Beas. At first Indian Punjab was called East Punjab; now it is simply Punjab. The Pakistani portion is also known as just Punjab.

Indian lore tells us that the *Mahabharata* bloodshed of mythology was preceded by another genocide in Kurukshetra: the elimination of the entire Kshatriya race by a Brahmin, Parasurama, who avenged the killing of his father by a Kshatriya. A particularly treacherous killing in the (later) Mahabharata war is of the Brahmin teacher Drona, whose son Ashwatthama then takes brutal revenge, killing women and children in their sleep. Ashwatthama is India's most vivid symbol of revenge. He is said to be always alive – forever miserable and hideous but unable to die because of a curse earned by his atrocities.

Yet Ashwatthama is not the only spirit alive in the Punjab. Indian lore also informs us that Kuru, the king and farmer who founded Kurukshetra, wanted to cultivate eight virtues there, two of which were forgiveness and compassion. Later in the Punjab's history, several Buddhist, Hindu, Muslim, and Sikh voices also advocated compassion, tolerance, and pragmatic commonsense. Two thousand years ago, the great Buddhist University of Taxila hummed with the conversation of international students on a site on what today is the northern border of Pakistani Punjab, not far from Islamabad, the Pakistani capital. The 10 Sikh Gurus were Punjabis, and several parts of the Punjab gave birth to Sufi saints honored to this day by Muslims, Sikhs, and Hindus. This other legacy

R. Gandhi (✉)
Center for South Asian and Middle Eastern Studies, University of Illinois at Urbana-Champaign, Champaign, IL 61820, USA
e-mail: rgandhi@illinois.edu

may have helped in 1947 when a wicked wind set off terrible cruelty in different parts of the Punjab, for at that time the soil of the Punjab also appeared to show instances of compassion and courage.

Watered by life-sustaining rivers and divided since 1947 between India and Pakistan, the soil of the Punjab has indeed seen much violence over the centuries. But humanity and courage are also among the crops, as was found in interviews conducted in Lahore, Pakistan, and New Delhi, India, with over two dozen persons having memories of the bloodshed of the 1947 partition. Among the stories told to us were those about oft-forgotten helpers from the ranks of the Other. These recovered memories can be a source of healing to teller and listener alike. When recounted to other Punjabis, such stories triggered from many a listener the remembrance and recital of another story in the same vein. Indeed, the publication of several of these stories in *The Tribune*, prominent daily newspaper of Indian Punjab, generated a similar reaction. We found, moreover, that the stories were perfect mirror images: Muslim Punjabis spoke of Sikh and Hindu helpers and Hindu and Sikh Punjabis of Muslim helpers.

Silence about what was experienced and witnessed during the violence of the Partition was the norm for decades after 1947. Now, finally, people in their seventies and eighties are willing to speak. Their memories – of pain but also of rays of humanity – should be recorded before it is too late. Many in Indian Punjab and Pakistani Punjab have access to such stories, which live in the memories of grandfather or grandmother or old uncle or aunt who experienced such help, or perhaps even rendered help, or witnessed an act of brave or ingenious assistance. Hidden under layers of silence or pain, these stories are waiting to be unearthed. As they are heard, they are likely to perform a healing role. This chapter is about these recovered memories.

The Project: From Myth to History to Remembering to Healing

History records many a period in the Punjab when Ashwatthama was not only alive but active, when a frenzy of revenge ended innocent lives, and none perhaps more gruesome than the year 1947, when a quarter of a million, or half a million, or a million (there is no consensus on the figure) were killed in the Punjab, most of them in the months of August and September, as India and Pakistan emerged as independent nations (see Gopal Das Khosla 1950 [1989]: 289–299 for the standard Indian account). Non-Muslim deaths equaled Muslim deaths.

The killings were accompanied by one of the greatest migrations known to history, with about six million Hindus and Sikhs moving from Pakistan into India and an equal or possibly larger number of Muslims moving from India to Pakistan, and by the loss of homes, lands, and all possessions.

Following the cruelties and mass migrations of 1947, the struggle of starting life afresh in a new place after having lost everything also meant (in many cases) a resolve not be paralyzed by memories, which were pressed down firmly under a lid. However, in order for healing from trauma to be accomplished, the lid must be lifted. Writing about the experiences of that year, Menon and Bhasin (1998:18) observe: "For most of the women remembering was important, but as important was *remembering to others,* having someone listen to their stories and feel that their experience was of value." We sensed in our research a similar value in the telling and hearing of stories of the opposite of cruelty. That humanity showed its face in 1947 was known but not talked about.

Catching and recording glimpses of this face was our project in the summer of 2005, when we conducted 9 days of research in Lahore, July 16–25, and later on interviews in New Delhi. We had informed friends in Lahore of our wish to record evidence that mercy, too, had surfaced in 1947, and they welcomed our proposed exercise. But we did not know how we would find persons possessing such evidence, or whether, if found, they would be willing to share it with us. We knew that they would see us not primarily as neutral academics but as Indians and Hindus.

Fortunately the task was made easier shortly after our arrival in Lahore. A close friend there, Dr. Mubashir Hasan, mentioned our intention to Nazir Naji, a columnist in a popular Urdu newspaper of Pakistani Punjab, *Jang,* in whose July 20 column was added a note asking readers possessing accounts of help given to the "Other" during the Partition to phone Dr. Hasan's telephone number, for the benefit (Naji added) of researchers from India (who were not named). We met most of our interviewees as a result of phone calls received in response to Naji's note. The rest were reached through friends. We called on most interviewees in their homes or place of work, but some came to meet us in our accommodation in Lahore. A few who were far from Lahore spoke to us over the phone. Aware that we intended to publish our research, all interviewees affirmed their willingness to go on record.

Our interviewees spoke (as many in Lahore do) in a mix of Urdu and English. Here their remarks are presented in English but with the retention, where they seemed telling, of Urdu expressions, which are translated in the text. We do not claim that these accounts and findings provide a fair and accurate representation of what occurred in 1947. In fact we did not set out to obtain "a fair and accurate representation." Such a goal is likely impossible. What we sought, and in our view were able to receive, was an illustrative and, we believe, helpful picture. We also fully realized that interviews in Lahore could not indicate the story of all of the Punjab. Interviews in, for instance, Amritsar, Jullundur, or Rawalpindi were perhaps capable of yielding other perspectives. On the other hand, we hoped that in Lahore we would find people connected to different parts of both Punjabs and with memories of help in both directions, from non-Muslims to Muslims and vice versa. An Indian daily, *The Tribune,* carried a report of our research on three successive Sundays in October 2005. We present four previously unpublished stories and have selected four other stories reported in *The Tribune*. Analysis and conclusions follow.

Four Previously Unpublished Stories

Ahmed Hayat Kalyar About Sargodha

We interviewed Ahmed Hayat Kalyar in Lahore on July 23, 2005. He was born after the killings, in 1949, but he told us of what he had learnt from his father, Mian Mohammed Hayat Kalyar, who was born in 1926. The family had lands in the district of Sargodha, about 120 miles northwest of Lahore, mostly in a village called Mir Ahmed Sher Garh. (In Pakistan and India, a "district" connotes a large geographical and administrative unit that roughly corresponds to a county in the United States.)

In answer to questions Kalyar said:

> Only one Hindu family owned land in our village—the family of Bhogaram Chugh. Three or four miles from the village was the big village – or small town – of Faruka, where Sikhs, who had served in the area for a long time, had established the Khalsa High School in 1906–07. One of the schoolteachers was Master Tara Singh, a Sikh, as the last name indicates. He was well liked but in 1947 he decided to go to India. The family left for Silawalli railway station, which was nine miles from Faruka. The army was protecting a camp in Silawalli where Hindus and Sikhs intending to leave for India had gathered. Two miles from Faruka, on the way to Silawalli, the entire family of Tara Singh, six or seven people, were slaughtered on a bridge over a drain. That was the reward given to a great man.
>
> But my family was able to save the family of Bhogaram Chugh. Soon after the Tara Singh incident, *tongas* [horse-driven cart with seats and a small roof] and guards were arranged and the Bhogaram family reached the Silawalli camp. His son Tilak Raj became a dental surgeon in Chandigarh. He sent photos of the family. In 1985 or 1986 my daughter Fatima (born in 1973) had correspondence with Dr. Tilak Raj's family. [We learnt afterwards that] Tilak Raj put Fatima's letter to his eyes and cried.
>
> After 1947 my father took control of the Khalsa school and ran it. He died in 1998. *Dil karta hai, khwaish hai* ("I have this wish, this desire"), why not give the name back to the school – Khalsa or Guru Nanak School, or name it after Master Tara Singh?"

Maqbool Elahi of Ropar, East Punjab

Retired colonel Maqbool Elahi, 89, and his wife Nusrat Elahi welcomed us on July 24, 2005 into their home in Lahore's Defence Housing Area. They were clearly part of the Pakistani elite. The drawing room had a picture of the colonel's father as a student in London. At Partition, Maqbool was a young army officer posted in New Delhi. His father, Mehboob Elahi, was an engineer from east Punjab who became a prominent Muslim League politician; he was staying with his son, the colonel, at the time. Other relatives were in Ropar in east Punjab.

Maqbool Elahi said:

> When violence started in Delhi, 80 Muslims moved into the space I had rented, which was an annex to a New Delhi house. I attended some of Mahatma Gandhi's prayer meetings in Birla House. A Sikh civilian came everyday on a motorcycle to bring

rations and milk for us. He did this until 17 September (1947), when we left for Rawalpindi (Pakistani Punjab's second biggest city, after Lahore). When he heard that we were going to Rawalpindi, he said, 'My sister and brother-in-law and children are there.'

Continued Elahi: "I found the (Sikh) family in Rawalpindi, put them on a train, and later heard that they had reached Delhi."

By now Maqbool's father was in Ropar with the rest of the family. Maqbool returned to India to take the father and other relatives to Pakistan. He and his father did make it to the new country, but 28 relatives were killed on a train that was to take them across the border. The train was attacked at Sirhind station in east Punjab.

Mohammed Saeed Awan of Hoshiarpur, East Punjab

We interviewed Mohammed Saeed Awan on July 24, 2005. He is originally from the village Khanpur in sub-*tehsil* Mukerian in *tehsil* (three to six *tehsils* formed a district) Dasooya in Hoshiarpur district in east Punjab. He was born in 1925. His father was a headmaster, presumably of a junior-level school, in Khanpur village. The family had lived for generations in Hoshiarpur district. Awan said that there was a substantial Muslim presence in Khanpur village and in the towns of Mukerian and Dasooya. Many in the Awan clan were in the army. In the early 1940s, Muslims of the area had the impression that Hindu moneylenders were gaining control over Muslim lands.

Awan related:

I went to Arya High School in Mukerian. [The name "Arya" establishes the school as Hindu-run] I led a campaign in the school after a Hindu *mithai*-seller (sweet-seller) roughly shook off a Muslim boy who had touched his tray of sweets, saying, '*Bharasht kar diya*' – 'You have polluted the sweets.' Dogs could lick his cooking vessels but a Muslim boy could not be allowed to come close. After the agitation led by me, the headmaster, Agya Ram Bhalla, got the *mithai*-seller to apologize in front of the whole school.

In 1945, Awan moved to near Lahore and found a job as a clerk in an office of the Public Works Inspectorate [PWI] near Baddi Nali railway station between Lahore and Narowal. He continued:

The inspector, Tikka, and the assistant works inspector [AWI] were both Hindus. The AWI was a Pandit [a Brahmin]. A day before August 15 I learnt that Tikka had fled, leaving behind everything. There was a plan to kill the Pandit. I asked him to move to my house. He was reluctant, perhaps even suspicious. I took out the Qur'an and promised, 'Before you die, I will die.' He moved in, with two or three families of relatives. I told the others that the Pandit had vanished and got the police to seal his house. Then I arranged for him and the relatives to go to a camp in Lahore, and said to him, 'Don't tell me where you are going.'

Awan said that after sending the Pandit and his party to the Lahore camp he managed to journey to the family's village in Mukerian in east Punjab and to escort three of his sisters to the Pakistan border, which was 30 or so miles from Mukerian.

He claimed that because the Awans of Mukerian were strong and united, not a single Awan girl was abducted by non-Muslims. Speaking of a fight in August 1947 between the Awans of Mukerian and Sikh groups, he said that before the Awans were forced out, they had dreamt for a while that they could "win" Mukerian for Pakistan. But saving the Pandit and his relatives near Baddi Nali was the story he had come to us to tell – it was his bridge to Hindus and Indians.

Dawood Pervaiz, "From He Knows Not Where"

One of the phone calls in response to the note in *Jang* was from a woman who insisted that she had to meet us even though she did not have a story of "help from the Other side." Her home was in the "township" area on Lahore's outskirts. We did not know what to expect when we arrived there and thought we might confront anger. Instead, there was a warm welcome and a generous spread accompanied by tea in the modest, neat, rented apartment where Nayla and her husband Dawood Pervaiz lived and where we also met other members of the family, including Nayla's sister. It was her husband's story that Nayla wanted us to hear. Dawood was two-and-half years old in 1947 when he was brought, with his head and elbow slashed, to one of Lahore's refugee camps ("the Walton camp, I think," Nayla said).

"He knows nothing about his family. We do not know if anybody came with him. We don't know of any relatives of his. Can you help find out?" This was Nayla's pressing plea.

Dawood showed us the large furrow on his scalp and the scars on the elbow left by the childhood wounds – inflicted by kirpans (daggers carried by Sikh males), so they had heard. The child Dawood had been adopted by Nayla's aunt, and in due course Nayla and Dawood got married. Nayla obviously longed for her husband to find his roots, and though there was nothing we could do to help, she seemed glad for the chance to express her wish to people from across the border, where – somewhere – Dawood's origins lay.

The gash on Dawood Pervaiz's head and his wife's unanswerable plea underlined for us the tragic fact that the bulk of 1947s stories will remain unknown and unrecorded – and therefore also underlined the value of gathering what *can* be recorded. And there was a sunny side even to their story of loss. Dawood smiled as Nayla told us of his comment that Pakistan had been created so they could marry: "*Pakistan bana tha hamaari tumhaari shaadi ke liye.*"

Four Stories Selected from *The Tribune*

Chaudhry Muhammad Hayat of Gujrat tehsil

Chaudhry Muhammad Hayat is a retired squadron leader in Pakistan's air force who had played for the joint services cricket team. We met him in his small first-floor office room in a crescent-shaped complex in Lahore's Defence

3 Partition Memories: The Hidden Healer

Housing Area. Aged 76 in 2005, Hayat now worked as a consultant. He came originally from village Snauk Khurd, about four miles east of the town of Gujrat on the road from Lahore to Jalalpur Jattan.

Hayat recalled:

> North of Snauk Khurd was the village of Nichra where lived many Nichra Jats. [They were Muslims. The numerous Jats living in India and Pakistan can be Muslim, Hindu, or Sikh.] There was one *dera* (settlement) where five or six Hindu families lived, some of whose members were educated and had found jobs in Rawalpindi. Everyone lived in *aman* and *chayn* (peace and security) and took part in each other's joys and sorrows.
>
> One (Hindu) boy of my age, Chunni Lal, studied with me. I used to visit his home and well remember his father Haveli Ram. His two brothers were working in Rawalpindi. Chunni Lal and I sometimes ate in each other's homes.[1]
>
> Two miles south of our village was a big village called Snauk Kalaan. In this village one-fourth were Hindus – hardworking and educated. One of them was Narain Das, an affluent man helpful with donations.

But Hayat's hero is the Sikh schoolteacher "Bhagat Saab" (*saab* or *sahib* being a suffix for the powerful or the eminent in India and Pakistan):

> Nobody knew or needed to know the real name of Bhagat Saab. I first met him in 1939 when I was in the fourth class. He was 60–65, had a short beard, a white turban, a pink-and-white complexion. He enjoyed smoking the *hookah* [water-pipe]. We boys kept the *angithi* [clay oven] burning for his *hookah*. He knew all the principals and headmasters of Gujrat *tehsil* and used to get tuition fees excused for poor boys, especially poor Jat boys. I was with him once in Snauk Kalaan when he said something in Narain Das's ear. Narain Das then asked his son to bring some money. He brought thirty rupees. Bhagat Saab gave the money to me.

Hayat broke down while narrating this incident. But he added: "Bhagat Saab also said to me, '*Hisab rakho*' ('Keep an account')."

Hayat's father removed him from school in the sixth class but on Bhagat's persuasion re-enrolled him after 4 or 5 months. Hayat went on to matriculate in the first division and start a successful career. "Had it not been for Bhagat Saab," he said, "I would just have been cutting grass in my village." And he added: "I will never forget what [Bhagat Saab] said when we sat with him one day: 'God sends us to different homes with different religions. We get our religion through God's choice. Can we be blamed for it?'"

But when Partition was announced, Sikhs and Hindus in west Punjab and Muslims in east Punjab felt suddenly endangered. Recalled Hayat:

> On August 10, 1947, people said to Bhagat, '*Bhag jao*' ('Run off!'). 'I will not leave,' he said. He was living alone, as his wife was dead. Two sons and a daughter lived elsewhere (in west Punjab).
>
> He moved to live with our family, in a shed near our well. One day he heard that his daughter and son-in-law had been killed... Then news came of a train arriving from the east (from India) with bodies of dead persons – *poori gaddi katal ho gayee*. [The whole trainload – of Muslims trying to reach Pakistan – had been murdered.] After this, Bhagat Saab, now 70 or so, became very shaken and ill.

Hayat says he carried Bhagat Saab on the back of a bicycle to a *hakim* (doctor in traditional medicine) in the town of Sialkot, which was about 25 miles southeast. The ride to Sialkot and back took two nights and a day. But there was no improvement. Then a train with Hindu refugees heading for India was stopped near Gujrat town. "All on the train were killed," said Hayat. "I saw the scene." Here Hayat could not hold back his tears. He added: "After two or three days, Bhagat Saab *gayab ho gaye*. (He just disappeared.) *Inse achha insaan maine nahin dekha*." ("I haven't seen a finer human being.")

After Bhagat vanished, there were attacks by outsiders on Hindus and Sikhs still left in the village but the villagers refused to join in the frenzy.

> Leaders of the village sheltered the Hindus and Sikhs and at two in the night took them four miles on foot to safety at a camp for Hindus and Sikhs in Gujrat town. I walked with the party. In the camp I looked everywhere for Bhagat Saab. *Lekin Khuda ka banda tha, oopar chala gaya*. ("But, God's good man, he had gone up to heaven.")

Hayat was moved, and so were we. Reflecting on the painful events he had just recalled, Hayat observed that in 1947 a *zahreeli hawaa* – a poisonous wind – had hit the Punjab. Among the things it destroyed was a deep relationship between a Sikh teacher and a family of Muslim peasants. But the wind could not obliterate memory, and Hayat was able to recall that relationship for today's Muslims, Sikhs, and Hindus.

Abdur Rab Malik of Quetta, Balochistan

The family of Abdur Rab Malik, 84, a retired director in the excise department, originally belonged to Batala in Gurdaspur district in what is now Indian Punjab. "But I was born in Ziarat (a hill station near Quetta). Father had settled in Balochistan."

We interviewed Malik on July 22, 2005, in his house in Lahore's Model Town, where many well-off Hindus and Sikhs resided before Partition. A Hindu temple stood near the house, but with no sign of worshippers. Malik was happy to learn that coauthor Usha Gandhi's Sindhi (and Hindu) parents had lived in Quetta before leaving for India in 1947. Recalling events in Quetta, he spoke of his Sikh subordinate, sub-inspector Sardar ("chief," a term for a Sikh man) Rajinder Singh, whom he had called to his home to prepare a raid on a cinema house. "Rajinder Singh came at about 8.30 p.m. By this time riots had begun in the town and we could hear sounds of an uproar outside. The Sardar got frightened. I said, 'You are in safe hands, I'll take care of you.'"

Malik took out a *burqa* (the cloak that completely covers a woman, including head and face) for the Sardar to wear and accompanied him to his house, which was nearby, along with his own wife, also in a *burqa*, and two constables in uniform. He warned the Sardar not to leave his house.

The next morning Malik went to his subordinate's home and "personally took Sardar Rajinder Singh, his wife, and son to the railway station. Again, all were dressed in *burqas*. We went in a hired car and saw that they sat in the train. From Quetta to Lahore my people traveled with them. They reached their destination (in India), Darwaza Ram Bagh in Amritsar, from where he wrote a letter of thanks."

Malik also spoke of a Hindu, Seth Hemal Das – "the biggest sweetmeat merchant in town" – who lived three or four houses away. "The Seth served *mithais* free of cost to poets in his store." (These poets would have been mainly Muslims.)

One night, at the peak of the riots, the Seth's son Lilaram arrived at Malik's house with a bunch of keys in his hand – these were the keys to their shop. "I went to the Seth's shop, opened his safe, took out 24,000 rupees and the jewelry inside, brought the stuff home, put a *burqa* on Lilaram, accompanied him to his house, and delivered the valuables to his father." The next day Malik, along with his sergeants, accompanied the Seth and his family to Machh railway station, 50 miles from Quetta, and put them on a train. "They reached Karnal (in Indian Punjab) safe and sound."

But there were those, said Abdur Rab Malik, that he could not save:

> Sardar Ram Singh owned a furniture shop. Mr. Scott, the [British] superintendent of police, shot down dozens of rioters. I saw 20 bodies on the road. Going on a bicycle with a friend – I used a cycle those days – I saw Sardar Ram Singh coming in a Morris Minor. He was stopped by a crowd of Hazaras and Pathans, who pulled him out by his hair and burned him, placing him on the engine of his car... My own eyes, these sinful eyes have seen that sight.

Prem Pandhi, "Tennis Star"

Samina Akram Sayed, daughter and wife of police officers, told us in Lahore of her father's role in 1947 in protecting Prem Pandhi, one of India's tennis stars in the 1940s and later a leader in industry and education. Samina's account put us on a trail that led to a first-floor office in New Delhi's Connaught Place where, at the end of July 2005, we met 86-year-young Prem Pandhi and elicited his story.

A son of Chamanlal Pandhi, a lawyer from Lyallpur (now Faisalabad, about 100 miles west of Lahore), Prem graduated from Lyallpur, excelled in tennis and other sports, did a master's course in history at Lahore's Government College, and later also obtained law and education degrees. He received a teaching assignment at Lahore's prestigious Aitchison Chiefs' College, the tennis circuit continued, and then came a job in Lahore with a British firm, Bird & Co. An older sister, Bimla, was married to police officer Narinder Nath Chopra. Narinder lived in Lahore's Fort area, which was overwhelmingly Muslim, along with his brother Kedar Nath, also a police officer, and their mother.

On August 10 ("just before the peak of the carnage"), Prem's parents, his sister Bimla, Bimla's two young sons, and other relatives left for India. Prem stayed on in Lahore, thinking that "the madness" that had affected Lahore from June or so would soon end.

A week after Partition, around August 22, the two brothers, Narinder Nath and Kedar Nath, came in their police uniforms to Prem Pandhi's office on Mall Road, announced that they had been transferred to cities in India (Panipat and Delhi), and asked Prem to take them and their mother (who they said was waiting in a *tonga* on the street) to their Fort house in his car. Pandhi's car was parked on Mall Road. The plan, the brothers said, was to remove their belongings from the Fort house. Three or four *tongas* had been hired for the purpose. But 28-year-old Pandhi tried to dissuade them. The times are dangerous, he said. They insisted and added that the head of the police station in their area was a friend and had promised assistance. Prem took the brothers in his car to their Fort home. In 3 or 4 hours the *tongas* were loaded. But a couple of policemen came to the house and said that a big crowd had collected near the car; it was dangerous to go there. "Don't worry," said the brothers. "We are police officers and have revolvers."

Walking to the car, the mother, her two sons, and Prem Pandhi saw that the car's tires had been deflated. A crowd of 100 or 200 persons carrying *lathis* (metal-tipped bamboo staves) and daggers surrounded them, and many pounced on the two brothers. Prem Pandhi: "One brother was killed on the spot, the other seemed to have still some life left (but he soon died), and the mother, too, was hurt (she was rescued by the police). But nobody touched me. I was dressed in *shalwar kameez* [long loose shirt hanging over baggy ankle-length trousers; worn by many Muslims and some non-Muslim males in northern parts of the subcontinent] and Peshawari *chappals* (sandals) and taken for a Muslim."

Policemen took Pandhi to the police station and asked if he wanted to contact anyone. He phoned Anwar Ali, the deputy inspector-general of police, or DIG, whom he knew. Anwar Ali (father of Samina Sayed, whom we met in Lahore) said he would come immediately and instructed the station officer to protect Pandhi. Arriving with two jeeps and policemen with Sten guns, Anwar Ali took Prem in one of the jeeps, guns pointing outward, to his home. As they were leaving the station, Anwar Ali said to Pandhi: "By now the crowd knows you are a Hindu. My men will shoot and kill, but I cannot guarantee that you will remain alive."

He reached the Ali home and after 2 or 3 days there (for safety Pandhi was locked up in the bathroom whenever the DIG was not at home), Anwar Ali said to him: "You had better go away. It is impossible to keep your presence a secret, with servants and all. I have found you a seat on a plane to Delhi. Here is your ticket. You will go confidently to the airport, driving my car. It will be safer that way. No attention will be drawn." Pandhi recalled to us: "I drove to the airport, left the DIG's car there with the key inside, boarded the plane and reached Delhi." After a brief pause he added, "I don't think I have paid Anwar Ali for the ticket."

Samina Sayed visited India earlier in 2005 and managed to meet Prem Pandhi. In Lahore she told us: "We were in tears when we met. In 1947, I was a very young girl. All I knew then was that this man who seemed in trouble was staying in our home and there was an air of secrecy about his stay."

The 1947 killings occurred in both Punjabs despite the presence of police and army officers (Indian and British) and of political leaders. Officials did not – they felt they could not – prevent the outbreak. Yet some lives were saved even while many perished.

Sughra Rasheed About Jalandhar (Jullundur)

Years earlier we had learnt from Aroona Kamal, a friend in Pakistan, that several persons related to her family had died in east Punjab in 1947. On July 19, 2005, we went to her mother's home in Thokar Niaz Baig in Lahore and met others from her family, including an aunt, Sughra Rasheed, who had been connected to the city of Jullundur (now Jalandhar) in east Punjab, and who, Aroona told us, had lost close relatives in 1947. Sughra Rasheed told us that in 1947, she was a young wife and mother in Delhi. Her husband, Abdur Rasheed, was a railway officer from a family from the villages Singhpura and Uggi near Jullundur. The husband's brother was a young doctor, also Delhi-based. The husband's father (a retired railway officer) lived in the railway colony in Jullundur city. We asked Sughra Rasheed for the names and ages of those who had been killed in August 1947 in Jullundur. Her answer, which was given clearly, calmly, and solemnly, and filled with brief pauses as she tried to remember with precision, follows.

> Dr Badruddin, the father of my husband. He was 60. Fatima, his (my husband's) mother. She was 55. Jamila, their newly married daughter, my husband's sister. She was 25. Tahira, their younger daughter, who was 22. Qutubuddin, my husband's *nana* (maternal grandfather), who was also my *dada* (paternal grandfather). He was 80. Idu, a *mulazim* (employee or servant). Idu's wife Fateh. Five children of Idu and Fateh.

Aroona and her mother were present when Sughra Rasheed spoke these sentences in their Thokar Niaz Baig home. It seemed that they too were hearing the names recited for the first time. We were greatly moved by this brief re-creation, through naming, of the dead, and perhaps specially by the naming of the servants. Like the vast majority of the killed in 1947, the servants had lacked the means or the critical contacts – in the military, or the police, or the railways – that made escape possible for many of the better-off, though not, in this case, for Sughra's relatives.

> The family was living in a Hindu *mohalla* [locality or neighborhood] on the main road with only two Muslim homes. *Amne-samne* (directly in front of us) was a Hindu family who had said to my husband's family, 'Don't go away.' I remember two girls from that family, Sheela and Dhannu. I don't think the family could have been involved. I think they were helpless before the attackers.

Sughra also had a "good" story to tell. Her husband's older brother Sharif was in Solan (also in east Punjab) with his young wife and 2-month-old daughter. Their lives, said Sughra, were protected by Hindu friends who then helped them to move across to west Punjab. But Sughra's *nani* (maternal grandmother), Ayesha, who was part of a walking caravan trying to reach Pakistan, died on the way, as also the *nani's* sister Jeena.

After recounting these events, Sughra said: "*Itna Jullundur yaad aata hai. Jab koi Jullundur ki baat karta hai, dil mein kuch ho jaata hai.*" ("I remember Jullundur so much. Whenever anyone speaks of Jullundur, something happens inside my heart.")

The Power of Stories

After the Lahore interviews, we offered our stories to *The Tribune*, the best known of the Punjab's newspapers. Started in 1881 in Lahore, the newspaper moved to east Punjab after Partition. Today it is published from Chandigarh (the city designed by Corbusier; it was built after Partition) and also from New Delhi, which became in many ways a Punjabi city after Partition and the arrival of Sikh and Hindu refugees. (Chandigarh serves as the joint capital of Indian Punjab and the adjacent Indian state of Haryana.) Our articles had been accepted but not yet been published by *The Tribune* when, in September 2005, we presented some of our research at the University of Illinois. At that presentation it was asked whether, given continuing Muslim/non-Muslim and India/Pakistan mistrust, the articles were likely to get a positive or a negative reaction. We did not know and said so. But, in fact, the response was entirely positive.

The Tribune carried our three-part report on October 16, 23, and 30, 2005. The series was entitled "Insaniyat amidst insanity." A word common to Hindi, Urdu, and Punjabi, *insaniyat* means humanity or humaneness. Four letters to the editor were published in response, all indicating an impressive if intangible spirit.

From the city of Patiala, Aneet Randhawa wrote in *The Tribune* on October 30, 2005:

> My grandmother often narrated to me incidents related to the Partition which describes the benevolent acts of my great-grandfather Biswedar Basant Singh, better known as Hakeemji, during the Partition mayhem. My native village Lakha Singh Wala in Fatehgarh Sahib district, in east Punjab, had a considerable population of Muslim peasantry. As the communal hatred spread, Muslims became vulnerable targets. They often had to take refuge in sugarcane fields. Basant Singh personally delivered food and other necessities to the hiding Muslim brethren. Post-Partition, some of the Muslims regularly corresponded with my great-grandfather and expressed their gratitude. I would like to dedicate an Urdu verse to such saviours of humanity. *Maine us waqt bhi baanta amrit subko/Jis waqt tha fizaon mein bhi zahar ghula hua* (I distributed nectar at a time when even the environs were poisoned to the core)."

Subhash C. Tajeja wrote from Rohtak on November 8:

> I honestly could not control my tears at the pathetic situation that prevailed at the time of Partition. The persons who were living like brothers became bitter enemies and there was bloodshed on both sides. But it is also on the record that *lakhs* [hundreds of

thousands] were saved by the members of both communities in Pakistan as well as in India. They remember each other for these acts of timely help extended to them at very crucial and dangerous moments. Now both countries are taking steps towards peace. May good sense prevail forever and feelings of hatred perish.

From Hoshiarpur, Professor Parveen Rana noted on November 20:

> Thousands of families perished during Partition within no time... Though the unruly mob did not spare anyone, even then there were some families who, at the risk of their lives, saved their neighbors of other faiths.

Brigadier H.S. Sandhu wrote from Panchkula on December 11:

> In our own case, our grandfather refused to leave our village, Manian Kalan, near Barki, in Lahore district during the riots. He was protected by our Muslim neighbors for four days despite repeated warnings by the attacking mobs. Ultimately, our grandfather was brought to India [against his will]. The shock of leaving behind his home and hearth affected him mentally and he passed away within a month of coming to India. The writers have done a commendable job by providing a healing touch to millions who continue to relive the scenes of those dark days.

Though containing an exaggeration ("millions" did not read the articles), the last sentence is indicative of the healing and hope experienced through a reminder of the humanity that defied, and reduced, the inhumanity of 1947.

In a letter that *The Tribune* forwarded to us, P.S. Bhatti from Dera Beas in Amritsar District wrote of how in 1947 he was saved in Dheri near Rawalpindi by a Muslim colleague who gave a timely warning not to go that evening to the card game that had become a regular feature of his evenings. A group had "arranged to kill all the three Hindu members of the cards team, including myself. Altaf Hussain came to know about this plot and saved the three of us. Such a kind and noble friend I had in Altaf Hussain Akhtar."

Since each person actually sending a letter to a newspaper represents many others who think like him or her but do not take the trouble to write, we assume that the *insaniyat* stories passed on by us through *The Tribune* reminded a fair number of people of the *insaniyat* they had experienced, witnessed, or hoped for.

On returning from Lahore to our home south of New Delhi in Palam Vihar, Gurgaon, we related portions of our research to Rajinder Das and Prabha Mathur, who have been our friends for decades. We were aware that Prabha Mathur had spent her early years, before Partition, in Lahore, but what came out on July 26, 2005, was totally fresh to us:

> My father was an officer in the Prisons Department of Punjab. We lived in Model Town, Lahore. My father had good relations with his Muslim colleagues who told him around August 10, 1947 that Hindus were no longer safe in Lahore and that he should leave with his family for India at once. I was thirteen and the eldest of six children. Within hours we packed our belongings and managed to reach the railway station. A Hindu family we knew came to the station with food for our journey. As our train rolled away the father of this family was stabbed on the platform. He must have died. I saw it happening. But my father's Muslim colleagues had saved our lives.

We moved to Simla. In our home we hid for several days a young Muslim man, a servant. We had known him in Lahore but he happened to be in east Punjab when Partition occurred and somehow turned up at our place. It was difficult to keep him without people getting to know. After some days we had to ask him to leave. Fortunately he was able to reach the other side – we heard from him.

In September 2006, in a living room in Urbana, Illinois, we were told the following story about a Lahore area village and Jullundur after we had spoken of our Lahore interviews. At our request it was written out by the narrator, Indra Aggarwal:

I am narrating one of the most memorable events in my life. This is a true story of a little Hindu girl by the name of Paro, who lived in village Bachiko, one of the villages near Lahore City during partition time of India and Pakistan. She was around six years old when her family was killed during riots but she survived due to help given to her by a passerby who happened to be a Muslim. The day her family was killed, she had gone alone to buy something and while coming back, she noticed from a distance that her house and nearby houses were being burnt. Out of fear she tried to hide behind a big tree but was seen by a Muslim man who took her to his place. He was afraid that if Paro stayed there, she would be killed.

This Muslim man (whose name is not known) worked as a gardener in the house in Lahore of a Hindu engineer with the army, who was planning to leave Lahore for India. The gardener asked his employer to take Paro with him. This Hindu officer, who was leaving Lahore for Jullundur, happened to be my father's colleague. While in Jullundur, he had to go to another town to take care of his family, so he decided to bring Paro to our place with the intention of coming back after a few days and take her with him.

For some reasons, he got delayed and could not come back for several days. Meanwhile, Paro started having a good time with us (five sisters and two brothers close to her age). She came from a poor family and was very much fascinated by a big house and a lot of food to eat whenever she wanted. During that period, my parents had sheltered several refugees which was another source of excitement for her. When that officer came back to get her she did not want to go with him. My parents suggested that she could stay with us and he agreed happily. She became part of our family and eventually got married. Now in her mid-sixties, she is living with her son in Meerut.

Conclusions

What have we learned? Our project confirmed that 1947 provides two kinds of stories, not the story of cruelty alone. That help came from the Other was known but seldom expressed in most accounts. When mentioned, it was as an aside and in general or hazy terms. Specific instances and details were rarely recorded. Often we noticed that close relatives present at our interviews were hearing the stories for the first time. And we saw that relating the stories did something for tellers *and* listeners. The study underlined the fact that the mirror image is a powerful reality of the Partition story.

There was parity not only in the numbers of Muslims and non-Muslims killed in 1947 but also in the numbers of refugees who moved in opposite directions; Muslim Punjabis spoke of Sikh and Hindu helpers, and Hindu and

Sikh Punjabis spoke of Muslim helpers. *Insaniyat* wore a Hindu face, a Sikh face, and a Muslim face. And insanity too wore all three faces. The story was not of the "infidel" Hindu or Sikh facing the "flawed" Muslim. It was of humans facing other humans, of persons who terrifyingly fall and also of persons who nobly save. We (Indians and Pakistanis, Hindus, Sikhs, Jains, and Muslims) were the same in cruelty and also, mercifully, in kindness. There was a frightening and yet consoling symmetry.

We found that the Punjab is, both Punjabs are, blessed with an intangible heritage of humaneness, which gets enriched as stories of the sort related here are recovered. This heritage is part of what many Punjabis on both sides of the border call *Punjabiyat*, which can be translated as Punjabiness, or the Punjabi way. Music, food, and a common language are vital parts of *Punjabiyat*, but so is *insaniyat*, or help of a timely, brave, or ingenious kind.

We also learned that numbers and dates are essential but insufficient. There is a vast difference between knowing how many were killed and when, and sitting with and listening to Punjabis with memories of 1947. The face of suffering lives long after numbers and dates are forgotten. So often it is a face also of hope.

The poor were the vast majority of the killed and perhaps also of those who saved. But their stories are harder to catch, their names more difficult to record, and their faces harder to fix. It is a challenge to wrestle with.

Some discoveries were less broad but also interesting, such as finding Muslim appreciation of the role of Sikh teachers in Muslim-majority parts of the Punjab. But perhaps the most important lesson is that for many in both parts of the Punjab, a healing process is near at hand. Waiting to be told are stories that will heal. Before the well dries up, all who can draw water should do so. All who can should record what they, or another person not far away, may recall about mercies in 1947.

Acknowledgments We are grateful to Friedrich Naumann Stiftung, New Delhi, for supporting our travel to and stay in Lahore.

Notes

1. This statement indicates that the commensal act was unusual. The notion of a Hindu home being polluted if a Muslim ate there came up in more than one interview.

References

Khosla, Gopal Das
    1950 *Stern Reckoning: A Survey of the Events leading up to and following the Partition of India*. Reprinted in 1989. Oxford University Press, New Delhi.
Menon, Ritu and Kamla Bhasin
    1998 *Borders and Boundaries: Women in India's Partition*. Rutgers University Press, New Brunswick.

Chapter 4
Gardens and Landscapes: At the Hinge of Tangible and Intangible Heritage

Michel Conan

Gardens result from the interlacing of nature and culture. This explains that their conservation might be concerned by three systems of norms for heritage conservation already promoted by UNESCO. These are the UNESCO Convention on the Protection of the Natural and Cultural World Heritage of 1972, the UNESCO Convention on Biological Diversity of 1992, and the UNESCO Convention for the Protection and Promotion of Cultural Diversity of 2005, which stresses the protection of cultural diversity through time and space, as well as the protection of intangible heritage, and which follows on the heels of the Convention for the Safeguarding of the Intangible Heritage (2003). Additionally, the Florence Charter, written in 1982 by ICOMOS, addressed gardens and garden preservation; because it was not issued by UNESCO, it lacked official clout. Until recently, the convention of 1972 was the unique reference for the whole architectural and garden heritage. However, since 2003, with the official acknowledgment of an interest in the intangible heritage of the human world, new questions are coming to the fore which should be discussed. Moreover, in these there are new questions regarding cultural assumptions of what constitutes heritage and how it should be preserved. This chapter will respond to these questions from cultural perspectives belonging to a few Asian cultures, as a reminder that Western cultural approaches may be unwillingly biased.

An Example of Garden Conservation in China

Numerous Chinese and foreign visitors to Suzhou nowadays enjoy a stroll in some of the famous historical gardens of Jiangnan, which have been recently restored to their material form during the late Qing period. The surge of garden restoration during the last decades in Suzhou has fostered a development of garden crafts, called "making mountains and waters" in Chinese. The development is often hailed as the recovery of the Chinese garden tradition and is

---

M. Conan (✉)
Landscape Studies, Dumbarton Oaks, Washington, DC 20007, USA
e-mail: michel.conan@gmail.com

currently exported to Canada and the United States, among others, where new Chinese gardens have been created in Vancouver, Montreal, Portland, Los Angeles, and New York City. This has produced the construction of a contemporary view of garden traditions resulting from mutual interactions between Western and Chinese scholars and professionals. It follows a pattern similar to the invention of the authentic Zen garden in early twentieth-century Japan demonstrated by Dr Miyuki Manabe-Katahira (2003) or the invention of a traditional garden in colonial India following the publication of *Gardens of the Great Mughal* by Constance Mary Villiers-Stuart in 1913 (Wescoat and Wolschke-Bulmahn 1996:17–18). These inventions of a garden tradition proceed from a sample of historical gardens presented as prototypical and proclaim that their material form stands for an embodiment of the essence of a long-lasting national *zeitgeist*. Each contributes to contemporary culture in their respective context, leading both to invented traditions and so-called garden style revival, but also to modernist interpretations of a fictitious past, as in the case of the dry gardens created by Shigemori Mirei (1896–1975) for his own house. However, Chinese classical culture no longer blossoms in these gardens. The *kunqu* – the Chinese opera style studied by Isabel Wong in this volume – provides one among many possible such examples. This kind of dramatic performance, which has been recently registered as part of UNESCO World Intangible Heritage, is most typical of the Suzhou region.

Since the Ming dynasty, wealthy families in Suzhou used to build a stage in their gardens, often on the bank of the garden pond, which allowed representations of *kunqu* dramas as an intimate family entertainment. This is no longer possible: *kunqu* dramas are now presented on public theater stages built outside the renovated gardens for the entertainment of foreign and Chinese tourists, as just outside the Tuisii Yuan, the "Garden of Retreat for Thinking," near Suzhou. The renovated gardens are no less important; to the contrary, they attract unending crowds of visitors. But clearly something of the cultural life of traditional Chinese gardens has been lost. This means that recent reconstructions of historical gardens should not be seen, despite their explicit reference to the past, as contributions to cultural conservation because they fail to allow the pursuit of cultural modes of reception to which the historical gardens they purport to represent owed their existence.

Cang Lang Ting, regarded as the oldest existing garden in Suzhou, provides an example that has been studied in great depth by Xu Yinong (Fig. 4.1). It was established in 1045 by Su Shunqin (1008–1048), a poet and scholar-official who temporarily retired to Suzhou after being dismissed from office. He built a pavilion (*ting*) on a stream bank in the abandoned garden of a noble dignitary who had died 60 years earlier. He named it the Cang Lang pavilion, an allusion to a well-known line in a Confucian classic, the *Mencius*: "When the *cang lang* waters are clear, I can wash my hat strings in them; when the *cang lang* waters are muddy, I can wash my feet in them" (Xu 2007:15, and note 34). It is traditionally understood as an encouragement (to the mandarin wearing the official stringed hat) to contribute to government when court life is virtuous and to walk away when it becomes corrupt.

4 Gardens and Landscapes

Fig. 4.1 Cang Lang Ting: the pavilion at present (photo: M. Conan)

Five centuries later, in 1544, the monk Wenying, whose monastery occupied the site of the former garden, erected a new pavilion – the old one had vanished – naming it "Cang Lang Ting." On his orders, a scholar wrote an account of the conservation of the "Cang Lang Ting garden," thus shifting from the earlier emphasis on the pavilion to an emphasis on the garden where it stood. However, the major restoration of the garden did not take place until 1695 when a scholar-official, Song Luo, restored the garden and erected a new pavilion, not on the banks of the stream but atop an artificial hill (where the Cang Lang pavilion stands at present). He did this while publishing a complete edition of the poems of Su Shunqin (Xu 2007:22–23). This example of garden conservation was not predicated upon material continuity but upon the memory of Su Shunqin's personal engagement with nature on this site. It should be noted that there is still a small pond in the garden, but it cannot even be seen from the pavilion. Each following renewal of the garden proceeded from a similar interpretation of the cultural import of Su Shunqin poetry tinged by specific concerns of the patron conducting the restoration.[1] Thus the successive renovations of the garden contributed to the continuity of a lively scholar-official's culture expressed through poetry, painting, calligraphy, and gardens. It is illustrated in the pavilion's interior (Fig. 4.2) where a miniature landscape, a vase with garden decorations, flowers, bamboo, floral decoration on the screen and the furniture, and poems inscribed on the blinds of a recently restored pavilion can be seen.

Fig. 4.2 Interior view of a pavilion in Cang Lang Ting (photo: M. Conan)

The successive renovations of Cang Lang Ting did not aim, however, at representing the past garden, but rather at inscribing evocations of the poet's presence in the garden into active personal responses of the renovator to issues of his own lifetime. They illuminate the typical Chinese approach to garden renovation during the five centuries that preceded the Cultural Revolution. The first aim of the approach is to conserve the memory of the ethical attitude of a Confucian scholar toward politics and nature. Second, the garden name as well as some physical features of the site, such as the Cang Lang Ting entranceway across the river on which Su Shunqin used to come to this place, constitute a major source of continuity. Third, however, material transformation – rather than conservation – of buildings and garden features was considered legitimate when it enhanced the engagement of scholar-official with the memory of Su Shunqin. Fourth, the older garden built by an aristocrat in the tenth century is neither remembered nor regretted; to the contrary, it serves as a foil that contrasts the gardens that deserve to be remembered because they contribute to the long history of Confucian saints with those that can be forgotten because they were a testimony to aristocratic greed.

Other gardens in Suzhou have been conserved for different motives and Xu Yinong insists that we should not make the history of the conservation of Cang Lang Ting into a testimony of a supposed essence of garden conservation in China (Xu 2007). Instead Xu observes that the history of the conservation of each garden, such as the Lions Grove, rests upon a sequence of reinterpretation of a particular cultural attitude toward nature and that it addresses a specific audience, which is thus enabled to pursue the development of the corresponding cultural attitude.

The audience consisted of not only scholar-officials but other groups as well. The gardens in Suzhou and in other cities of the Chinese empire were often open to the common public, which lacked the subtleties of scholar-officials' thought. Untutored commoners did not engage in sophisticated appreciation but simply "rambled in crowds" to watch the flowers, the pavilions, kiosks, watersides, and scenic views while eating "fragrant sweets" and fruity cakes" or buying "gimmicks and toys" for children (Gu Lu 1830, in Xu 2007:221–222). This indulgence in consumption and sensual pleasures may seem comparable to the unsophisticated appreciation of Jiangnan gardens by contemporary crowds of Chinese tourists. Yet even the quest for sensual pleasures by commoners living in earlier centuries is quite different from the pursuit of self-representation in a famous place, through a purely visual and photographic culture, that can be observed in the renovated gardens of today.

Ancient gardens addressed different audiences of elites and commoners who responded differently to them with the passing of history – the elite in ethical, the commoners in hedonistic terms. Garden conservation in premodern China made a continuity of these cultural responses possible through time and dynasties. Today, in contrast, the contemporary pursuit of a fixed material image of these gardens has radically changed their cultural reception. The newly restored places are new gardens under an old name.

Defining the Historic Garden

We should not accept the definition of a garden as "a living monument" proposed in the Florence Charter for the conservation of all historic gardens. This remarkable oxymoron, which implies that life in nature can be reified, fails to take into account that gardens are cultural transformations of nature that enable humans to renew cultural bonds with nature, and thus with life itself.

A sixteenth-century painting by Nasuh Matrakçı provides a topographic representation of the Ottoman city of Konya, where a celebrated medresa is depicted at the bottom of the image just outside the city walls, while a celebrated garden, praised by the seventeenth-century Ottoman traveler Evliya Çelebi as one of the most marvelous gardens in the world, stretches over the two hills in the background, as indicated by the flowers, shrubs, fruit trees, and buildings (Atasoy 2007:202, 210–211). It does not fall within our usual understanding of either a garden or a landscape, since this place where the inhabitants of Konya came to spend the summer comprised hundreds of houses with orchards, as well as mosques, bazaar, and baths. This should alert us to the differences in the concept of a garden throughout history and space.

At various historical periods, cities such as Damascus, Kaifeng, Hangzhou, Suzhou, Marrakech, Granada, Isfahan, Genoa, Paris, London, Vienna, and Stockholm have been celebrated for their gardens to such an extent that some of their gardens set their mark upon the image of the city and are still remembered (see multiple essays in Conan and Wanghong 2007). Although the forms and design of these gardens are only partially known, we know how the cultural uses of nature they afforded to the inhabitants transformed the usage of the city, the habits of its inhabitants, and the skill of some categories of craftsmen. Yet there is no universal definition of gardens. They do not play a similar function in every city life and economy, and it would be wrong to generalize about the roles of gardens in city life and culture from any particular example of a historical city. The gardens also resulted from the initiatives of different groups of people, ranging from aristocrats and official administrators to horticulturists and commoners. The variety of gardens throughout world history prevents any generalized interpretation of the significance of their forms, habitual practices, and reception. Even the word "garden" is inadequate, because it does not translate clearly the different cultural forms of transformation of nature that allow a renewal of cultural bonds with nature. The various types of appropriation of natural space are given specific names in each language. In Chinese, the Suzhou gardens are called *yuan lin*, which means garden and grove, and very often they are designed to display miniature landscapes, *san shui,* at various scales. Any study devoted to a specific culture should use vernacular categories, and multicentered studies have to consider a broad category of space that enhances cultural bonds with nature. I use the phrase "gardens and landscapes" being fully aware that particular forms of space corresponding to this phrase should be specified according to each culture when engaging with specific examples.

Gardens and landscapes afford humans not only a renewed bonding with nature but also a renewed contact with horticultural, poetic, literary, musical, and pictorial uses of gardens in the past of their own cultures. Because gardens and landscapes contain time, culture, and nature and engage not only the senses but also the whole body, the mind, and the heart, they enable us to express our immersion in the flow of changing nature and culture. These bodily responses can be achieved through ritualized actions, such as a poetic response to a borrowed scenery, *jiajei*, in a Chinese garden; mystic appreciation of the scent of roses in a Persian garden; *hanami*, the ritual visit to cherry blossoms in the *meishos* of Japan; or the sacred processions around the groves of Braj in India. It is important to note that these rituals refer to a variety of spaces.

With respect to gardens in the Ottoman world, Walter Andrews (2008) observed that gardens and landscapes can be characterized by (1) forms of nature and its transformation (the material dimension), (2) ritualized as well as ritual practices (the embodied dimension), and (3) the reception by the audience. Thus gardens and landscapes partake of a three-tiered existence, even though each of these terms varies with the cultural context. The reception in particular can only be described as an interlacing of knowledge, beliefs, and imagination, three terms that vary for different cultures in meaning and importance. From this, I propose that we can define gardens and landscapes as places that enable a renewal of bonds with nature and of their poetics through material transformation of nature, ritualized as well as ritual practices, and cognitive as well as imaginary receptions (the intangible aspects of garden existence). Thus the existence of gardens and landscapes is embedded within social and cultural practices. It contributes to their historical development, and we may wonder whether gardens and landscapes can survive the demise of cultural practices for very long. Three examples from India, the Caribbean, and Britain demonstrate in what sense gardens articulate tangible and intangible heritage.

The Garden Groves of the Braj

A festival established in 1517 in the Braj region of India along the Yamuna river, the region where Krishna is thought to have spent his youth, celebrates the passionate love of Radha and all the cowherds for the deity. A popular theme in Indian painting is the image of Krishna who appears among the *gopis*, the cowherds of the Braj region, set against a flat landscape scattered with sacred groves. The 3-weeks-long festival was codified in 1543 by a text in Sanskrit "that enumerates the groves and their constitutive features and prescribes the rituals and itinerary of pilgrimage" (Shah 2007:153–172). Behula Shah (2007) has described how, on the first day, pilgrims leave the city of Mathura and cross the Yamuna river for a long clockwise tour of the region that lasts 23 days in August and September during the monsoon period. Every day they walk together, sing, pray, and celebrate a different moment of the history of Krishna in the Braj, following a specific itinerary to the corresponding grove, which they circumambulate ritually. The whole sacred landscape is comprised within a conceptual mandala forming an intangible square with a perimeter of about 143 miles, within which are located more than 50 groves of very different sizes (indicated as black dots on the map). Within the groves themselves, there are smaller consecrated garden groves "characterized by a cluster of trees that surround a water feature," which may be natural, agricultural, or built for the ritual. Building upon studies of performative action performed by rituals by Stanley Tambiah (1985), Shah explains that the pilgrims bring the sacred landscape and gardens into existence by walking and singing together along the ritual paths (Fig. 4.3). Here the Western categories of "garden" and "landscape" provide only a rather vague and inadequate way of describing precise differentiations of space that depend more upon the ontological status of place than on its material form or its conditions of creation. At the festival, each space is ontologically differentiated by the moment in Krishna's life to which it is consecrated. For 3 weeks the pilgrims circumambulate the whole of the sacred area, and everyday clockwise circumambulation of each grove and its interior garden groves constitutes an essential part of the ritual. The act of walking together through the ritual itineraries and attending the moments of sacred intensity in the narrative, as they reach the inner sanctum of the groves, transforms the agricultural into the sacred landscape of Braj. Everyday brings a new mystic experience and contributes to the building up of the whole landscape within the virtual mandala as a deeply sacred place. Finally, on the day after the end of the festival, the whole of it returns to its agricultural and pastoral existence. Thus the landscape and the gardens vanish out of existence as soon as the intangible meanings and emotions attached to the rituals come to an end.

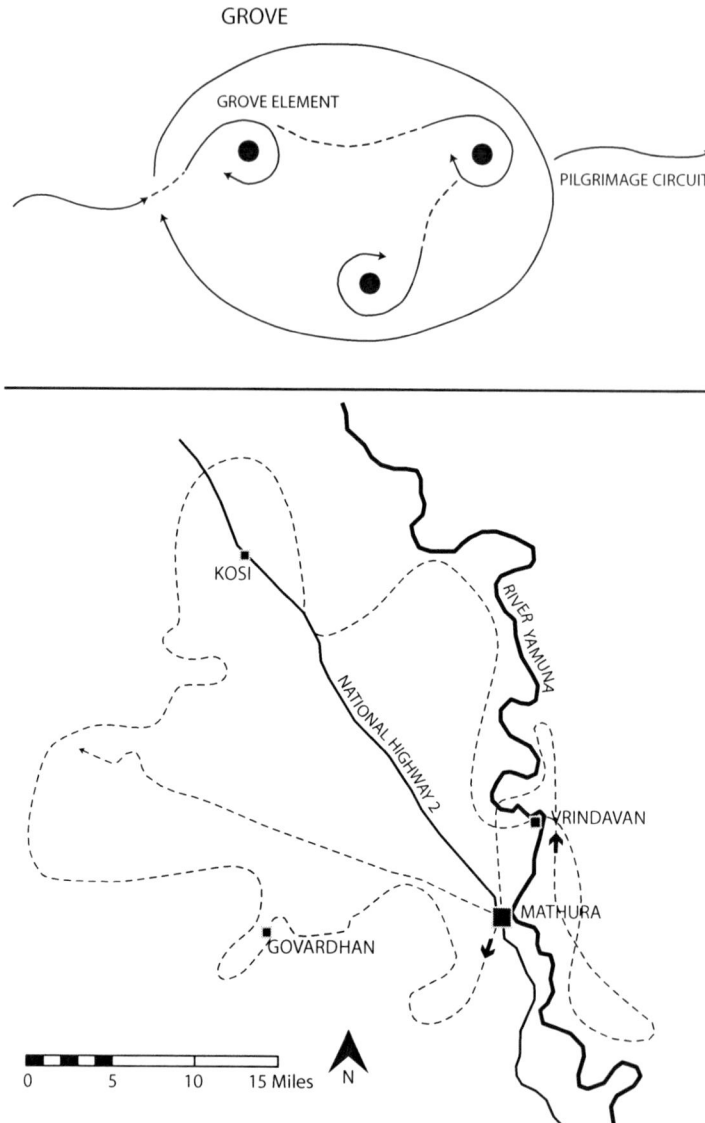

Fig. 4.3 Braj region, pilgrim itinerary and principle of circumambulation (P. Jain after Behula Shah)

Gardens of Slave Descendants in Guadeloupe

The gardens of slave descendants in the suburbs of Pointe-à-Pitre in Guadeloupe provide a completely different example of a deep metaphysical and personal significance of gardens for Creole islanders following their own version of the Catholic creed (Fig. 4.4). These are the gardens around their houses,

4 Gardens and Landscapes

Fig. 4.4 A garden in front of a cabin in Guadelupe (photo: Catherine Benoît)

and they look like abandoned ground, since they have no wall or fence around and they seem invaded by lush tropical weeds. Yet Catherine Benoît (2007), when studying vernacular medical practices, discovered that these gardens play a central role in the protection of the life of the house dwellers from attacks by evil spirits of dead souls floating in the air and pushed by the winds or the hostile intentions of sorcerers. Each garden contains a number of plants that have a particular apotropaic function and are planted in order to protect the windows and doors of the house. One of them, the *piésizé*, is mostly located to shield the master's bedroom from the evil spirits of the dead souls blown by the *alizé* wind. Their existence has to remain unspoken of, because speaking of evil spirits might summon them to the place. Moreover, because either neighbors, passersby, foreign visitors, or anthropologists may be sorcerers, it is necessary to conceal these magic plants within untended bushes of innocuous plants. The efficacy of their sacred geometry rests upon invisibility.

Moreover, Benoît discovered that the garden was part of the body of the dwellers, since their bodily existence was bound to plants and hidden caches in the garden. For instance, after child delivery, the placenta is buried at the foot of a tree in the garden and the child's life thereafter is bound to the life of the tree itself. Thus the garden is inextricably tied to the most intimate perception of self. However, when, in spite of all these protections, the sense of threat is too strong, some people resort to Protestant conversion. In that case, they change the form of the garden altogether, erasing the old, apparently derelict garden. Here again the intangible features of the garden are essential to its existence.

These examples of gardens in India and the Caribbean show that gardens are not purely material objects, as they are usually treated in the West. Moreover,

I would like to challenge the idea that gardens in the West can be reduced to their material components and show that, like the examples above, even British municipal parks give rise to rituals and to an ensuing intangible heritage.

Municipal Parks Bring Civility and Civilization to British Cities

Reception is a vital dimension of the meaning of public space, and it can vary significantly according to the identity of the users. David Lambert (2007) has demonstrated that a single municipal garden in a British city existed through not only one but two conflicting intangible forms of reception. It raises interesting questions about the conservation of cultural heritages resulting from social class conflicts. In mid-nineteenth-century England and Scotland, large cities such as London, Birmingham, Stoke on Trent, Bristol, and Glasgow developed public parks, because in the words of a politician in 1833 "the want of recreation generated incipient disease, discontent; which in its turn led to attacks upon the Government" (speech by Richard Slaney, MP for Shrewsbury, quoted in Lambert 2007:198). The contact with refined nature that these municipal parks offered was meant to civilize the urban poor, and yet, from the start, the parks were used in ways that deeply disturbed wealthy urban dwellers. As a consequence, municipalities hired guards and enacted laws to promote civilized behavior. The penalties for offenders were serious, and yet they failed to remove altogether some groups of city inhabitants such as young smokers and lovers from the working classes who insisted on using public benches to engage in courtship. Administrative reports attest that police spies were perfectly aware of the rituals of transgression and used this knowledge to try to catch people red-handed. In these parks, both civilized and transgressive behaviors were highly ritualized and promoted very different ways of understanding and imagining the use of the municipal park. There were deep conflicts about the propriety of games (such as soccer), public rallies, and bathing, all of which were activities of the working classes. Lambert shows that municipal parks were centrally concerned with educating the poorer classes into a newly invented tradition of gentility in public space and that these classes responded by attempting to appropriate the parks to their own views of legitimate public behavior. Thus, the parks were sites of social tension and ongoing cultural confrontations, and they were designed to curb popular mores and disseminate bourgeois ideals of public behavior. Any history of these parks that would simply describe their design, planting, iconography, and architecture would entirely miss their cultural significance.

These examples point to the great differences in the roles gardens and landscapes have played in the life of cities in different parts of the world. They demonstrate the relationships between habits, ritualized practices, and rituals in these parks and the meanings, emotions, and fantasies that were part and parcel of these gardens and landscapes. They also underline the strong ties between the cultural context and the intangible dimension of gardens and landscapes that command the life of these places and their profound transformation even when their material existence is unchanged.

The Dynamics of "Gardens and Landscapes" Culture in Japan

As noted earlier, the relationships between, on the one hand, immaterial, ritual, and cognitive, and, on the other hand, material aspects of a vernacular garden may break down under the impact of Westernization. In order to ponder the possibilities of a conservation policy that would not ignore the intangible aspects of the existence of gardens and landscapes, the impact of Westernization upon local cultures of place must be considered. This demands an understanding of the dynamics of the local culture of gardens and landscapes. In this respect, Japan provides instructive examples in Edo's cherry blossom festival, a garden in Ibaraki prefecture in the city of Koga, and a landscape in the city of Hiroshima.

The history of Japanese culture is unique and the observations made in this context should not be applied to the history of another culture. However, like other societies Japan has gone through large social and cultural changes that are reflected in the changing significance of its bonds to nature, and as a consequence in the changes of its gardens and landscapes. The study of the history of *hanami*, the ritual appreciation of cherry blossoms, by Sylvie Brosseau (2007) reveals an interlacing of changes and continuities of the material and the cognitive as well as imaginary aspects of landscape places predicated upon a very slow change of ritualized practices. *Prunus Sargentii* and *Prunus serrulata* variety *Spontanea* are two native varieties of cherry tree in Japan, which are largely distributed through the countryside (Kuitert 2007).

Hanami is an ancient practice of rural villagers who went into the countryside to meet the *kami*, the Shinto gods coming down from the higher mountains where they lived in the spring. Rural people were purified by these encounters at a most important time of the year, just before the beginning of the agricultural season. Later, between the eighth and tenth century, the practice of *hanami* was borrowed by aristocrats at the same time that they adopted models of courtly life and garden making from the Tang dynasty in China. In the eighth century, they also adopted a Chinese tree, the *prunus mume*, and they began to write poetry to capture their experience of its blossom, and in the ninth century, an urban court life (Brosseau 2007:96–97). Thus court practices conserved the rural *hanami* while transforming it. All of these innovations resulted in a development of *hanami* for purely aesthetic reasons in urban court gardens as well as in the mountain places around the city of Heian-Ko, where wild cherry trees blossomed.

These practices went through some slight changes such as the choice of a new favored tree variety and the codification of the rituals in the courts of Kyoto. A major change occurred at the end of the Japanese middle ages when the Tokugawa shoguns took power and established their seat in Edo, ushering a new era of Japan history, the Edo Period (1615–1847). The cherry trees from Yoshino became the favorite variety until the present day (Kuitert 2007:132). Starting with the third Shogun, Tokugawa Iemitsu, many *meisho* (famous places) were created by planting large numbers of Yoshino cherry trees and inviting the public. Thus, from having been a poetical practice of courtiers, *hanami* became a leisure activity enjoyed by the numerous urban dwellers of Edo. This form of appreciation of nature was extended to other nature phenomena in the *meishos*: enjoying prunus and peach blossoms in the spring, looking at wisteria and lotus blooming as well as listening to insects' chirping in the summer, watching red maple leaves in the autumn. Despite some changes in ritual, these practices provided a sense of continuity between the past and the present and between city, court, and rural life.

Sylvie Brosseau (2008) explains how the *meishos* and the practices of *hanami* evolved during the Edo period, but she also shows the transformation that resulted when Japan was opened to Western culture in the Meiji era (1868–1912). The government in the Meiji period attempted to transform Edo into a modern city, shifting from Chinese to Western models in its quest for cultural development. Most of the old *meishos* were destroyed to leave room for new forms of land use; only later did the creation of the new public park in the Western manner at Hibiya, and the designation as park of a few other places – some of them on the site of former *meishos* – allow a renewal of *hanami*.

More parks have been created since, enjoyed by large crowds of Tokyo dwellers who celebrate the New Year by enjoying the cherry blossom. The experience may call to mind memories of ancient agricultural rituals, and yet it is completely different. Tokyo inhabitants nowadays practice *hanami* not only during the daytime, but more importantly as an evening outing with family, friends, fellow students, or business colleagues (Fig. 4.5). Groups of people

Fig. 4.5 Hanami in the evening in Ueno Park, Tokyo (photo: Sylvie Brousseau)

engage in a ritual of purification during an evening spent under the cherry blossoms while drinking and exchanging memories about events of the past year, thus preparing a fresh start for the social, educational, and business opportunities of the New Year. During the whole night, the boss of the company listens to exchanges between the employees venting their feelings about events in the firm during the past year (Brosseau 2008). These rituals give rise to shared dramatic experiences in which everyone is both actor and spectator. It is a time of collective and public renewal of self that transposes the ancient rural ritual into a modern urban context, thus anchoring the new self in both the deep (almost mythical) and the recent past. The spontaneous practice of *hanami* went through periods of drastic change, even of disruption, and yet its survival demonstrates that it has maintained significance and still provides memories of intangible past attitudes toward nature.

While the *hanami* is an example of adaptive continuity, an example of deliberately maintained conservation of the traditional Japanese attitude toward nature can be seen in the public park of Koga and the reconstruction of an embankment on the Otogawa river in Hiroshima.

The Re-creation of a Garden at Koga

In spite of the ongoing reinvention in contemporary Tokyo of the enjoyment of nature during the Edo period, rural practices binding a sense of nature to bodily experiences tend to be less and less understood by younger generations of city dwellers. This has prompted the development of several interesting initiatives by citizens of the city of Koga, north of Tokyo, which has strongly impacted the design, uses, and meanings attached to the newly created public park of Koga.

This park was initiated by the municipality in the 1970s to re-create a famous local site, a palace with a pond later planted with thousands of peach trees that had been created by the Ashikaga family in 1455 when they established the shogunate of Koga. The site endured until the 1920s when it was last enjoyed by crowds coming there for the spring festival. Thereafter it was abandoned, the pond turned into a marsh, and the marsh drained for rice fields. By the mid-twentieth century, the Ashikaga Park was but a memory. In 1972, Japan's economic growth led to a policy of reduction of the rice fields, and the space once occupied by the pond reverted to the state of marshland. It prompted the mayor of Koga to move toward a re-creation of the historic park as an evocation of the Shogunate years. But since the Ashikaga Park had developed over several centuries, the restoration could not return to a single point in time: instead a pastoral landscape, the conservation of the ruins, and the construction of an historical archive inside the park were planned to evoke the historical presence of the former park. Between 1972 and 1977, a peach grove with an iris paddy and a lotus pond, and a hydrangea garden and a play facility were created, and two old farm houses were transferred to the site to add a note of staged authenticity. The unfinished park was opened to the public, but due to political changes in the city, few other site developments occurred until 1988 when Professor Yoshio Nakamura (from the Technical University of Tokyo) was asked to conduct a public review of the park and revise its master plan. Nakamura discovered that some groups in the public had appropriated the park during the interregnum period, with little attention for the attempts at creating a rehabilitated image of the Shogunate past. And he prepared a project for resuming the construction of the park based upon his interpretation of the public attitudes revealed by his investigation of actual practices in the park.[2]

The ensuing project had four interesting aspects. First, it was built upon the already existing park amenities while introducing radically new designs (Fig. 4.6); second, it was undertaken to restore the ancient pond ; third, capitalizing on initiatives clearly taken by local associations, it was proposed to make the park into a civic center where people could engage in the discovery of ancient ritual practices of agriculture and aesthetic appreciation of nature, under the aegis of local associations devoted to one or the other of these activities; and fourth, it created the position of "Parkmaster" in charge of supporting programs to enhance the "citizen's life in the park." This last aspect points to the clear awareness in Koga's official circles of the importance of public reception as a constituent of the park itself. Later, in 2003, a park management committee of local citizens was established to work with the Parkmaster in discussing management issues and planning events, in particular with the 12 citizen groups active in the park (Suga and Iwahori 2004:5).

The aim no longer was the construction of a park in the manner of Western historical gardens, that is, a mythical image of a fixed past. Instead, it presented

Fig. 4.6 Entrance to the newly redesigned park at Koga (photo: M. Conan)

a place where local town people could discover and bodily experience the historic link to nature of their rural ancestors. The view at the entrance showed a newly created pond that could bring to mind memories of the ancient pond and its traditional use by local people, such as fishing.

Professor Nakamura's philosophy of landscape design developed to a large extent as a result of the dynamics of this project, which developed slowly during the different tenures of Koga's Mayor Ogura (1988–1991 and 1995–1998). During this last period, Japan's financial crisis aggravated the economic difficulties of city governments, leading Professor Nakamura to propose that an even greater emphasis be given to local initiatives in giving shape to new forms of cultural appropriation of the park. The 20-hectare park developed around a reconstructed pond surrounded by marshy banks and spanned by a modern suspended bridge. A small number of specific places were created, such as hills for viewing the distant landscape of Mount Fuji or the sunset, a visitor's center, and a series of symbolic gardens on which it opens. The hill has been spontaneously appropriated by children as a sledding slope during the winter: this is detrimental to some of the planting but it has been accepted as an aspect of the park's vitality. Moreover the design of the *Jelateria* and teahouse is unhesitatingly modern and the gardens in front of it deliberately mix Western-style lawn and flower beds and representations of both traditional and contemporary Japanese landscape. In particular, they introduce spectacular techniques of modern landscaping presently used by civil engineers in Japan, together with a traditional use of miniature trees in a garden and a bonsai in the foreground (Fig. 4.7).

Fig. 4.7 The garden at the Jelateria with European and contemporary landscape features (photo: M. Conan)

Local Koga citizen associations had no nostalgia for the times of aristocratic rule but lamented the great divide between the rural past of Japan and the urban present, because it implied a loss of the ancient sense of nature. They wanted to retrieve the lost link to water, seasons, and cultivation that had been at the heart of many cultural developments in Japan including the enduring habit of quoting and composing poetry and catching insects to engage poetically with them at home. Thanks to their proposals and practical activities, the park once again became a place for experiencing traditional links to nature. At present, these activities include angling, kite flying, haiku writing during the peach blossom season, planting and reaping rice fields, cultivating tea trees, and ritually reaping, drying, and selling the young tea leaves. Of course none of these practices reflect the everyday life of Koga town dwellers. The inhabitants are no longer full-time rice or tea farmers. Rather, the traditional activities of the agricultural season are selectively enacted by the general public under the guidance of members of the associations. These dramatic moments constitute rituals that allow people to watch or engage in a representation of rural activities (Fig. 4.8). However, the fact that the city people of Koga are the actors of these representations makes the link with nature that they symbolically express their own. The young children who tramp in the rice field to replant seedlings engage momentarily in identification with rural rice farmers, experiencing the cold of water,

Fig. 4.8 Children replanting rice at Koga (photo: Yoshio Nakamura)

the thud of slimy earth, the toil of field work in their bodies, their feelings, and their minds in a way that is far more memorable than any media representation. Their own bodies are the register of their memories.

These are only a few of the possibilities of engaging with past practices of nature. Some are rather traditional community rituals: flying kites, enjoying peach blossoms, or cutting reeds for the autumn festival. Others, like place naming, derive from practices to be found in a few Daimyo gardens (Fig. 4.9). This is how the park at Koga has developed as a cooperative enterprise between the municipality and independent local associations focused on the conservation of various aspects of the intangible heritage of cultural bonds to nature. It is a very popular place and has helped fuel the development of a new historical consciousness in Koga of the relationship of humans to nature that is historically Japanese.

Fig. 4.9 "The Meadow of Spring Grass," a place name along the Goshonuma pond (photo: M. Conan)

The Otagawa Embankment Project in Hiroshima

The Koga Park example illustrates a popular response to changes in rural practices in Japan. Yet these are not the only changes in social practices that have radically altered the Japanese engagement with nature. Civil engineering – the making of roads, bridges, canals, waterways and harbors – has introduced a view of nature developed by Western engineers that reflects the reductionist view of material nature developed by Western science. Engineers consider this to be the necessary and sufficient horizon of understanding and transforming nature; however, it clashes with traditional Japanese engineering techniques, ritualized practices of places by the common people, and their horizon of perception and imagining nature. Its impact is pervasive because it is ubiquitous. It introduces new human–nature relationships that are taken for granted at present but which make some of the ancient bonds to nature impossible.

Because Hiroshima is located on the river Otagawa's delta, it is exposed to devastation by typhoon tides that flood the embankment of the river. This problem has been made ever more pressing by large urban developments in the center of the city. A project to make a solid uniform bank that would allow a swift flow of the water caused a wide range of debates in the municipality because it would have prohibited any use of the bank for public walks. Professor Nakamura was called for advice in 1976. He knew that walks along the river have been a source of public delight for many centuries in many Japanese cities but conducted a study that revealed that local inhabitants no longer perceived the river as part of Hiroshima's cityscape. He studied the river banks to discover some traces of their historical uses and meanings (Fig. 4.10). Finding traces of traditional jetties that had been used in the past to abate the force of the water flow, he proposed to re-create and shape them in such a way that people could walk on them in order to enjoy proximity to the water (Fig. 4.11). He also advocated tree planting and preservation, in opposition to the rules of the river management administration that prohibit planting trees on its domain. Finally, he drew attention to the proximity of the memorial dome where a

Fig. 4.10 Proposed re-creation of ancient jetties (courtesy: Yoshio Nakamura)

4 Gardens and Landscapes

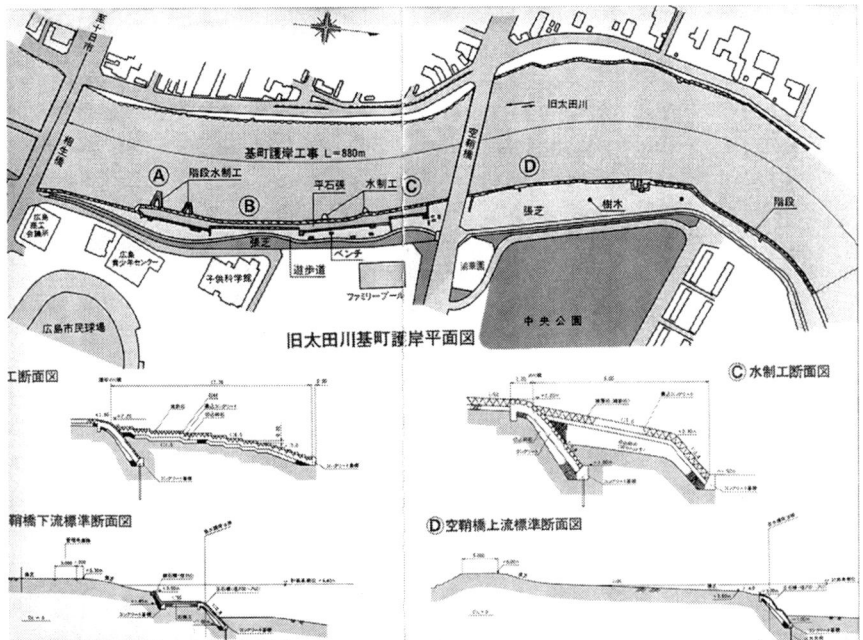

Fig. 4.11 The Project by Yoshio Nakamura (courtesy: Otagawa work office, Hiroshima)

commemoration of the city's destruction by an A-bomb takes place every year on August 6. Thus, following the "inventive analysis method" of the French landscape artist Bernard Lassus (1998:57–59), he proposed three different modes in which the city could relate to the past along this bank: a technical heritage that was largely ignored, the living presence of ancient trees, and a cultural observance of a historic human drama.

None of these was acceptable to the flood-control authorities. But Professor Nakamura engaged in both technical and cultural designs and negotiated with the port authority for a scheme comprising several parts. Each of them followed a specific design that responded to the city landscape close to the river and the forces of erosion caused by typhoon floods. On the part close to a high-rise center and very exposed to erosion, he proposed a lower bank of round stones, leaving enough room for a long promenade alley, with a higher part made of a granite wall above it, then leading to a gentle green slope. Under this lower bank he reconstructed four small dikes using the same technique as traditional protection dikes. Upstream where the green hills are silhouetted against the sky, he proposed only the construction of a simple gentle green slope with the single poplar tree that could be saved, protected at waters edge by a round stone wall (Fig. 12). In the last zone, close to the A-bomb memorial dome, he created five waterfront terraces for meditation, and a longer terrace stepping into the waters was built for praying and for the lantern-flowing ceremony when lanterns are put on the water in remembrance of the victims of the A-bomb (Fig. 4.13).[3]

Fig. 4.12 General view of the project with the single tree and the lawn used by the associations with the cherry trees they planted in the background (photo: Otagawa work office, Hiroshima)

Fig. 4.13 One of the terraces near the A-bomb Memorial Dome (photo: M. Conan)

It took much negotiation with higher authorities and a clear demonstration that it made sense from a flood-control perspective and not only from a cultural one in order to get the first two parts of the project completed. The next parts were easier because these embankments soon became one of the most haunted outdoor spaces in the city, being used for the spring festival after a local group donated a row of cherry trees to be planted along the bank. Another group was formed to save the poplars along the river. The tree was blown out by a hurricane in 2004, and they mobilized to have it replanted and make sure it gave rise to more trees on the spot. They also mapped its DNA in order to trace its natural history. The dikes have become places to achieve a close experience of the river, and mostly the terraces along the A-bomb memorial dome have become the places for solemn commemorative rituals for the repose of the souls on the night of August 6.

This project has triggered changes in local attitudes toward the river, which do not necessarily follow from the intentions of the landscape designer. It is not certain that the traditional technique of dike protection against erosion is perceived as such by people who enjoy walking on them. And it is too soon to know whether the river authorities will adopt the ancient dykes as part of their own historical heritage. What is clear, however, is that contemporary design may contribute to the conservation of tangible and intangible cultural heritage of gardens and landscapes whenever it gives rise to an autonomous process of development of traditional culture.

Conclusion

In the preceding examples, some ritualized practices were reinstated while at the same time new leisure practices developed. Some visitors are directly engaged as actors in these activities, while others are merely spectators, and yet for all of them these gardens and landscapes offer a link between past and present cultures, forms, and practices of nature.

Let us return to the definition of gardens and landscapes to demonstrate this point about the Koga and Hiroshima projects. (1) Their forms and material appearance are largely modern, but they display features belonging to or evocative of the past; (2) they give rise to habitual and ritual uses some of which are traditional, others modernized versions of a tradition, and still others quite new; (3) they imbue nature with meanings attached to the past and the present, and they invite flights of imagination either to the past or the future. This observation applies equally to Koga, Hiroshima, and to the public parks of Tokyo studied by Brosseau even though the form, rituals, and cultural reception of each of them is different. These examples suggest that the conservation of gardens and landscapes does not depend so much on their material continuity with the past, but rather on the existence of strong cultural symbols and citizen's initiatives – their intangible heritage.

These conclusions apply to Japan; in any other context, the processes of cultural change of ritualized practices and renewal of attitudes toward nature and the cultural responses to Westernization would have to be analyzed before we could hope to engage in the conservation of the intangible heritage of gardens and landscapes. The two Japanese examples, however, present some bewildering aspects. It is tempting to think that historic garden culture would be easier to keep alive in the context of historically protected gardens. And yet, the Otagawa river bank conservation and the Koga park example call attention to the possibility of conserving intangible aspects of local culture attached to gardens and landscapes in physical contexts where only a few traces of ancient design remain. The embankment of the Otagawa river has become a new linear park in the center of Hiroshima, and yet in spite of its novelty, it has also revived the old cultural pleasure of enjoying the river and thus is directly linked to the past cultural bonds to rivers and waterways in Japan. The same applies to the marshes in which the Koga Park has been created. Moreover, unlike historical gardens which are entirely devoted to aesthetic appreciation of the garden as historical artifact, these newly revived parks are less scripted and thus are open to unspecified popular uses (Fig. 4.14). These paradoxes call into question the utility for contemporary communities of the more static restoration criteria by the Florence Charter.

Fig. 4.14 A family rest area in Koga Park (photo: M. Conan)

Interestingly, one of the few Daimyo parks still surviving in Japan is located a few hundred meters away from the meadow planted with cherry trees along the Otagawa river. It was established in 1620 by Asano Nagaakira, the newly appointed Daimyo of Hiroshima. It was called *Shukkein* (miniature garden), and the *Takuei* pond around which it was planted (Fig. 4.15) may have been an attempt at representing the celebrated West lake in Hangzhou. The other miniature landscapes in this garden present among many other scenes, a small tea orchard and miniature rice fields. The Shukkein garden was burned to the ground by the A-bomb and restored in 1951. At present it is maintained as a historic monument. Japanese people enjoy visiting the garden, and some learn how to read the ancient cultural symbols, such as the ubiquitous daoist symbol, the Turtle Island (Fig. 4.16), while others simply indulge in the sensual pleasures of a beautiful place and the opportunity for making memorable photographs. Western culture has been adopted by Japanese people to such an extent that reified images of the past are now thoroughly enjoyed. The attitude toward historic gardens as monuments reflects contemporary Westernized Japanese culture and as such will pursue its course of development whatever the critiques that purist historiographers may raise.

Visiting this rehabilitated garden and its miniature landscapes is enjoyable, but while the sense of cultural continuity that it gives with respect to gardens and landscapes in Japan is satisfying, it is not historically accurate in the sense

Fig. 4.15 View of Takuei pond in the Shukkein (photo: M. Conan)

Fig. 4.16 Turtle Island in the Shukkein (photo: M. Conan)

of the Florence Charter. Yet, at the same time, Japanese people experience a sense of cultural loss – of alienation from long-lasting cultural bonds to nature – that is not addressed by the strict conservation of ancient gardens as historic monuments. Once the circumstances of cultural renewal and continuity are understood, the re-invention of some traditional uses of historic fabric together with the development of new gardens and landscapes for the sake of keeping alive more intangible aspects of gardens and landscapes culture seems to be a possible answer to this dilemma.

The Hiroshima and Koga examples suggest the powerful cultural dynamics that may result from interactions between citizen groups oriented toward the pursuit of traditional ritualized practices and local authorities (Brosseau 2007). The riverbank lantern-flowing ceremony also demonstrates the possibility of absorbing new urban concerns within the frame of traditional practices, as it would happen in any living tradition. The variety of cultural initiatives triggered by these two landscape creations calls attention to the embedding of garden ritualized practices in a network of other cultural practices such as writing and quoting poetry, enjoying flowers and insects, practicing floral art, participating in season rituals, naming of places, and appreciating calligraphy. The conservation of the intangible heritage of garden and landscape culture cannot be separated from the conservation of these other aspects of intangible culture. On the other hand, the enactment of these activities in public parks may allow their dissemination and their reinterpretation with respect to contemporary issues or concerns of everyday life, as in the contemporary practice of *hanami* in Tokyo or the mourning for the dead in Hiroshima. Thus in Japan, at least, the conservation of the intangible heritage of gardens and landscapes may gain from any policies encouraging traditional cultural practices and allowing local associations of their supporters to demonstrate them in ritualized circumstances in newly created public parks or promenades.

There are, however, many limits to the conservation of intangible heritage of gardens and landscapes. One of them is our distaste for cultural confrontations in public places, and another is the conflict between contemporary practices predicated upon technical models and ancient tradition-based practices of transformation and engagement with nature. Participating in ritualized practices such as planting and replanting rice transforms labor into festivity, making a mere representation of traditional agricultural work that in practice was arduous. Participants may develop an intense emotional experience when acting out this dramatic representation of the past, but they cannot escape the radical difference between an experience and its representation: the work of daily life cannot be dissociated from the pain of the whole life, whereas a representation can be aestheticized and cherished for itself.

These are powerful dimensions of the preservation dilemma: the complex interconnection of the garden as a historical material entity, as a site for historical cultural practices, as a site satisfying new practical needs (for fresh air, pleasure, beauty), and as a site for the reinvention and reinterpretation of past meanings through representative practices.

Notes

1. Yinong Xu writes (2007: 9): "It was not until 1695 that the place was reused as the site of a garden. The most important part of this event was the construction of a pavilion on top of the hill by Song Luo, who was appointed as the provincial governor of Jiangsu 3 years earlier. From then on, Cang Lang Ting has undergone a series of major repairs or restorations in 1827, 1873, 1928, 1941, 1953, and 1979, and each time, except the ones in 1953 and 1979, a *ji* essay was composed to record the event."
2. The following analysis is drawn from personal observation.
3. The "Floating paper lantern ceremony," Toro Nagashi, is a Buddhist event held in August. Paper lanterns are floated down rivers to allow the soul of ancestors a safe trip to the other world. In Hiroshima, this ceremony is held on August 6 to help the soul of the victims of the A-bomb.

References

Andrews, Walter
    2008 Gardens—Real and Imagined—in the Social Ecology of Ottoman Culture. In *Gardens and Imagination: Cultural History and Agency* (Dumbarton Oaks Colloquium Series in the History of Landscape Architecture, XXX), edited by Michel Conan. Dumbarton Oaks, Washington DC.

Atasoy, Nurhan
    2007 Matrakçı Nasuh and Evlyia Çelebi: Perspectives on Ottoman Gardens (1534–1682). In *Middle East Garden Traditions: Unity and Diversity* (Dumbarton Oaks Colloquium Series in the History of Landscape Architecture, XXXI), edited by Michel Conan. Dumbarton Oaks, Washington DC.

Brosseau, Sylvie
    2007 Tokyo's Modern Parks: Spaces and Practices. In *Performance and Appropriation: Profane Rituals in Gardens and Landscape* (Dumbarton Oaks Symposium on the History of Landscape Architecture, XXVII), edited by Michel Conan, pp. 95–116. Dumbarton Oaks, Washington DC.
    2008 The Promenades and Public Parks of Tokyo: A Tradition Permanently Re-invented. In *Gardens, City Life and Culture, A World Tour*, edited by Michel Conan and Chen Wanghong, pp. 229–246. Dumbarton Oaks, Washington DC.

Kuitert, Wybe
    2007 Political Change and Cultural Values of Plants: Origins of Cherry Hybridization in Medieval Japan. In *Botanical Progress, Horticultural Innovations and Cultural Changes* (Dumbarton Oaks Garden and Landscape Symposium, XXIIX), edited by Michel Conan and John Kress, pp. 129–146. Dumbarton Oaks, Washington DC.

Lambert, David
    2007 Rituals of Transgression in Public Parks in Britain, 1846 to the Present. In *Performance and Appropriation: Profane Rituals in Gardens and Landscapes* (Dumbarton Oaks Symposium on the History of Landscape Architecture, XXVII), edited by Michel Conan, pp. 195–212. Dumbarton Oaks, Washington DC.

Lassus, Bernard
    1998 *The Landscape Approach*. Pennsylvania University Press, Philadelphia.

Lu, Gu
    1830 *Record of the Pure and the Fine*. Reprinted, Nanjing, 1986.

Manabe-Katahira, Miyuki
    2003 Approaching Zen Gardens: An Anthropological-Phenomenological Approach. *Analecta Husserliana* (theme issue on "Gardens and the Passion for the Infinite") 78: 69–84.

Shah, Behula
    2007 Braj: The Creation of Krishna's Landscape of Power and Pleasure and its 16thC Construction through the Pilgrimage of the Groves. In *Sacred Gardens and Landscapes: Ritual and Agency* (Dumbarton Oaks Symposium on the History of Landscape Architecture XXVI), edited by M. Conan, pp. 153–172. Dumbarton Oaks, Washington DC.

Suga, H., and Y. Iwahori
    2004 A Study in changes of the park management–organization of Koga park in Ibaraki prefecture in Japan. Unpublished paper presented at the 2004 IFPRA World Congress in Hamamatsu.

Tambiah, Stanley
    1985 A Performative Approach to Ritual. In *Culture, Thought, and Social Action: An Anthropological Perspective*, edited by S. Tambiah. Harvard University Press, Cambridge, Mass.

Wescoat, James L., Jr., and Joachim Wolschke-Bulmahn
    1996 Sources, Places, Representations, and Prospects: A Perspective of Mughal Gardens. In *Mughal Gardens: Sources, Places, Representations, and Prospects* (Dumbarton Oaks Symposium on the History of Landscape Architecture, XVI), edited by James L. Wescoat and J. Wolschke-Bulmahn, pp. 5–29. Dumbarton Oaks, Washington DC.

Xu, Yinong
    2007 Gardens as Cultural Memory in Suzhou, Eleventh to Nineteenth Centuries. In *Gardens, City Life and Culture, A World Tour*, edited by Michel Conan and Chen Wanghong, pp. 203–228. Dumbarton Oaks, Washington DC.

Chapter 5
Preserving the Cultural Landscape Heritage of Champaner-Pavagadh, Gujarat, India

D. Fairchild Ruggles and Amita Sinha

Champaner-Pavagadh, designated a World Heritage Site in 2004, is an example of the multivalent nature of the spirit of the place. Its hyphenated name denotes the split identity between Pavagadh Hill as the abode of a Hindu goddess, and at its foot Champaner with the remains of a historic Islamic city. While the tangible heritage of historic architectural monuments receives institutional protection, the sites of pilgrimage—temples and shrines, some nearly a thousand years old and others recently built—are kept alive through popular participation and the support of sectarian establishments. The current emphasis on architectural preservation overlooks the dialectics between these tangible and intangible forms of heritage. As important as it is to preserve significant material remains from the past, the knowledge base and skills that produced them should be preserved as well in order to support a living heritage tradition. It is the human efforts, guided by cultural knowledge and traditional technologies, that produce the material world. A broader and more comprehensive framework for conservation would focus on this inhabited cultural landscape, which is a dynamic entity rather than a fixed object, to integrate the architectural monuments, sacred places and associations, and multiple forms of heritage of Pavagadh and Champaner. These efforts would be based on an understanding of the cultural habits of perception and ritual patterns of movement, of traditional design vocabularies that reified natural forms into architecture, and of the intimate knowledge of the terrain and site hydrology that sustained the historic settlements.

Champaner-Pavagadh: Past and Present

Historic Champaner-Pavagadh, 78 miles southeast of Ahmadabad, consists of a sacred mountain—a Hindu pilgrimage destination—and the archaeological remains of a fifteenth-century Islamic capital city at its foot (Fig. 5.1). Its

---

D.F. Ruggles (✉)
Department of Landscape Architecture, University of Illinois at Urbana-Champaign, Champaign, IL 61820, USA
e-mail: dfr1.illinois.edu

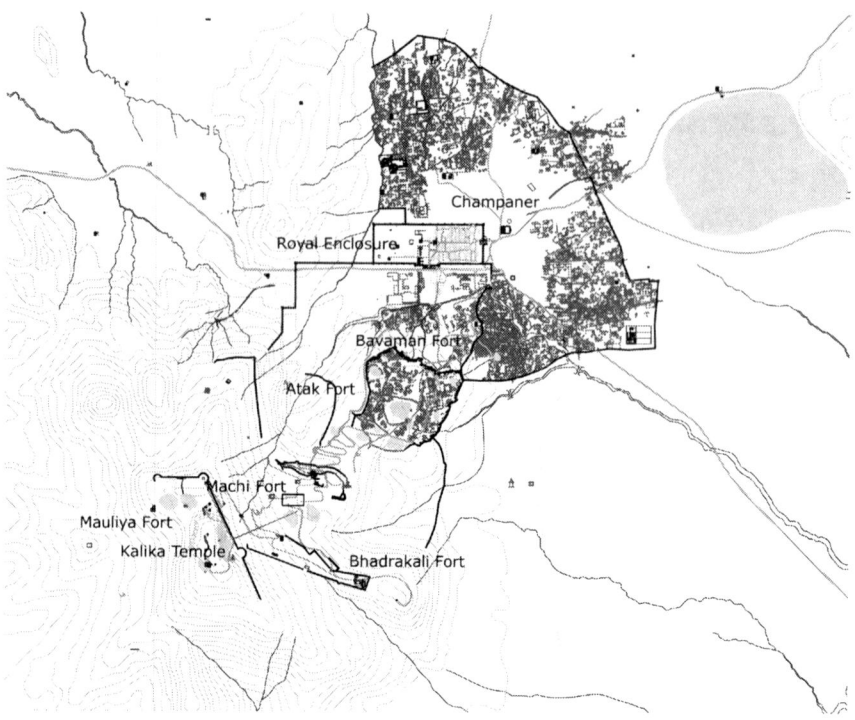

Fig. 5.1 Site plan of Champaner-Pavagadh (plan: Sinha)

preservation presents a distinct challenge because it is an enormous site (42 km^2) inhabited by combined population of 6,000 people and visited by over 2 million pilgrims annually. Moreover, although the site resonates with historic political significance and religious meaning, its history is a complex layering of both Muslim and Hindu periods, which requires political sensitivity in its interpretation. A plan for Champaner-Pavagadh was proposed by Nalini Thakur in 1987 (Thakur 1987). A new study was made by faculty from the University of Illinois at Urbana-Champaign and the Heritage Trust of Baroda with the objective of proposing it as a World Heritage Site to UNESCO, a goal that was successfully realized by the Heritage Trust in 2004.[1]

The site has a topography that is extraordinary for the region: above a flat plain, a hill rises 830 m above sea level (Fig. 5.2). Its built fabric includes hundreds of buildings that reflect multiple phases of habitation and a rich cultural history. Historians date the founding of the first urban settlement—Champakdurga—in the eighth century. The city served as a political and economic capital for the Chauhan Rajputs from approximately 1300 through most of the fifteenth century and for the Begara (or Begada) dynasty of Muslim sultans from 1484 until the Mughal conquest in 1535 (Hajji al-Dabir 1970: 29–30, in Saxena 2003: 339).

5   Preserving the Cultural Landscape Heritage

Fig. 5.2 Pavagadh Hill with the Kalika Temple at its crest (photo: Sinha)

Both before and after that period the hill was a spiritual center for devout pilgrims worshipping the Hindu goddess Kali at its summit. The very oldest and the most recent buildings are the temples and other structures associated with this cult.

Champaner city began as a siege camp by Sultan Mahmud Begara, who made it the capital city of Gujarat in 1484 until it was ransacked by the Mughals in 1535 (Sahrfuddin, in Saxena 2003: 341). It consisted of a walled, large fortified city with nine gates that included the Royal Enclosure where the king and his retinue resided amidst pavilions, stepwells, and mosques adorned with fine stone carving and a mighty outer fort wall enclosing the dwellings of 50,000 persons (Fig. 5.3). Most of the residential architecture from that period has vanished, but many of the mosques and tombs still stand, revealing a style characterized by exquisite stone detail, especially carved screens and surface relief, and harmony of proportions. These include the Jami Masjid (the congregational mosque, built ca. 1508) and its courtyard; at 72 × 60 m, it is the largest complex in the urban enclosure. Of its three entrance pavilions, the east (main) pavilion is unusual in its adornment of pierced stone screens, capped with *chhatris* (open-sided cupolas) (Fig. 5.4). The portal of its 22-m-high sanctuary façade is flanked by niches. The nearby stepwell (Fig. 5.11) would have provided water for the mandatory ablutions prior to prayer.[2] For monuments such as this, the architectural historians E. B. Havell, Percy Brown, and Herman Goetz singled out the architecture of Champaner as representing the finest of Islamic buildings in Gujarat from the sultanate period and the most indigenous in style, derived from regional traditions (Havell 1913; Brown 1964; Goetz 1949).

Fig. 5.3 Champaner, the Royal Enclosure (photo: Ruggles)

Fig. 5.4 Champaner, the Jami Masjid, entry pavilion (photo: Ruggles)

While today much of the formerly handsome architecture is in ruins and many of its greatest monuments are quarantined by the protective fences erected by the Archaeological Survey of India, the urban plan can nonetheless be discerned and offers a rare opportunity to study the original spatial context of medieval Islamic monuments. After the Mughal sack, the capital was moved to Ahmadabad and Champaner was forgotten. Today it is a small village of about 2,000 residents (UNESCO Advisory Body Evaluation, no. 1101).

Additionally, there were older palaces and fortifications built by their Rajput predecessors up on the mountain to which Champaner's people could retreat in perilous times (Hajji al-Dabir 1970; see also Bayley 1979 and Nizam al-Din Ahmad 1942:148–149). Its natural defenses were enhanced by thick rubble and ashlar walls that cut across the valleys, effectively blocking them and funneling human movement through a succession of mighty gates piercing the imposing fortifications (Fig. 5.5). Most of these fortification gates and walls survive and some of them, such as the Sadan Shah Darwaza and the Budhiya Darwaza with the sheer, merlon-capped walls of the Sat Kaman looming above them, can be read not only as individual defensive works but also as an interconnected, planned fortification system in which the massive stone and the succession of

Fig. 5.5 Pavagadh Hill's fortifications: The Budhiya Gate with steps cut into the bedrock (photo: Ruggles)

tiered walls along the steep slope are only one element within a much larger protective strategy. The other, equally important element was the exploitation of the natural topography to take advantage of opportunities for surveillance.

In a flat landscape, Pavagadh is an odd volcanic hill that looms in sharp contrast to its surroundings, and perhaps because of this geographic anomaly, it came to be worshipped as a Hindu sacred site. The eruption occurred some 500 million years ago, and the site was revered as the abode of the goddess since the second century, attracting human settlement. Today it literally has hundreds of heritage structures such as temples, shrines, forts, a few mosques, and tombs and it continues to be an important pilgrimage destination.[3] Besides the temple to the goddess Kali (or Kalika), the patron deity of the Rajput chieftains, there are numerous Devi temples—a Kali temple stands in Champaner at the base of the hill, and a Khudiyar (a tribal goddess) Devi shrine is located where the pilgrim path begins its ascent. The goddess temples at the foot of the hill serve those who are unable to climb to the top. Ambaji Temple is located on the lower Machi Plateau, a shrine to Khappar Jogini, Bhatiji, and to Bahachur Devi is near the upper reaches of the pilgrim path, and Bhadrakali (elder sister of Kalika) temple is on Bhadrakali plateau. In addition, small shrines to Kali are housed in the many ashrams functioning in Pavagadh. Bhadrakali Temple is built at the edge of steep Elephant Valley in the vicinity of Rajput palace ruins. Bahachur Devi is housed inside a natural cave, just below the top. While the Kalika Temple is the primary destination, the goddess's other manifestations find a home in the landscape for their worship to take place.

Not surprisingly, Shiva temples also abound. The oldest structure in Champaner-Pavagadh is the temple known as Lakulish (another name of Shiva) on the edge of Chassiya Talao built in the eleventh century (Fig. 5.6). It is now in ruins and no longer a site of active worship. The ruins of another Shiva shrine are found inside the Royal Enclosure of Champaner and a new temple has been built adjacent to the old one. On the pilgrim path that winds up the hill, Shiva is worshipped as Dattathreya in a cave shrine and as Mahadev Annapurna in a built one. There is only one temple to Krishna, known as Ranchor-Raiji Mandir on the path. There are shrines to Bhairva, who protects the site, and to local deities such as Tithariya Dev on Bhadrakali plateau. Unusually, a mausoleum to the Muslim Sufi saint, Sadan Shah Pir, superimposed on the Kalika Mata Temple, attracts both Muslim and Hindu devotees, their ritual circumambulations encircling both goddess and Sufi in the same circuit (Fig. 5.7).

The Jains consider the hill to be one of the four sacred regions where *moksha* (release from the cycle of birth and death) may be obtained. There are three Jain temple complexes at the base of Pavagadh Hill, with temples, rest houses for pilgrims (*dharmashalas*), and even an old-age home, and on Pavagadh Hill itself there are seven Jain temples. The group on Mauliya Plateau, built on the remains of historic structures, offers a striking composition against the hill and the sky. Collectively, these temples are the focus of pilgrimage and worship for the more than 2 million pilgrims who come every year to climb to the Kalika Temple at the top of Pavagadh Hill, and they are complemented by a built fabric of stone-paved roads, monumental gateways, impressive fortifications, water tanks, and watercourses.

Fig. 5.6 Pavagadh Hill, Chassiya Talao, and the eleventh-century Lakulish Temple (photo: Sinha)

Fig. 5.7 Pavagadh Hill, Kalika Mata Temple with domed Muslim shrine on top (photo: Sinha)

While archaeological study has revealed many of these individual structures, the site is simply too vast and too diverse to be treated solely as an archaeological or architectural precinct. An appreciation of its drama and splendor must take into account the fact that it is both a natural and a humanly constructed environment. Some of its most enduring material character comes from the natural basins that were used for catching and storing water, the views from precipices across densely forested valleys, and the contrasting colors of blue sky, reddish-orange rhyolite boulders, and green vegetation. Moreover, the various people who lived there in the past and who reside and visit there today attribute a range of different meanings to those places and structures. For some, the site was a powerful stronghold against enemy attack, while for others it was a productive landscape that yielded crops, minerals, and animals for hunting; for yet others, it offered a path to an encounter with the goddess Kalika and the enlightenment of her presence. Today the site is also

Fig. 5.8 Sadhu dressed as the monkey god Hanuman (photo: Ruggles)

studied for its historical and ecological fabric as well as the intangible heritage of its festivals, ephemeral shrines, *sadhus* (including one man who in recent years has dressed and painted himself as the monkey god, Hanuman), and the palpable atmosphere of joy among the pilgrims who flock there (Fig. 5.8).

The pilgrims describe their beliefs about Kalika in terms of "*shakti*" (remover of obstacles), "fulfiller of wishes," and "one who rewards hard work." [These observations were conducted by Sinha in 2004]. They state that "whoever comes with faith, his work is done," "*shraddha* (faith) brings people here," and "she draws people-they walk as far away as 300 km, singing *garba* (folk song) and carrying a *ratha* (chariot) as they walk." A female devotee said: "at one time all representatives of the government were women and Kali was at the head." A few describe Kalika as their *kuldevi* (family goddess) and say that their belief in her will make all their work successful. The Dudhiya Talao acts as a threshold to the temple, and pilgrims voice regret that in its present dilapidated and unhygienic condition, it is difficult to bathe in its waters for physical and moral cleansing.

The upper stretch of the path is lined with shops that sell images of the goddess, flower garlands, incense, coconuts, and other ritual objects; also food, bottled water, film, tape cassettes, and plastic sandals. The teeming hordes of people and the commercial activity that caters to them are to some extent distractions from the spiritual purpose of pilgrimage, with the regrettable side effects of trash, human waste, water pollution, noise, and vehicular traffic, but they are also as much a part of the historic character of the site as the temples and their priests. Yet it is precisely this living aspect of Champaner-Pavagadh that is ignored by the typical heritage management plan. While the archaeologist R. N. Mehta (Mehta n.d.) was successful in excavating the historic city of Champaner, and the Archaeological Survey has preserved 39 heritage structures, no agency has yet addressed Champaner-Pavagadh as an integrated, living heritage *landscape*.

Cultural Landscape

Rather than focusing on Champaner-Pavagadh's endangered buildings or landmarks per se, it is important to try to address the entire landscape as the frame for heritage inquiry, because "landscape" encompasses the full physical, social, political, economic, ideological, and ecological context of the built environment. The field of landscape is often dismissed as belonging to the realm of nature, rather than culture. But any landscape architect, historian, or geographer knows that landscapes are never purely natural, despite the common insistence on a primordial paradise that existed before or apart from humankind. Landscapes are the result of an ongoing historical encounter between nature and culture, in which neither can be experienced in isolation from the other. Unlike a building or an artifact, landscape is not an inert object. It is a living, dynamic, and often contested space that demands an approach that differs from that of architectural preservation.

In Champaner-Pavagadh, for example, there is an enormous amount of fabric *between* the architectural structures that requires preservation and maintenance: roads, paths, and steps that guide human movement; the bodies of water (necessary for ritual immersion but alarmingly polluted); the walls and spontaneous places for rest stops, and the viewsheds. Unlike the insistent presence of buildings, these are spaces and objects that lose their significance if unused, or disappear altogether. They gain meaning by virtue of being inhabited. Human beings are as much a part of a landscape as its vegetation, native fauna, and structure.

Champaner-Pavagadh provides the opportunity to study the interrelationship of architectural, urban, and landscape features in a complex historical settlement together with local and extralocal communities. More than an object, the landscape comprises a network of interconnected *systems*—pedestrian movement, water flow, habitats for vegetation and animals, viewing strategies—that are hard to contain within a "quarantine" model of preservation within fenced enclosures. It is not only the architecture that merits conservation, but also the landscape's visual structure of viewsheds and vistas afforded by the natural topography, and the visual focal points combined with axes of movement that produced its urban design. Likewise, the site hydrology provides visible evidence of the interconnectedness of built architecture and managed ecology (Sinha et al. 2005).

Another reason that Champaner-Pavagadh cannot be treated as a fixed object is that it is constantly changing with respect to its human inhabitants, plants, and natural resources. The vegetation differs from season to season, and in some years drought causes the water tanks to dry up. Not only the plants but also the buildings are subject to change. Some of Pavagadh's temples are regularly repainted (renewed as a sign of religious respect); others are treated to cleaning and preservation measures by Archaeological Survey of India (ASI) workmen (a different form of respect accorded by scientific method). Moreover, scattered throughout the site are small shrines whose character and meaning are entirely dependent upon ritual activities such as the donation of flower garlands, the application of butter or presentation of a coconut, the presence of a beautifully draped cow or the man whose vivid body paint transforms him into the monkey god. Landscapes constantly evolve, changing daily, seasonally, through the years, and in response to weather and cultural pressures (such as pollution, poverty, and changing human values). A landscape cannot be delimited to a specific historic moment and cannot be stabilized with fixed forms and meaning. Instead, it is a dynamic and interactive environment that is both a physical entity *and* an ongoing process, a dialectic of intangible and tangible heritage.

Human values and belief systems, ways of relating to nature and thinking about time and space, and building traditions handed down from one generation to the next without being codified into a canon are all intangible aspects that interact with the material world of nature to produce the tangible landscape that presents itself to the eye. The two interact in myriad ways to give rise to heritage to be treasured and protected for posterity. The transformation of raw nature into a cultural landscape occurs as a result of human actions over time that are guided by a worldview within which nature is assigned meanings, ranging from transcendental to utilitarian. The building traditions and skills associated with them that develop to implement that worldview form the core of instrumental knowledge transmitted orally and through continued practice within artisanal communities.

The most prominent feature of the visible landscape is its historic building structures. But even these have a dimension of intangible heritage with respect to the traditional design vocabulary that is mimetic of nature, as well as the building skills that implemented it. Ostensibly, the Hindu and Jain temples of Pavagadh and the mosques of Champaner use very different languages of design and are expressions of faiths that have little in common. However, they share not only contiguous locations but also artisanal building traditions that draw upon a shared iconographic program of depicting nature in building ornamentation. Water management was crucial in the sustenance of many medieval settlements in Champaner-Pavagadh. The knowledge of local hydrological systems and the building skills necessary for collecting, storing, and distributing water constitute an ephemeral intangible heritage, the tangible reminder of which is the *talaos* (ponds), *kunds* (tanks), and *vavs* (stepwells), which were formerly the lifeblood of the community but now lie semiderelict (Sonal Modi 2002). The cultural habits of perception and ritual patterns of movement have shaped the landscape and are manifest in the acts of pilgrimage as well as in the layouts of historic settlements. The internalized patterns of viewing and traversing the landscape are a significant, although seldom articulated, aspect of intangible cultural heritage.

Architectural Forms and Ornamentation

Pavagadh's numerous Hindu and Jain temples reflect a building tradition dating to the tenth and eleventh century (possibly even earlier), while Champaner's Islamic buildings reflect a distinct regional architectural style responsive to local site exigencies, which developed a few centuries later (Sumesh Modi 2004). The Hindu temple symbolized the cave in the mountain in its inner sanctum *garbha griha* (womb house) below the *shikhar* (mountain crest) (Michell 1977), while the Islamic congregational mosque evolved from the courtyard archetype of the Prophet's house in Medina (Creswell 1958: 1–6) to other distinctive mosques types characterized by the four-iwan plan or large domes. In the Maru-Gurjara architectural style in Gujarat and Rajasthan can be seen an evolving relationship between the two forms, as the mosque developed into a distinctly Indic version. The *mandapa* (hall) of the temple became a modular unit in the large spacious sanctuaries of the mosques in Champaner (and elsewhere in Gujarat) (Patel 2004). For example, the Jami Masjid had a central octagonal bay with ribbed and corbelled domes, with clerestories bringing light and air in the dark interior. On the roof of the prayer hall, these clerestories are surrounded by ornamental balustrades and benches, akin to *mandapa* seats (*asanapatta*) and seat backs (*kakasana*), which invite one to sit, enjoy the refreshing breezes, and view the stunning panorama of Pavagadh Hill (Fig. 5.9). In this as well as the Kevada and Nila Gumbad Mosques, nature was thus visually integrated into the architecture in a manner that was rare elsewhere in the Islamic world (Ruggles 2008: 98–101).

Fig. 5.9 Champaner, Jami Masjid's dome and second-story terrace (photo: Sinah/Ruggles)

The built temple reified natural form, while the mosque paid homage to nature in its vistas and in its rich building ornamentation, borrowing from the preexisting repertoire of temple iconography. Artisanal communities responsible for building Champaner's mosques in the fifteenth century practiced the regional style of architecture, offering their skills to the reigning patron, regardless of his faith. Even though figural representation—a mainstay of temple embellishment—was prohibited in Islamic religious buildings, the artisans had many opportunities to practice their trade in the profuse aniconic ornamentation. The stone *mihrabs* in the Jami Masjid and other mosques had recessed frames with lintels topped by aedicular niches within which were

Fig. 5.10 Jami Masjid, detail of stone relief with pot-and-vine motif (photo: Ruggles)

carved symbols of plenitude: the sun, pot, and foliage (Fig. 5.10). Besides the pot motif (*purnaghata*), the mosque and tomb surfaces were ornamented with the vine (*kalpavalli*), the bands of diamond motif (*ratnapatta*), and lotus medallions (*padmasila*), which had adorned the surfaces of earlier temples.

Although the stone carvers and masons worked within a regional design tradition, learned by imitative practice and passed down from one generation to the next, their knowledge and skills were employed with a degree of flexibility and inventiveness. The building patrons and users were identifiably Hindu, Muslim, or Jain, but while the workers themselves also had specific religious identities, their art was not limited by sectarianism but could be adapted as needed (Asher 1992: 246; Inayat Khan 1990: 205–206). Their building knowledge and skills were a living tradition imbibed from their forefathers, not a codified and static text that would prove irrelevant with changing times and patrons of different faiths.

Water Intelligence

The sacred and utilitarian dimensions of water use are evident in the many historic *talaos*, *kunds*, and *vavs* dotting the landscape.[4] Water is essential for any settlement, and the ability to collect, store, and distribute it locally was crucial to the survival and self-sufficiency of communities residing in Champaner-Pavagadh, especially when besieged. Pavagadh has only one rivulet, Vishwamitri, and even that dries up in summer. However, "creative water intelligence" was demonstrated in the ways the rainwater and runoff on the hilly slopes were caught and conveyed into an elaborate system of macro- and microcatchments (Sonal Modi 2002). Champaner was called a "city of thousand wells," and Pavagadh may be similarly designated as a "hill of hundred pools." In the hot arid region of Gujarat, it is a marvel that the inhabitants could enjoy such water abundance.

The large and small tanks were the nuclei of settlements on the hill, while Champaner residents depended upon wells and large water basins, most of which lay outside of the city walls. Their water served a gamut of needs from spiritual, aesthetic, recreational to utilitarian. The tanks located in the successive plateaus on the northeast part of the hill (Dudhiya, Chassiya, Annapurna, Teliya, and Medhi Talaos) served those climbing the pilgrim path and their ritual needs as well as the residents of numerous forts built by the Rajputs on high ground. The western side of the hill was another watershed where rainwater was harvested in the huge embankments and conveyed to stone cisterns: the Ganga, Yamuna and Saraswati Kunds on the edge of the Mauliya Plateau. The large Kasbin Talao on the city's western edge was fed by damming ephemeral streams and river tributaries and diverting the water into a channel to the reservoir. The largest water body, the Wada Talao, to the east of the city, was fed by catching water from rivulets and runoff from the hills.

The ornate Gaben Shah tank and the Helical Stepwell were likely situated within public gardens at the entry to the city and the beginning of the pilgrim path. The remains of the summer pavilion in the Royal Enclosure, the magnificent stepwell in the Jami Masjid precinct (Fig. 5.11), and the water channels and wells in a wealthy noble's house, called the Amir's Manzil, are examples of superb workmanship of water structures, built by those responsible for the palatine and religious architecture of Champaner. However, the knowledge base went beyond building skills; it required an intimate understanding of the terrain and movement of water in it, precipitation and percolation rates in the soil, and water table and its recharge. The regular maintenance required to keep the systems of interconnected catchments–conveyances–reservoirs functioning would have been dependent upon a holistic knowledge of site hydrology. Water recycling at the domestic level of the kind in evidence in the extant water channels and tanks in the Amir's Manzil implied a sophisticated understanding of the integration of water in architectural layout. The traditional technologies of water management were efficient, easy to operate, and sustainable. Water was not just a resource but also a purifying element, integrated into sacred rituals that formed a part of daily life. It was a salient feature of the cultural landscape and contributed to its legibility.

When Champaner lost its importance and the population began to dwindle, the abandonment of settlements resulted in the loss of that knowledge base. The revival of goddess worship at Pavagadh has not brought about a revival of

Fig. 5.11 Jami Masjid stepwell (photo: Ruggles)

water intelligence. The tanks in the upper plateaus are no longer used for ritual bathing, only for washing, and drinking water is brought to the site in Municipality barrels and there is bottled water for sale (for those who can afford it). This fragmentation of the overall hydrological system has resulted in a loss of awareness of its workings.

Vision and Movement

Perhaps more than any other factor, habits of perception and patterns of movement shape the cultural landscape. Pavagadh Hill is perceived by the believer to be the metonymic form of the Great Goddess. The traditional Hindu explanation for the hill is that it was formed from the toe of the goddess Sati, a previous incarnation of Kali. Sati, the faithful consort of Shiva, was angry when her father slighted her husband, and in protest, killed herself. To prevent the mourning Shiva from going mad with grief over Sati's body, Vishnu cut it up, the parts of which fell to earth (Sonal Modi 2005; Sinha 2006). These sacred sites associated with Sati "exemplify the way in which the goddess is linked with the earth and this world, in complementary opposition to transcendent Vishnu and Shiva" (Fuller 1992: 44). In the Hindu pantheon, Sati is also Kali, an ambivalent yet primal goddess of energy, both in the sense of destruction and resurrection. Depicted with four arms that represent her total dominion, she is the Great Mother, the cycle of life itself, and was probably descended from a prehistoric fertility goddess.

Worshipped as the abode of the goddess since prehistoric times, pilgrimage has shaped the cultural landscape of Pavagadh Hill. Pilgrims climb the 5.28-km-long winding path for the *darshan* of Kalika in her temple on the crest of the hill (Fig. 5.12). The ascending movement signifies the transition from lower to higher realms, from the profane to the sacred. Ritual movement is also circumambulatory around the hill, shrines, temples, and *talaos*. This age-old movement pattern has inscribed a system of paths that are still used to this day by the devotees. The path up the hill, a major spine of movement, has been renovated recently. Pilgrims and laden donkeys are most likely to use it nowadays, since a modern paved road brings most travelers up to a point two-thirds of the way up the peak and mechanical gondolas lift those who are willing to pay for the last and most wearisome portion of the ascent. Gateways threading this path controlled the movement of people, animals, and goods and led to a network of paths within the settlements. Their location was strategic, coinciding with overlook points and natural barriers such as a narrow neck of land and natural ravine. Symbolically significant buildings were sited to be always visible: Kalika Temple on the pinnacle of the toe-shaped hillcrest proclaimed her supremacy and her transcendence. Palaces such as that of the Queen on Mauliya Plateau, Patai Rawal's Palace on Bhadrakali Plateau, and Khapra Zaveri no Mahal were deliberately placed to take advantage of spectacular views and also perhaps be closer to sacred sites of the hill. Khapra Zaveri no Mahal was directly in the line of sight of the sacred spring Panch Kuva (source of the Vishwamitri stream) and Kalika Temple would always be visible from the palaces on Mauliya and Bhadrakali Plateaus.

Fig. 5.12 Pavagadh Hill, with the pilgrim path winding up the steep incline (photo: Ruggles)

Excavations in Atak Fort on the hill and Champaner below reveal compact settlements enclosed by high walls: the Fort roughly circular in shape, and Champaner fan-shaped and much larger. The street network represents the landscape structure that held the communities together and focused on the seat of secular and sacred authority. The urban landscape was a largely pedestrian realm, with people traversing it mostly on foot and the occasional processions of the sultan and his nobles on elephants and horses. Physical proximity was essential as was the need to enclose the largest area within the walled perimeter. Streets led from the nine city gates to the high walls of the Royal Enclosure, the inner fort of the Sultan, and to the imposing Jami Masjid.

With the exception of the enclosure walls themselves, the settlements were not laid out according to canonical texts, but working knowledge of an optimal arrangement of building clusters minimized distances and kept the visual focus on seats of authority. Settlement growth was ad hoc and organic in nature, based on an unwritten code of privacy. This shared knowledge of the habitable city from the perspective of defense, commerce, centrality of power, and logic of movement represented a sustainable way of life, adapted to the terrain and the climate. It implied an organic unity between place and community and indicated the value placed upon living in proximity to power, divine and human, in uncertain times. The physical imprint that resulted was the tangible trace of a far more ephemeral set of social and political relations among humans.

Conservation Approaches

Preservation of such a site is by no means straightforward. The preservationist cannot employ the well-developed methodology of historic preservation (which in South Asia is usually limited to architectural preservation) because the site is not static: it is home to a living community in a ritual landscape that is continually recreated, and it is the site for the enactments of what UNESCO has categorized as "intangible heritage." All of these are profoundly affected by many layers of religious, cultural, and ecological significance.

The principal question at Champaner-Pavagadh is one shared by a great many site managers, curators, conservators, archaeologists, and designers: how to balance historic heritage with living communities (who may themselves contain considerable diversity) and the different values that they attribute to history and its material legacy. Moreover, the material fabric of the stone monuments, roads, and water tanks, although visible and clearly in need of stabilization, is only one part of a much larger heritage environment. There is the predicament of the stakeholder: who really owns and takes responsibility for Champaner-Pavagadh? Its current (impoverished) residents? The various local, national, and international agencies that seek to improve its ruinous condition? Or the people of the nation state of India, whose taxes will pay some of the costs of preserving the site and who may have an ideological investment in it as a site of Indian history and myth? Or the religious devotees who seek to experience the blessing of the goddess by visiting a place associated with her? Overlapping concepts of ownership are implied in the descriptive terms "Hindu shrine," "national treasure," and "World Heritage Site."

The historic structures fall under the purview of the Archaeological Survey of India, which, with limited funds, does the best it can to protect and preserve the 39 monuments under its wing (of the 114 identified by the Heritage Trust of Baroda). In its exclusive focus on architectural fabric, the Archaeological Survey ignores the relationship between the historic building and its site. The landscape is fenced and the immediate vicinity of the building is landscaped with lawns and shrubs, often in a style that has little to do with the historic significance of the monument (Fig. 5.13). The Forestry Department owns 93% of the land, making it the largest stakeholder with respect to sheer size. Temple trusts and *ashrams* (sectarian establishments) are other institutions that own shrines and temples and facilitate pilgrimage by providing boarding and lodging facilities. Each stakeholder group has its own interests and constituencies to serve, with the result that many heritage features of the larger cultural landscape lie neglected.

Fig. 5.13 Shehri Masjid (late fifteenth century) with enclosure fence installed by the Archaeological Service of India (photo: Ruggles)

A landscape conservation approach needs to address the dynamic, temporal aspects of the site and to resolve the contradictions inherent in the process. Landscape management should be less about "freezing" the site in a desired image and more about understanding and implementing the knowledge principles and associated skills that crafted the historic landscapes. This requires coordination and collaboration among stakeholders to meet the needs of the resident communities and plan for other kinds of visitors who may come to enjoy nature sports or study the site's history. It needs legislative protection and an administrative structure that can oversee the landscape planning and management process.

Conservationists could do much to preserve intangible heritage by creating suitable conditions for its enactment. This involves ensuring a physical locale for ritual movement and performing arts, craft production, and valued landscape experiences. Landscape architects could participate in that endeavor by designing appropriate settings, restoring degraded landscapes, and creating new landscape infrastructure. An essential first step would be to restore the "goddess ecology." Pavagadh Hill is the embodiment of *shakti*, the feminine principle such that divinity is inscribed in the landscape, in its topography, water bodies, and vegetation. Conservation of this landscape by desilting and dredging of *talaos* and restoration of their *ghats* (steps to water), planting of auspicious trees such as the *banyan*, *pipal*, and *neem* in the lower plateaus, preventing soil erosion on the hilly slopes through large-scale planting, and rehabilitating degraded sites will be steps toward restoration of the environmental health of the hill.

Landscape experience is produced by the senses in a human body that moves. Envisioning the hill as the form and site of the Goddess is the *raison d'être* of pilgrimage as is ritual movement around the hill and to its summit. The journey (*parikrama yatra*), that is, pilgrimage, is a vivid sequence of spaces that should be coordinated with adequate rest stops and clearly marked trails to all the sacred sites on the hill. Heritage planning should also provide facilities for ritual bathing in the *talaos*, ceremonial tonsure, *garba* (folk dance), and feasting. The new World Heritage Site designation has the potential to bring an influx of tourists that will tax the existing infrastructure at Champaner-Pavagadh. Planning for it can be an opportunity for community development and an occasion to reconsider the complex and multiple meanings of the site's intangible heritage.

Notes

1. Between the years 2000 and 2005, teams of students from the University of Illinois, Urbana-Champaign, worked with teams from the D.C. Patel School of Architecture, Vallabh Vidya Nagar; the Bhausaheb Hiray College of Architecture, Mumbai University; and Maharaja Sayajorao University of Baroda in design workshops sponsored by the Heritage Trust of Baroda. Karan Grover, President of Heritage Trust, Sumesh Modi, Sonal Modi (Surat), and Ghanshyam Joshi (Champaner) contributed to the workshops. Funding for the Illinois portion of the project was provided by the Ryerson Fund in the Department of Landscape Architecture of the University of Illinois at Urbana-Champaign, the Max van Berchem Foundation of Geneva, Switzerland, and the Heritage Trust of Baroda. We wish especially to acknowledge the collaboration in those projects of James Wescoat, Jr. and Gary Kesler.

2. Today the courtyard has been treated as a *chahar bagh* (four-part garden), a classic Islamic garden type. But this is historically incorrect. While some Islamic mosques did have gardened courtyards, the *chahar bagh* layout was reserved exclusively for palaces and tombs.
3. A great many of these have been catalogued by Sumesh Modi and published in *Impressions of a Forgotten City: Architectural Documentation of Champaner-Pavagadh*. Heritage Trust and Archaeological Survey of India Publication, 2004.
4. In this analysis of water in this section, we have relied heavily upon the contribution of James Wescoat to the University of Illinois's second and third coauthored planning reports (Sinha et al. 2003, 2005).

References

Asher, Catherine
    1992 *Architecture of Mughal India*. Cambridge University Press, New York.
Bayley, Edward C.
    1979 *The Local Muhammadan Dynasties*. 2nd ed. Delhi.
Burton-Page, John
    1998 Mosques and Tombs. In *Ahmadabad*, edited by George Michell and Snehal Shah, pp. 20–119. Marg Publications, Mumbai.
Creswell, K. A. C.
    1958 *A Short Account of Early Muslim Architecture*. Pelican, Middlesex.
Fuller, C. J.
    1992 *The Camphor Flame: Popular Hinduism and Society in India*. Princeton University Press, Princeton.
Goetz, H.
    1949 Pavagadh-Champaner. *Journal of the Gujarat Research Society* XI (2): 1–67.
Hajji al-Dabir, Abdullah Muhammad al-Makki al-Asafi al-Ulughkhani
    1970 *Zafar al-walih bi muzaffar wa alihi: An Arabic History of Gujarat*, translated by M. F. Lokhandwala. Oriental Institute, Baroda.
Havell, E.B.
    1913 *Indian Architecture: Its Psychology, Structure, and History from the First Muhammadan Invasion to the Present Day*. S. Chand, New Delhi.
Inayat Khan
    1990 *The Shah Jahan Nama*, edited by W. Begley and Z. A. Desai, based on an earlier translation by A. R. Fuller. Oxford University Press, New York.
Joshi, G.
    1999 *Pavagadh Darshan*. Chiragh Printers, Ahmedabad.
Mehta, R. N.
    1977 A Christian prayer hall of Champaner. *Indica* 14(2): 111–116.
    n.d. *Champaner: A Medieval Capital*. Heritage Trust, Vadodara.
Michell, George
    1977 *The Hindu Temple: An Introduction to Its Meaning and Form*. Elek, London.
Mirat-i Sikandari
    1979 Translated as *The Local Muhammadan Dynasties*, by Edward C. Bayley. 2nd ed. Delhi. 1st edition, 1961, edited by S. C. Misra and M. L. Rahman. Baroda.
Modi, Sonal
    2002 Water intelligent city: Champaner-Pavagadh. In *Landscapes of Water: History, Innovation and Sustainable Design*, edited by U. Fratino. 1: 113ff. Politecnico di Bari, Bari.
    2005 Intangible Heritage—Tales of Yore. *Architecture+Design*, India, 22(2): 34–37.

Modi, Sumesh
    2004 *Impressions of a Forgotten City: Architectural Documentation of Champaner-Pavagadh.* Heritage Trust and Archaeological Survey of India Publication, Vadodara.

Nizam al-Din Ahmad
    1942 *Tabaqat-i Akbari*, trans. Brajendranath De, vol. III. Delhi.

Patel, Alka
    2004 *Building Communities in Gujarat: Architecture and Society during the Twelfth through Fourteenth Centuries*. Brill, Leiden.

Ruggles, D. Fairchild
    2008 *Islamic Gardens and Landscapes*. University of Pennsylvania Press, Philadelphia.

Saxena, Adhya Bharti
    2003 The Making of Pavagadh-Champaner City Complex: A Gaze into the Historical Geography from the Earliest Times to the Nineteenth Century. *Proceedings of the Indian History Congress*, 63rd session (Amritsar, 2002). Indian History Congress, Kolkata.

Sahrfuddin
    n.d. *Tarikh-i Gujarat*. Maulana Aazad Library of Aligarh Muslim University, Aligarh.

Sinha, Amita
    2004 Champaner-Pavagadh Archaeological Park: A Design Approach. *International Studies of Heritage Studies* 10 (2): 117–128.
    2006 Cultural Landscape of Pavagadh: The Abode of Mother Goddess, Kalika. *Journal of Cultural Geography* 22 (1): 89–103.
    2007 Forts on a Sacred Hill: Champaner-Pavagadh, Gujarat, India. *Architecture+Design* (India), 24 (8): 128–134.

Sinha, Amita and Gary Kesler with the Baroda Trust
    2001 *Champaner-Pavagadh Archaeological Park*. Department of Landscape Architecture, University of Illinois at Urbana-Champaign, Champaign.

Sinha, Amita, Gary Kesler, D. Fairchild Ruggles, and James Wescoat, Jr.
    2003 *Champaner-Pavagadh-Cultural Sanctuary*. Department of Landscape Architecture, University of Illinois at Urbana-Champaign, Champaign.
    2004 Champaner-Pavagadh, Gujarat, India: Challenges and Responses in Cultural Heritage Planning and Design. *Tourism Recreation Research*, 29: 75–78.

Sinha, Amita, D. Fairchild Ruggles, and James Wescoat, Jr.
    2005 *Panch Yatras in the Cultural Heritage Landscape of Champaner-Pavagadh, Gujarat, India*. Department of Landscape Architecture, University of Illinois at Urbana-Champaign, Champaign.

Sinha, Amita and Yuthika Sharma
    2006 Urban Design as a Frame for Site Readings of Heritage Landscape of Champaner-Pavagadh, India. *The Journal of the Indian Institute of Architects*, 71 (7): 45–48.

Thakur, Nalini
    1987 *Champaner: Draft Action Plan for Integrated Conservation*. Heritage Trust, Baroda.

UNESCO
    Advisory Body Evaluation, no.1101: Champaner-Pavagadh. www.unesco.org/archive.advisory_body_evaluation/1101.pdf

UNESCO
    2003 Convention for Safeguarding the Intangible Heritage. www.unesco.org/culture/ich/index.php?pg=00006

Chapter 6
Governance and Conservation of the Rapaz *Khipu* Patrimony

Frank Salomon and Renata Peters

In the village of Rapaz, high in the Andes Mountains of Peru, villagers have preserved a unique walled precinct containing the only known functioning Andean temple. Inside it is a remarkable collection of *khipu* or "cord records" (Ruíz Estrada 1981; Salomon et al. 2006). There is also a disused communal storehouse, whose contents were controlled by the ceremonial chamber. The village has cared for this heritage on its own, without dependence on national cultural institutions. The Rapaz ceremonial precinct and its contents have fascinated anthropologists and archaeologists who are struck by its apparent relevance to *khipu* use in various pre-Hispanic societies of the Central Andes, especially the Incas. The village of Rapaz has gained regional fame among Peruvians through media coverage and has become a minor tourist destination for Lima-area weekenders. For visitors, the Rapaz precinct has become an emblem of Peruvian or regional authenticity.

But to Rapaz villagers, the *"khipu* house," the old community storehouse, and other features comprise an active ceremonial and political venue, not an extinct archaeological site. The ceremonial precinct is used for ritual service to *wakas* (Andean superhuman beings). Ritual is fused with regulation of land and water use, and civil authority. The buildings of the precinct are accordingly revered and restricted, cherished and feared. The precinct and its contents are "sacred," taking that term in a sense that the *Oxford English Dictionary* attests from 1548 onward: "Secured by religious sentiment, reverence, sense of justice, or the like, against violation, infringement, or encroachment."

Outsiders might assess the ceremonial precinct's activities as "intangible heritage" in the meaning of the 2003 United Nations Convention for the Safeguarding of Intangible Cultural Heritage. But villagers never treat their practice as a reified "genre" or "performance" that ought to be "preserved." Rather, they see the use of the tangible patrimony as a pragmatic way of getting things done.

With the collaboration of Carrie Brezine, Gino de las Casas Ríos, Víctor Falcón Huayta, Rosa Choque Gonzales, and Rosalía Choque Gonzales.

F. Salomon (✉)
Department of Anthropology, University of Wisconsin, Madison, WI 53706, USA
e-mail: fsalomon@wisc.edu

It is sacred, but its sacred power is part and parcel of the local web of politics and economy. Dealing with it is part of practical know-how rather than a special domain sealed off and objectified as unchanging heritage. Some villagers are optimistic, while others are anxious, about reconciling the scientific, touristic, and sacred uses of the Rapaz patrimony. What does the encounter between researchers and villagers suggest about the means of doing so?

This chapter reports on a scientific inquiry into the archaeology and ethnography of the precinct. As a precondition to scientific work, the village required an initiative to conserve patrimonial objects and buildings so as to assure their continued communal functions. The patrimonial objects are tangible elements of inward-looking self-knowledge and cultural continuity. But at the same time they are resources for outward-looking ventures: tourism and the search for an acceptable public identity at regional and national levels.

We hope to convey an ethnographic idea of the paradoxes involved in such a complex conservation context. Villagers themselves are involved in three different projects converging on the same materials. First, Rapacinos (except the Protestant minority) are committed to protecting traditionalistic and inward-looking ritual use of the patrimony. Second, they also want to make outward-looking, pragmatic use of it. And third, they, like the conservators, are concerned to stabilize and protect the *khipu* material fabric, despite the stresses of the first two. These three cultural frames make different material demands on the Rapaz legacy. Our experience was not that of solving a conservation problem but rather of learning to work through an imperfect, open-ended practice so as to achieve a modus vivendi among irreducibly different, equally legitimate frameworks and interests.

The Village of Rapaz and the Rapaz Research Project

The village of San Cristóbal de Rapaz and its *comunidad campesina* (peasant community or corporation of the commons) of the same name are located on the west slope of the Sierra de Raura, in the upper Huaura River drainage, Province of Oyón, Department of Lima. The nucleated center lies between 4,000 and 4,050 m above sea level, on a spur high over the uppermost reach of the Checras River. This densely built village (whose origin reaches back centuries into the colonial period) is located a little below the boundary between spacious puna pasturelands and restricted farmlands. Peru's Instituto Nacional de Estadística e Información 1993 census registered 707 inhabitants. Inhabitants speak Quechua (in declining use) and Spanish.

Rapaz upholds a notably strict regimen of the commons, long since eroded by privatization in the majority of comparable villages. Only those born in the village may have land and water rights. These rights are usufructs, not property, and the community retains right to redistribute them. Formerly, a sector of land for common production, as opposed to the plots allotted for households, formed the biggest food-producing holding in each agricultural zone. In the livestock area of the high slopes, this still holds, and common fields to grow alfalfa for the community herds also still exist. The agricultural sector includes a band of dry-farmed fields under sectoral fallowing (Guillet 1981; Hervé et al. 1995) and an irrigated lower band near the river. Sectoral fallowing entails an elaborate ceremonial and technical governance, for which the patrimonial complex is key.

The Polish archaeologist Andresz Krzanowski (1977, 1978) heard reports of *khipus* in Rapaz in the 1970s, but Peruvian archaeologist Arturo Ruíz Estrada (1981) was the first to verify them. Later reports (Alva Salinas 2006; Capurro 1995; Kaufman Doig 2005; Necochea 2004) merely repeat and garble Ruíz's findings. Peruvian historian Pablo Macera (Macera et al. 1995[?]) published a photographic book about the seventeenth and eighteenth-century murals in Rapaz's remarkable painted church, now under the care of specialists (Estabridis Cárdenas 2004). A teacher born in Rapaz printed a "local monograph" of interest for its "*costumbrista*" coverage (Valentín Montes 1996). The village has also received a good deal of attention from journalists and tourism promoters, one of whom, Cecilia Raffo (2005), offers outstanding photographs. A publication by Salomon et al. (2006) contains the first detailed description of the "*khipu* house."

The ceremonial precinct is the patrimony of Rapaz, belonging to the *comunidad campesina*, which protects it earnestly. The "*khipu* house" is especially sacred, but the associated ancient storehouse that it governs is also a site of sacrifices. Nobody may approach the precinct without a legitimate reason. Any visit requires the offering of coca leaves and invocation. Most Rapacinos firmly believe that the complex is their vital channel of communication with the deified mountains, whose gift of rain is their greatest need.

At the same time, Arturo Ruíz's work made villagers aware that outsiders are also interested. Because they regard scientific interest as legitimate and because they see the *khipu* as a glory of their village, they do allow the vice president to show visitors around. Villagers feel that maintaining the site's dual status, as a working ceremonial center and as a tourist venue at the same time, sets a challenge. The pact that underlay the present project was an offer of scientific access in return for help in protecting the physical patrimony vital to both communities.

The Patrimonial Buildings and Their Contents

The ritual-administrative precinct of traditional governance occupies an area of 346.17 m^2, close to the eastern edge of the village, on the same block as the church (see Fig. 6.1). One side of it lies along the boundary between the two traditional moieties, Allauca and Lamash. The precinct is protected by walls and gates: on two sides by fieldstone masonry, on the other two sides by *tapial*

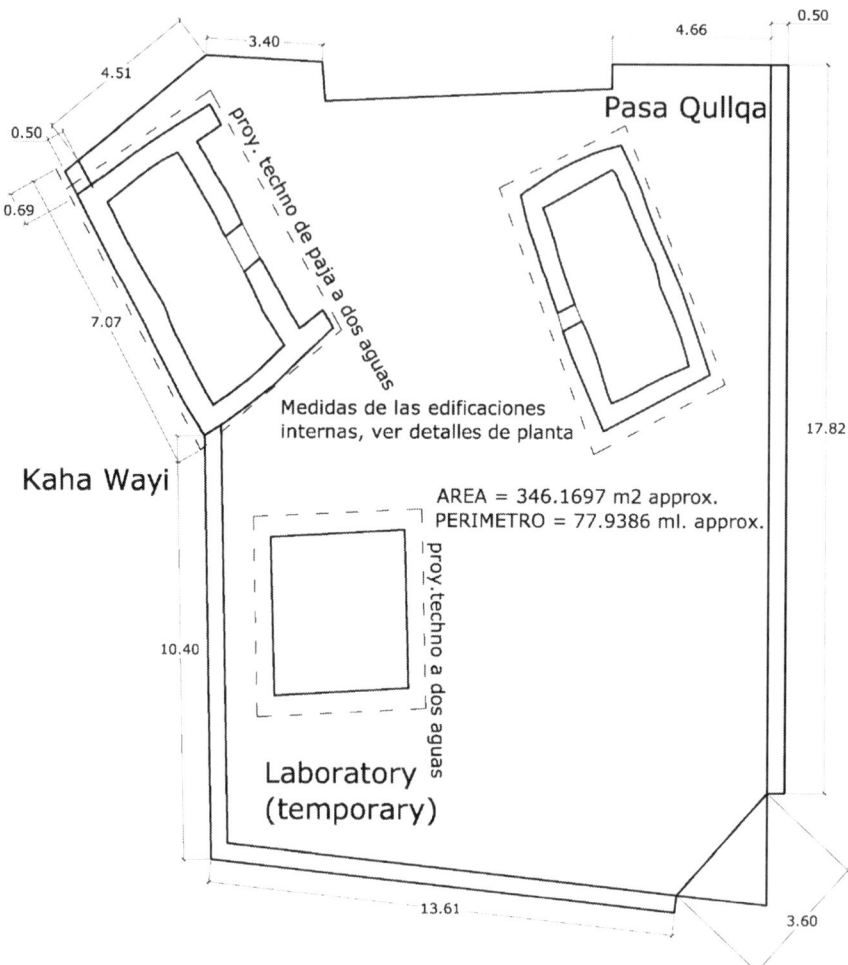

Fig. 6.1 Plan of the Rapaz ceremonial precinct

(rammed earth) walls backing onto private residences. The precinct's two buildings are the "*khipu* house," *Kaha Wayi* (Fig. 6.2), and the storehouse, *Pasa Qullqa* (Fig. 6.3). The two are roughly aligned, facing each other along a northeast–southwest axis, which forms an angle to the street grid. In Fig. 6.1, the gate at lower right is the northeast corner. Excavation showed signs of heavy plaza use, both recent and historic.

The name *Kaha Wayi* consists of a Spanish root, *caja* "treasury," and a Quechua one, *wayi*, cognate to *wasi* in southern Quechua, meaning "house." *Qullqa* means "storehouse." The adjective *pasa*, cognate to *pacha*, means "time, season, weather." Asked to translate the name, villagers render *Pasa Qullqa* as *depósito del tiempo* ("storehouse of weather") or *depósito estacional* ("seasonal storehouse").

Fig. 6.2 The precinct's *Kaha Wayi* or "*khipu* house" before conservation

Fig. 6.3 The storehouse or *Pasa Qullqa* in December 2005

Kaha Wayi (described more fully in Salomon et al. 2006) is the more frequently used part of the patrimony. It functions as the meeting place of the traditional authorities, particularly for the important New Year's meeting described later in this chapter and for the *tinka* or *mesas calzadas* in which the designated ritualist (*aukin, vendelhombre*) communicates with the owners of rain. It is rectangular, with walls of irregular stone and earth mortar and with adobe gables. A single northwest-facing door gives access to the main chamber.

A smaller opening in the southwestern gable, 2.8 m over the inside floor level, opens into the now-empty attic. The endwalls project past the main façade to form two buttresses. A low stone bench of a type common in regional pre-Hispanic architecture runs along the base of the façade. It afforded seating for officers whose low rank allowed hearing but precluded seeing the rituals within *Kaha Wayi*. The main entry, a "Dutch" door, allowed sound and the smoke of incense to reach these persons. Long eaves sheltered the outside bench.

The floor of the main chamber is compacted earth. Thick trunks of *quinual* (*Polylepis racemosa*) sustain the upper floor, 17 cm thick, whose top surface was finished with a layer of smoothed clayey earth. A small cross made of puna straw was discovered sealed under this layer.

All around *Kaha Wayi*'s interior in the main or lower chamber run built-in benches for the officers and ritualist. A niche high on the northwest wall holds candles and remains of flowers.

In 2003 and 2004, the collection of *khipu* was draped in seeming disorder over a stick hanging from the woodwork of the upper floor. This hanging rack lay parallel to the southeast or rear wall. Contrary to often repeated assertions about a unitary "giant *khipu*," it is, in fact, an assembly of 263 discrete cord objects. They are of a different basic design from Inka *khipu* (see Quilter and Urton 2002 for an overview), having no pendants but rather a single cord along which significant objects such as wool tufts, pompoms, rawhide tags, and figurines (Fig. 6.4) are attached.

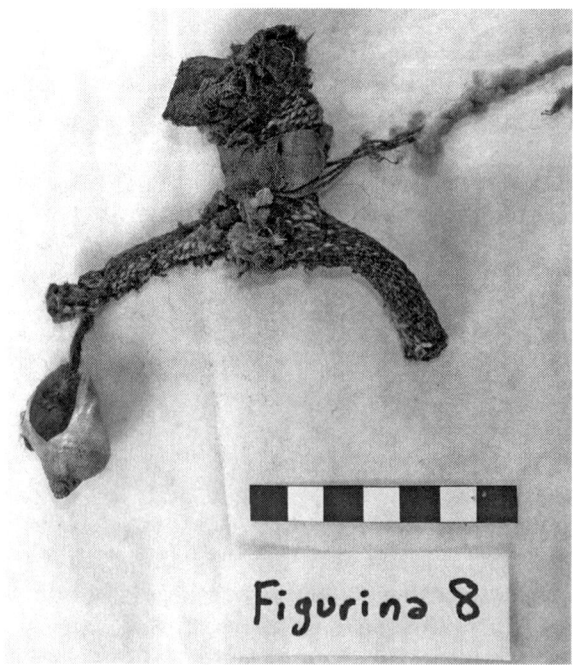

Fig. 6.4 Figurine KR08 is attached to a single "*monokhipu*" cord along with other significant objects

Even more important in the eyes of Rapacinos is the altar or the offering table, which stands in the westerly part of the chamber. Covered with a double cloth, it permanently holds three small gourds for liquid offerings (*jurka*), a coca bag (*walqi*), and a small lime gourd for consuming coca. A large pile of coca leaf obscures most of the surface. From the ceiling hang 26 diverse objects dedicated as past offerings. A large broken pot on the floor serves as a censer for burning llama fat with the aromatic herb *kunuk*. Dry plant remains under the altar attest to the *Raywan* ceremony described in a later section.

Pasa Qullqa, the storehouse, resembles *Kaha Wayi* in its overall shape and size, but is constructed differently. It neither contains furnishings now considered sacred nor functions any longer for storage. It is, however, still used frequently for nighttime community rituals.

Pasa Qullqa's exterior shows traces of having been plastered with earthen mortar and lime. It is rectangular, with three levels. Built in a style similar to that of nearby pre-Hispanic sites, it has double stone lintels and stone gables not found in colonial buildings. Around all four walls runs a projecting cornice of flat stones at 2.86 m height. This feature is also common in local late pre-Hispanic (ca. 1000–1470 AD) pre-Inca villages, which are numerous. (Indeed Rapaz seems to stand atop one such ancient village.) The masonry is less than regular but stones are consistently placed with flattest side outward. There are no exterior buttresses or benches.

Two of *Pasa Qullqa*'s three openings are on the southeastern side, facing *Kaha Wayi*. The lower of two southeastern openings gives access to a low-ceilinged semisubterranean chamber. Heavy trunks of *quinual* seated upon reinforced wall segments sustain the middle floor, which retains its surface of smoothed earth. The access to the middle floor is through the higher of the southeastern openings. The top floor was built like the middle one, but it has collapsed. Access to it was through an opening in the southwest gable, reached by an exterior stairway. Parts of the third floor's wooden door and jambs remain. Overall, *Pasa Qullqa* was more robust than *Kaha Wayi* and was designed to sustain great weights.

The Agenda of Conservation

The Rapaz complex presented novel and delicate issues of research practice. In 2003, when Salomon began negotiating terms of scientific access with the community officers and the Assembly, they expressed concern about the poor condition of the *khipu* (damaged by moths, fungus, smoke, moisture, and physical stress; Fig. 6.5). Twenty years earlier, they had tried to make a protective display case (which was discarded because it did not fit). The Assembly voted study access in return for conservation work that would allow uninterrupted dual use. They asked for scientific conservation and repair of damaged cords, and a secure display case to protect the *khipu* from smoke, moths, harmful treatment, or earthquake. Improving *khipu* protection also had a moral purpose insofar as it would imply displaying the *khipu* as respected patrimony and vindicating the community as responsible custodians.

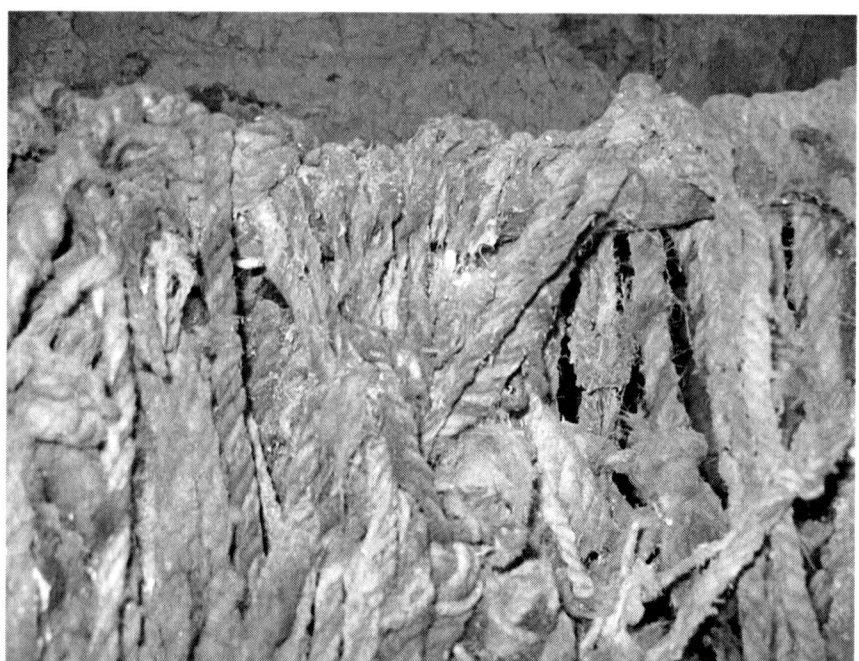

Fig. 6.5 Previous damaged condition of the *khipu*

Because living cultural knowledge is a large part of the site's value, and because it is thought to be relevant to the archaeology of storage and ceremonial places, the project was framed to include the widest possible range of anthropological subdisciplines. The decision-making process of conservation was constructed within this framework; it is intended as a specifically anthropological contribution to conservation. The archaeologist Lic. Víctor Falcón Huayta studied the immediate surroundings of the buildings. Renata Peters supervised the conservation work and coordinated some of the consultation sessions. She also provided training and support on a range of technical and scientific issues, making sure that the work carried out would be sustainable by the local community. The textile conservators Rosalía Choque Gonzales and Rosa Choque Gonzales cleaned and reinforced the *khipu*. They cooperated with Carrie Brezine, an archaeology graduate student with textile and mathematical expertise, in describing them. Salomon coordinated the project while conducting ethnographic interviews and studying the community archives. The conservation architect Gino de las Casas designed the repair and stabilization measures for the buildings, and a restoration technician, Edgar Centeno Farfán, carried them out.

At the start of fieldwork in May 2005, the community had reason to worry about the safety of the patrimony. There were cracks and fissures in the walls of both buildings. Stones and mortar were missing in many areas, allowing dust, water, and small animals inside. The interior walls were rough and dusty, and sooty with incense smoke. Both roofs were dilapidated. The top floor of *Pasa Qullqa* had collapsed after it went out of use, and its weight threatened the lower floor. The community had recently rebuilt the precinct walls and they were in good condition, but the gate to the precinct was problematic because the villagers had installed a huge steel double door so as to park the communal truck and bus inside the courtyard. Villagers agreed that the parking was undesirable but they lacked an alternative, because Rapaz has already filled all the usable space on its small hilltop. A plan that was developed by the villagers provided for relocation of vehicle storage and installation of a wooden gate at the precinct, together with paths and plantings.

The *khipu* ca. 2003 hung from the ceiling of *Kaha Wayi's* ground floor. As villagers often commented, this was not safe for the *khipu*. The ceiling over them, made of wood sticks covered with vegetable fibers and a layer of smoothed earth, had developed gaps and was covered with mold on extended areas. A large leak just above the *khipu* had allowed moisture to percolate onto the *khipu* collection. Mold grew profusely around leaks. The village had not replaced the puna grass thatch of the roof in a decade, and holes appeared along the ridgeline. The earthen floor had no drainage way.

The most obvious problem on the *khipu* themselves was abrasion of the fibers where the *khipu* were hung over a stick. The top area of the *khipu* was the most damaged showing breaks and losses. At an unknown past time, villagers had made extensive repairs to damaged *khipu* by tying pieces of cord together or by joining or reinforcing them with blanket-stitch sewing, but nobody claimed to know who had done these repairs or when. It is likely, however, that they were carried out by different people in different times, as they showed different styles and used different materials. The cords were covered with a thick layer of dust that dulled the colors of the fibers and figurines. They were also darkened. The central area of the *khipu* had a darker color and some yellowish stains, possibly caused by urine of the animals that were once fed on the upper floor. There were signs of old insect activity in some cords but it was restricted to the cords made of sheep wool. The camelid wool was almost totally intact. Insect traps did not catch any live moths during 3 months of monitoring, but the sheep skins on the benches around the room showed signs of insect activity, and when the *khipu* were conserved, moth cases were found. There were also signs of old mold infestation, more noticeable in the area underneath the hole in the ceiling. Some of the figurines attached to the *khipu* appeared at risk of becoming detached and were crushed and deformed. Yearlong interior climate monitoring showed favorable conditions, with slight fluctuations of temperature and humidity.

Conserving the Precinct Collaboratively

The practice of conservation can have a great impact not only on material culture but also on society. Clavir (2002:95) has written that the "overwhelming impression given by First Nation statements about the preservation of material culture is that preservation of objects is connected to regaining identity, respect, and cultural well-being through practicing traditions and redressing historic power imbalances. Preservation of objects is defined as integral to maintaining the life of the community. In addition, objects housed in urban museums may remain in the museum or may be repatriated; however, in both cases the objects should be contextualized in such a way that First Nations are able to make decisions about them." Lowenthal (1985: 63) writes, "Every act of recognition alters survivals from the past. Simply to appreciate or protect a relic, let alone to embellish or imitate it, affects its form or our impressions." Selecting an object for conservation, that is, making it a "conservation object" (objects that are worthy of conservation, and not only repair, maintenance, cleaning, or care; Viñas 2002: 27) is one step beyond this alteration.

The last 20 years of debate about what kind of intervention conservation is has provoked significant changes in the way it is carried out. "The old certainties of a conservation profession based on a technical understanding of the material world have been changing towards an engagement with diverse cultural perspectives and the need to justify the conservation process to a broad range of interested groups" (Peters and Sully 2006:13). New voices are heard in decision-making processes that were once restricted to museum professionals. In trying to decide how best to care for objects, understanding cultural use and significance has become as important as expertise about the material fabric or the causes of deterioration. This shift of emphasis has provoked considerable disquiet within cultural heritage institutions worldwide. The case at hand, however, is one where the local use community is entirely in command, and the researchers, as cultural heritage workers, are bound to find ways to conform to it.

Debate on conservation philosophy has been fomented by a number of international and national conventions, charters, codes of professional ethics, and guidelines for conservation practice. They include NAGPRA (1990), the Nara Document on Authenticity (ICOMOS 1994), the Burra Charter (ICOMOS 1999), and the UNESCO Convention for the Safeguarding of the Intangible Cultural Heritage (2003). These have incited considerable debate and resulted in a number of important publications such as those by Avrami, Mason and de la Torre (2000), Clavir (2002), Viñas (2002), and Johnson et al. (2005). They inform the basic decision-making process of this project. For instance, the Burra Charter "is notable as a conservation policy argument because it states that spiritual values may take precedence over physical preservation" (Clavir 2002: 59). The Burra Charter is a departure from conservation practices that did not explicitly address culturally potent objects (Clavir 2002:59).

In order to respond to these challenges, we organized a series of consultations with the *comuneros*, and especially with their elected officers who have immediate responsibility for the precinct. In May 2005, Formas Aplicadas, a firm specialized in prefab construction for high-altitude mining sites, built a small temporary site laboratory inside the precinct. In 2006, it was removed. A lab in the precinct was needed because *Kaha Wayi* is too dark and small, as well as too sacred, to admit a *khipu* worktable, while spaces outside the precinct are too profane and too insecure. In frequent meetings both onsite and off we learned about village concerns and what *comuneros* expected from us. We accepted constant supervision by them, including exclusion from the site during weeks when ritual work was underway inside.

Rosa Choque Gonzales and Rosalia Choque Gonzales, conservators from southern Peru and *comuneras* in their own home village, promoted the first of several joint events with the community in early June 2005. The activities focused on Andean techniques of spinning and weaving. This proved a very popular event with ample attendance. With the help of spinners (normally women) we bought local camelid and sheep wool in all the natural colors available in Rapaz so as to optimize match with the original fibers where repairs were needed.

The cleaning and repair of the cords began in July 2005. The *khipu* collection was taken whole to the conservation lab by the *Kaha Wayi*. Each cord was assessed, studied, photographed, and treated separately. All the cords were mechanically cleaned with brushes, small tools, and light vacuuming. All signs of insect and mold activity were removed without use of solvents. Breaks and severely abraded areas were mended with threads of matching local wool. In most of the cases a new wool thread was introduced and spun around the area under repair in a fashion similar to the earlier repairs we found on the *khipu*. The figurines were also mechanically cleaned. Some of them had to receive reinforcing lining in sympathetic materials. The offerings hung from *Kaha Wayi's* ceilings, and even the fragile remains of floral offerings received similar treatments. The *khipu* were not removed from the hanger stick, but rather worked upon in the same tangled positions we found them in. In order to isolate the *khipu* one by one for study, we slid paper underneath each cord so as to isolate it visually only. Because this meant settling for less than 100% visibility, and because the tangled cords remained a topological puzzle, the task of describing the collection was quite complicated.

One of the biggest concerns was stress damage that the fibers along the hanger rod had suffered due to sustaining the weight of the *khipu* (10 kg) in vertical position. Horizontal display, on the other hand, would not be possible, because it would obstruct the space for seating ritual participants in *Kaha Wayi*. Together with the display designer, Nelly Faustino, and following decisions made during consultation sessions, we designed a support mount that would distribute the weight of the *khipu* more equally on its surface (Fig. 6.6). Placing it on a 60° slant reduced the stress on the top area of the cords considerably while minimizing obstruction in the ritual chamber.

The architectural conservation work went on concurrently. Only techniques and materials matching original construction were employed, even though others might have been more durable or more protective. Architect Gino de Las Casas directed it, coordinating with the Instituto Nacional de Cultura (National Institute of Culture). Preparations included a *mesa calzada* (invocation, oracle, and sacrifice) conducted by the community's contracted ritualist,

Fig. 6.6 The glass vitrine installed with the *khipu* returned. This new mount distributed the weight of the *khipu* so as to reduce stress on the top cords while permitting visibility without obstructing space in the chamber

Melecio Montes. Together with village workers and with the technician Edgar Centeno, we effected repair of masonry, replacement of broken adobes, removal of rubble, replacement of missing mortar, roofing of both buildings, and improvement of drainage both within the buildings and in their exterior courtyard. While the *khipu* were in the lab, the ceiling of the ritual chamber was removed. Infested and rotten wood was replaced with healthy material of the same species and worksmanship. During this period, the safety of the offering table was a cause of anxiety for many villagers, because disturbance to it would also disturb relations to the sacred mountains, who might withhold rain. We built a wooden shelter to cover it on all sides, and it was not disturbed.

As decided in consultation with the community officers, the floor was left untouched; direct contact with the earth is essential to the ceremonies. We did not install electric light because electricity is not allowed inside the *Kaha Wayi*. Insect traps were set in strategic areas for further monitoring. The sheep skins on the benches, which were foci of moth infestation, were burned and replaced. The inside walls were brushed and vacuumed.

In early August, as structural architectural repairs were advancing and archaeological work was ending, we consulted about how *Kaha Wayi* and *Pasa Qullca* should be readied for reinstallation of the *khipu* collection. The *khipu* chamber at that time contained miscellaneous unused material, which the traditional authorities divided between trash and unused but still sacred material to be resituated. Among the latter was a wooden cross that had been removed from its former outdoor site in the course of road repair and left in *Kaha Wayi* pending relocation.

The latter category also included large gunny sacks containing coca leaves, which had been sucked dry and set aside during years of ritual. Coca is never trash; on the contrary, used coca is called "the work," that is, the precipitate of good efforts. Ritualist Montes decided it should be buried in the remaining open archaeological excavation unit, so that in closing the unit "the work" would be united with the foundations of *Kaha Wayi*. Late in the dry season, we hired local herders to bring long puna grass, the traditional roofing material, down from the heights. Deteriorated thatch was removed from both buildings and given away or scrapped. A new roof was built under the direction of master roofer Melanio Falcón. The final phase included improvements to the drainage, gates, and path of the precinct, which had suffered damage because of occasional use as a parking space for the community truck.

Toward the end of the fieldwork, in December, a crew composed of villagers, display case fabricators, and project staff assembled the showcase inside *Kaha' Wayi*. The *khipu* collection was mounted on a plexiglass support panel, then packed, carried inside the chamber, and installed (Fig. 6.6). Having finished the conservation, we prepared a report and brochures of pictures of the process as community records; like most peasant communities, Rapaz is extremely strict about documentation. The report was presented at the New Year Assembly of 2006 and all of the keys of the case were handed over to the vice president or *Kamachikuq*. Discussion of the work at the Assembly was extensive, because anything that touches the precinct is taken as a solemn and vital matter. In particular it was necessary to dispel a rumor: Having seen the simulacrum cords that we made early in the process for self-training, some villagers mistakenly supposed that real *khipu* would be taken away and new cordage substituted.

The Patrimony at Night: Ritual Use

The ritual regimen of the patrimonial precinct is carried on alongside a typical rural Andean Catholic calendar of feasts and devotions, impressively performed within and around the village's famous painted church. At some point in the past, unknown hands created a hidden connection between the two ritual centers by secreting a small straw cross in the upper floor of *Kaha Wayi*. Modern Rapacinos knew nothing of it until it was accidentally revealed during floor repairs. Today, three-and-a-half centuries after the "extirpations of idolatry" hammered their district, the great majority of Rapacinos see no problem in coexistence between Christian and non-Christian sacred practices. (This is not true of the minority Pentecostal, Adventist, and Evangelical religious sectors, which despise the patrimonial tradition and profess a desire to silence it.)

But if villagers uphold coexistence of the two sacred places – which share the same block – they never mix them. Their respective occasions do not overlap. Neither have they common property nor is any object transferred between them. No trace of the patrimonial precinct is paraded in Catholic processions. The patrimonial precinct lacks visible symbols of Christianity. Indeed, Church and precinct coexist well precisely because their activities belong to different spheres of activity and discourse. Rapacinos neither speak of *Kaha Wayi* or *Pasa Qullqa* as religious places nor consider their dealings with the superhuman natural powers to be "religion." Rather, *Kaha Wayi* embodies a group of civic obligations to superhuman powers, and their discharge is entirely fused with the traditional political regimen.

Rapacinos conceive of themselves and their entire productive environment as a single hierarchy of living beings. (It is unclear whether the deities of Christendom belong within or "above" it; this would be a useless question, since a practical system for living with both already exists.) Not only people are ranked with regard to each other, but the same chain of rank also extends upward into the superhuman sphere. The superhuman sphere includes the deified mountains, the high lakes, and glaciers, all of which are spoken of as being quasi-persons. Relations with them are organized as relations of asymmetrical reciprocity, and they have most of the same social attributes as human relations with higher-ups: deference and gift giving, professions of dutiful obligation and loyalty, with frequent supplications, but, at the same time, a touchy readiness to stand on dignity and even to defy, should expectations of reciprocity be disappointed.

Superhuman rank has nothing to do with supernaturalism and involves no dualism of substance. The superhuman powers are in and of the material world; they have bodies and bodily needs. Indeed anything that has a physical body – a planted field or the buildings of the sacred precinct themselves – must be addressed as a person in ritual chant or song. The deeds of the powers are imputed to their purposes and material means; there is nothing miraculous or metaphysical about it from the local point of view. The reason the deeds of the high powers are harder to understand and deal with than those of people is that they are remote in hierarchy, haughty, and hard to talk with.

This framework is noticeable in relational terms connecting villagers to higher-ranking humans, and also humans to still higher ranking beings such as the sacred precinct and the nearby oracle places (springs and caves). These in turn had the great deified mountains as their superiors. Any actor speaks of superiors in the idiom of seniority using gender-bound relational terms. The villagers speak of superior officers, notably their contracted ritualist, as *awkin* ("elder, old man") or *vendelhombre* (*bien del hombre*, "human welfare," said in both Spanish and Quechua). But the ritualist in turn speaks of the superhuman beings to whom he is supplicant with the same terms. When the relation is female-focused, as in the case of the ritualist's wife, one uses the corresponding female term *chakwas*. *Awkin* and *chakwas* do not imply descent, for which there are separate generational terms. They do, however, imply power, especially the power to give or withhold the conditions of growth, so biological continuity, and hence the continuity of community, depends on them.

Powerful beings are imagined in variable degrees as strict and demanding, even punishing. The more senior the power one approaches, the more the danger involved. A great ritualist is a supplicant before them, but at other times a bold advocate. He must speak fearlessly for the collectivity's interest. In extreme moments it is his mission to roam the icy heights in a state of ritual asceticism and confront the mountains close up, upbraiding the peaks and punishing the glacial ice with slingshots for sending hail. The powers expect obeisance but respect valor and courage. Humans owe them deference rather than subservience. When reciprocal relations turn bad, it is right for people to defy or fight even the high powers.

Kaha Wayi functions as a central place – it would not be too much to say a temple – connecting the villagers, their fields, and their herds with the "owners of water" or deified mountains. It formerly also regulated the irrigation regimen and the storage of products of the commons. Those who enter *Kaha Wayi* enter a mediating position. From there, authority both voices the village's requests to superior beings and emits commands to the villagers.

The people authorized to enter *Kaha Wayi* are an annually chosen "agropastoral committee" who form an inner corp within the legal government of the recognized peasant community. "Agropastoral committee" is an updated name for the corps called *varayuq* ("staff holders" or "traditional authorities"), present or formerly present in most Andean communities. At the annual Community Assembly, these officers wear traditional Andean formal dress (brown poncho, flowered hat, and coca bag) in contrast to the urban styles of the "statutory" officers. As well as having a temple-like function, *Kaha Wayi* is something like a board room. It is the traditional place for deliberative discussion among the authorities (*rimanakuy*), and everything said inside it is confidential.

One person is necessarily a Janus-faced member of both the traditional and the statutory hierarchy. He is perhaps the most important member of the hierarchy, the hinge between its inner and outer or ritual and bureaucratic components. In the statutory hierarchy he is called the vice president of the community. As such he has charge of all intravillage transactions involving the commons, an immense administrative burden. (The President has charge of the community's external relations.) At the same time, he also holds the title of *Kamatsikuq* ("who animates and orders") within the Agropastoral Committee. In this capacity he holds the silver-clad staff of office, leads the traditional authorities into the patrimonial precinct, guards its key exerting sole decision about access, and organizes ritual work for the welfare of the crops. (A lesser but similar officer, the *Mayordomo* of the communal herds, has charge of the livestock productive sector.)

Sectoral fallowing means rotating of three successive crop groups through eight sectors (*anqi*). The agricultural cycle begins in October, with potato planting. The newly opened sector grows potatoes, the most esteemed and ritually salient crop. The sector in second-year use grows oca or mashua (other Andean tubers), and the one in third-year use grows barley or quinua. The other five sectors, including the newly closed one, are used for stubble grazing only. The Agropastoral Committee's members police this system. They allot usufructs, enforce participation in the collective labor days (*faena*) which repair infrastructure, detect illegal use, capture stray animals, monitor the health of crops, and give out permissions to harvest in proper sequence.

And the Agropastoral Committee is responsible for procuring rain. Ideally, rain arrives in October. But the wait for Rapaz's sparse and irregular rain causes intense anxiety. The "search for weather" (*búsqueda del tiempo*) is the most pressing reason why the vice president must annually contract a vendelombre or ritualist.

The political year, unlike the farming year, begins on the first of January. The incoming officers and their ritualist therefore take over crops that have already begun to grow, and they must care for them by both ritual and technical means (an extraneous distinction, from the local viewpoint). As soon as the Community Assembly adjourns, normally January 2, the vice president/*Kamatsikuq* leads the Agropastoral Committee into the sacred precinct and begins readying the nocturnal ritual that will install his new officers. They sit on the stone benches around the altar table, some with their backs near the *khipus* (Fig. 6.7).

There he dispatches officers to inspect the sectors where the new crops are growing: for each sector, a team is composed of one incoming and one outgoing officer. This is to make sure the new officer assumes responsibility for the condition of the crop as of the changeover, without incurring blame for any damage that occurred before it. Each team brings in a crop token called *raywan* ("mother of food"). A *raywan* is a living plant, complete with roots in a soil ball, selected as the representative of its crop sector. It should be one of the healthiest and handsomest. When all have reassembled in *Kaha Wayi*, the ritualist begins in earnest the rounds of libation, coca leaf sucking, and cigarette smoking, which accompany every series of invocations. The returning teams then report prosaically on the observed state of the plantings: height of growth, moisture, signs of fungus or larval infections, condition of the field fences and paths, etc., giving recommendations for treatment of any defect and correction of infractions. If any fault is found with a sector's condition, the outgoing officer is symbolically whipped. The ritualist authorizes the replacement of old with new *raywan*. The authorities remove from under the altar the withered remains of last year's raywan and set them in the area for deactivated ritual things, while installing the new ones. (In past times *raywan* were planted inside *Kaha Wayi*, where, because of the darkness, they grew into a tall, ghostly thicket of pallid stems.)

Fig. 6.7 New officers of the Agropastoral Committee are installed

The vice president dismisses the outgoing officers and yields to the ritualist, who begins a long series of libations, smokes, and coca rounds with invocations that gradually lead up to the *mesa calzada* or sacrifice dispatched to the mountains. Night falls; *Kaha Wayi* becomes cold and dark, lit only by the flicker of a candle and the flare of matches. The invocations, which are murmured in Quechua, address *Kaha Wayi* and *Pasa Qullqa*, the *khipu*, the nearby oracle spring of Tukapia, and the many superhuman places of the landscape outward and upward from the village all the way to the giant snowcap Waqrunchu. These beings each stand in a particular relation to the village. Some are allies in long-standing ritual friendship, but others, called *chúcaro* or "untamed" mountains, make no pact with humanity. These are touchy, vengeful, and violent and must be addressed with courage as well as tact. The invocations have a general format, namely semantic couplets, with a slight caesura between parts, which is varied to express the village's particular relation with each powerful place:

> Mountain [name], Mountain [second name],
> Forgive our mistakes, talk to us, converse with us
> So there will be good rain, so the plants will grow well.
> We ask for good rain, for good weather;
> Let there be no hail, let there be no drought,
> Let [the plants] not be blighted, let them not be wormy,
> Let all be for the best, let all be for the best.

While invoking them, the group prepares a special incense compounded of llama fat (*llama wira*) and aromatic sprigs from the high slopes (*kunuk*). The glowering embers are carefully watched, as their flickers express the powers' response to the invocations. With great care and deliberation the ritualist prepares three types of liquefied maize (*jurka*), of three different colors. They are poured into the three small gourd bowls on the altar and dedicated with blessings. Some 15 sacred places must be called upon, each triply using the three kinds of *jurka*, so the rite is long. The proceedings have a rhythm that allows relaxation between rounds of libation and invocation. But now, past midnight in the increasingly icy darkness, they take on a more solemn air as the ritualist readies himself for his confidential dialogue with the mountains and for the sacrifice of the offering. In the wee hours he leaves *Kaha Wayi* to make an animal sacrifice by starlight and voice a prayer, which nobody is allowed to witness. The final invocations must be finished before the first pallor of dawn, because it is important that no other villager see officers leaving the rites.

As the year proceeds, both *Kaha Wayi* and the former storehouse *Pasa Qullqa* will be the scenes of many more ritual actions. Their scheduling depends upon the weather and the degree of anxiety it provokes. Several times the ritualist will sequester himself in the precinct for days and nights, subsisting only on maize water, and coca leaf, so as to ready himself for further divinations and sacrifices, and, if need be, for pilgrimages to "search for weather." During these intervals the project was excluded from the precinct, as were the villagers. Other rites, such as the two sacrifices this project sponsored to safeguard *Kaha Wayi* and *Pasa Qullqa* during conservation, may be shorter and less exclusive. But in all cases, ritual events take place at night, and in all cases the physical integrity of the site by local criteria was anxiously considered.

The Patrimony by Day: Tourism and Other Outward-Facing Uses

Journalistic publicity, road building, and the rise of a thermal-bath circuit in the Checras river valley have connected the formerly remote village of Rapaz to the fringes of tourist orbit. Since 1978, when Ruíz Estrada began informing Limeños about the place, a slowly growing traffic of visitors has been arriving. A subsidy in the era of President Alberto Fujimori to hot-spring bathing facilities at the nearby village of Huancahuasi markedly stimulated it. The demand for visits prompted traditional authorities to work out a regimen for outside viewing of the *khipu* patrimony, albeit an unreliable one: visitors must find the vice president, and he must personally unlock the precinct and show them around. (This is unreliable because campesinos, including the officers, necessarily spend much of their time in remote fields and pastures.)

During the project reported here, over 300 people visited the patrimony and signed a guestbook. Many were peasants from other villagers in the region, some of whom understood the ritual inheritance well, while many more were Limeños on side trips from the baths. Groups of hikers, students from universities, and educated retirees arrived seeking knowledge of what has wrongly been publicized as an Inka inheritance. Only a tiny number of foreigners, all longtime Lima residents, arrived. Although it seems all but inevitable that Rapaz will eventually attract international "adventure tourism," this has not occurred yet.

Not all visitors are tourists. One or two times a month, rural technocrats such as agronomists from the Ministry of Agriculture and Livestock stop by. So do staff of the NGOs with which the community has contracted to improve veterinary medicine and preventive health care. Architectural conservationists employed by the Getty Foundation's project to stabilize endangered colonial churches in the Huaura river basin visit Rapaz every few months and take interest in *Kaha Wayi*. Teachers in the village's public schools usually have little taste for local culture but there are exceptions, and a few of these asked to visit. A mining company, which has been interminably trying to persuade the community to sell exploration rights, sends its representatives; on one occasion a mining trade magazine sent a journalistic team, preparing a cultural article as a way of public relations. And not least, the city-born descendants of emigrant Rapacinos often appear for village festivals. Village festivals create crowds of would-be visitors, a logistical problem because the tiny chamber of *Kaha Wayi* has space only for a few at a time.

In July of 2005, a Lima NGO called the "Alliance for Struggle Against Poverty and Memorial *Khipu* of the Fallen" organized a rally in Rapaz at which a well-known priest of the Catholic left spoke. ("Fallen" refers to those killed in the Shining Path war or dead of poverty-related illnesses.) The campaigners chose Rapaz for a stop of its caravan because *khipu* harmonized with its theme of memorialism. In the course of an all-day ceremony including a Mass, the campaigners had the villagers tie lengths of colored acrylic into a giant ersatz *khipu* for procession. Few, if any, villagers grasped the supposed connection to the *Kaha Wayi* patrimony, but the large crowd avidly visited the sacred building. The community, equally avid for politically potent Lima connections, slaughtered several of its cattle and fed the visitors a lavish *pachamanka* (an earth-oven feast).

Because of its unusual status as a self-curated, village-owned patrimony, the precinct of Rapaz has not been the object of direct intervention by any unit of government. But government agents at various levels do want to develop stakes in it. In most highland villages the Municipality propagates a Lima-emulating program of cement-built modernizations, and Rapaz is no exception. Its Mayor occasionally proposes to "coordinate" the precinct, over which he has no governance rights, with the faux-Inka décor he imposed on the main square. A semigovernmental organization called PROMPERU, responsible for promoting Peruvian tourism abroad and developing tourist resources, repeatedly stimulated tours by journalists and television crews. Peru's Instituto Nacional de Cultura, the powerful central bureaucracy governing archaeological research, has obtained wide powers over post-Inka patrimonies and required a detailed report on the project. An INC *declaratoria* proclaiming national protection of the site has not been sought. In the authors' opinion it would not be useful because it would inhibit the self-governing, active-use curation, which Rapaz has successfully evolved. INC "protection" at hundreds of sites amounts to an unfunded mandate, which increases legal burdens on local people without facilitating conservation.

Tourism raises fateful questions for Rapaz, exceeding the scope of this report. The village hopes it will afford chances for commerce, but no villager is familiar with the tourist business, and most of the necessary infrastructure (sanitation, lodging, restaurant) is lacking. The village has not yet developed a way to sell goods or services to visitors. Working out a harmonious touristic use of the precinct would provide an opportunity, but first, the traditional authorities will have to find a way of reconciling their busy peasant schedules with the need for scheduled attendance at the site – a site to which only one person may grant admission.

Conclusions: A Moving Equilibrium

Visitors to Rapaz are shown the *"khipu* house*"* as a cultural patrimony of historic interest. During the project the village allowed over 300 people, nearly all Peruvian, to view the patrimonial precinct. Villagers presented it to them as a memorial to local people's share in "Inka" greatness. Traditional authority at the same time asks tourists to acknowledge the site's other role, as a sacred place, by giving coca to its altar. For many urbanites this is a completely new experience, because it entails taking part in a culture they are taught to see as strange, backward, and racially "other." As a tourist policy this is novel, interesting, and positive. The generous donations visitors give show that it evokes engagement and good will.

Visitors are not told, however, that they are in fact entering the cardinal present-day ritual place of the village or that it is the modern scene of the same Andean worship that the Catholic Church strove to "extirpate" 350-odd years ago. Rather, the *khipu* collection, because it is a famous emblem of the past, offsets the encounter from the present. The premise of the visit is that the newcomer is entering the past, by encountering the space of an "Inka" relic. Nearly all the dialogue concerns this theme. The contemporaneity of the precinct is effectively silenced in tourist interaction.

This is a congenial working misunderstanding. Reticence about the present makes sense. It has to do with villagers' conviction that nocturnal rites have to be invisible, and also with awareness that Limeños associate the cult of the mountains with racially stigmatized "Indianness." (Rapacinos have yet to encounter the Indianophile mentality of tourists from North America and Europe, who romanticize Andean ritual as a source of "green" wisdom.)

In cooperating with scientists and conservators, village authorities hope to make the most of a patrimony, which is at once a cultural monument by day and a sacred center by night, yet not prejudice either function. Many or most Rapacinos feel that their village deserves more fame and would benefit by a growth in cultural tourism. They consider that outside specialists are valuable in materially stabilizing the patrimony, in publicizing it, and in providing information to underwrite the "educational" or secular-civic side of the visiting protocol. Without having worked it out sufficiently, they optimistically hope that these improvements will help them key into the hot-spring tourist circuit and attract much-needed cash business.

The project sketched above tries to serve this multiuse goal. Much was achieved: we learned how physical conservation, scientific study, tourism, and ritual could be combined within one small space and in closely apportioned time. But we also learned that any durable success in such radical multipurpose use can only be a moving equilibrium among practices that make contradictory demands on the patrimony. The legitimate interests involved are simply too incommensurable to be reconciled in a single, steady community policy. Site use is and will continue to be a historic process of negotiation and change.

One reason a fixed policy will not suffice is that Rapaz is itself diverse in its understandings of the patrimonial precinct. At the grossest level, one must take into account dissensus between Protestants and folk-Catholic Rapacinos. The former are willing to preserve the site, but only as historical monument. Nothing save their minority standing stops them from attacking what they call "satanic" nighttime rituals.

More subtly and more interestingly, however, folk-Catholic users of the site themselves differ in their views. Early in the project, Salomon failed to realize that in negotiating scientific access with the community board, he was hearing a biased sample of local discourse. Male villagers versed in metropolitan law, language, and rhetoric are disproportionately the ones elected to the directorate They are considered best able to engage outsiders such as academics, technocrats, lawyers, mine staff, tourists, and government personnel. By speaking for the village, these men screen outsiders off from the larger body of opinion held by less cosmopolitan villagers, particularly women, elders, and the many who spend most of the time in the high altitudes with herds.

The latter sectors take the ritual claims of *Kaha Wayi* and *Pasa Qullqa* literally. They see every material attribute of the precinct – including dirt, contaminants, insects, and moisture – as the visible precipitate of working relations with the *aukin* and *chakwas* powers. They are sure that any disturbance to these materials also disturbs delicately achieved relationships, and therefore threatens crops and herds. They are the strictest of "conservators:" their idea of conservation means not changing anything at all, not even a rotten roof, unless the *aukin* should tell them to. Such people became anxious about the roofing of the two patrimonial buildings. Since the site brings rain, they felt rain could not come until the site was restored to its former condition, preferably with dirt and bugs.

A similar paradox occurred with regard to transparency about the work in progress. Rapacinos, like highlanders in general, distrust outsiders and foreigners. To allay fears about theft or mistreatment of the *khipu* collection, transparency was crucial. In an earlier patrimonial *khipu* project, Salomon had set his worktable along a main-traveled way so that villagers would continually witness the work. But in the case of Rapaz, transparency is also transgressive. The *"khipu* house" is an arcanum, and in the older regime (within the experience of everyone over about 35 years), outsiders were never admitted at all. Even now admission is far from public. The *khipu*-cleaning temporary laboratory provoked curiosity, and many wanted to visit (Fig. 6.8). Some visitors said they had never seen the *khipu* and feared them. We felt allowing visitors into the lab was crucial in alerting villagers to infestation and deterioration, as well as making sure sufficient witnesses could counteract rumors of *khipu* theft. But generous access also raised questions of ritual propriety. Villagers became anxious that possible transgressions in this unprecedented project would prevent rain from arriving. It did arrive, albeit late, just in time to dispel mounting tension. During Salomon's later visits (2006, 2007, 2008), ritualist Montes and other non-Evangelical villagers expressed satisfaction at the compound's good condition and climatic effectiveness. Nonetheless Protestant hostility to the site poses a conservation threat for the future.

No less paradoxical are the questions of "authenticity" that occur in the tourist–patrimony encounter. The old storage of the *khipu*, draped over a wooden rod, was rejected by the village leaders because it exposed wool to

Fig. 6.8 Elisa Falcón visits the lab

pollutants, infestation, and mechanical stress. It was they who (desirably, from a traditional museological viewpoint) requested a strong metal and glass case and even tried to build one in the past. However, the old installation had an "organic" and congenially low-tech feel. It gave a pleasant sense of closeness to the swaying, woolly-smelling textile treasure. This fitted a popular idea of authenticity. Replacement by the new display case challenges the taste of sophisticated visitors.

But there is room for doubt about whether satisfying this taste should be a priority. From the villagers' viewpoint, installing the case meant appropriating for rural society part of the prestigious technical power of the city and its museums. As a gesture, it stands against the all-centralizing acquisitive claims of the national cultural institutions. It is as if to say, "we do what no museum can do: we conserve things for ourselves, and we do it at home." From the viewpoint of innumerable rural groups (and not only in Peru), it would be helpful if museum audiences came to the country instead of demanding they release rural patrimony to cities.

Finally and most centrally, the ritual use of the *khipu* chamber goes against the main principles of preventive conservation care. The rituals smudge the *khipu* and other patrimony with smoke from incense and tobacco, invite moths because the members sit on sheepskins, propagate fungus because they spill liquids on patrimonial objects, and bring in foreign matter on plants. The revered cover of the altar, a small textile of the 1930s that is all but eaten away by fungus, is a good example of the paradox. To profane eyes, the reason for the damage is that the gourds holding *jurka* or liquefied maize offering sit on it. They are hygroscopic (hold moisture), so the textile underneath is often wet. But in ritual context the seepage is said to show that the deified mountains are drinking their offering. The textile conservators mended the cloth with partly synthetic fibers, which resist fungus, and with the ritualist's permission put porous ceramic saucers under the gourds so as to slow the seepage. But ritual outcome, not conservation policy, decides whether Rapaz accepts the measure. (Up to 2008, it had.) A conservation intervention like this represents only an interim measure, a proposal for practice. It should not be seen as the solution to long-term conservation problems or as an end point stopping material change. The altar cover exemplifies the need to view conservation as an ongoing process, rather than to focus on the statically conserved object (Peters and Sully 2006: 12–17).

The rituals are the patrimonial precinct's reason for being, no less so than its historic and anthropological worth. The intangible and the tangible parts of Rapaz's inheritance stand in a dynamic relationship, which defies the idea of permanent conservation. Intangible practices both consume material patrimony and produce it. Neither one can be expected to remain the same. Our approach was to try to minimize the incongruity between preservation and active ritual use, engaging the parties on their own ground and using the means, which would be locally acceptable rather than museologically optimal.

Any conception of heritage positing separable "tangible" and "intangible" parts that each ought to hold motionless in time is, in the end, unrealistic because it is born of a misunderstanding about how cultural things endure. The active and changing work of "intangible" ritual, hospitality, and politics are themselves what caused the patrimony to endure. If they are, at the same time, the things that put it at risk, that is a fact with which conservator-allies must work in good faith, and not some pathology they are authorized to cure.

Acknowledgments The authors gratefully acknowledge the support provided by the National Science Foundation under grant no. 0453965, the Wenner-Gren Foundation for Anthropological Research, the Fulbright-Hayes Commission, Fundación Telefónica of Peru, the Instutito Nacional de Cultura, and Centro Mallqui. Above all, we thank the Comunidad Campesina de San Cristóbal de Rapaz for allowing us the opportunity to study its patrimony.

References

Alva Salinas, José
    2006 Universo Rapaz, un desconocido tesoro colonial en la sierra de Lima. *El Comercio* (Lima), 12 febrero 2006:8–9.
Avrami, Erica, Randall Mason, and Marta de la Torre
    2000 *Values and Heritage Conservation*. Research Report to the Getty Conservation Institute. Getty Conservation Institute, Los Angeles.
Capurro, Hugo Ramón
    1995 El Quipu gigante de Rapaz. *Restaurantes y Turismo* 1(1):17–21. Lima.
Clavir, Miriam
    2002 *Preserving What Is Valued: Museums, Conservation and First Nations*. University of British Columbia Press, Vancouver and Toronto.
Estabridis Cárdenas, Ricardo
    2004 Iglesia de San Cristóbal de Rapaz: Análisis Iconográfica de la Pintura Mural. Unpublished report to The Getty Foundation.
Guillet, David
    1981 Land Tenure, Ecological Zone, and Agricultural Regime in the Central Andes. *American Ethnologist* 8(1):139–156.
Hervé, Dominique, Gilles Rivière, and Luz Pacheco
    1995 Communities and Collective Usage of Land Resources in the Andes. Paper presented at the Fifth Common Property Conference, Bodø, Norway, 1995.
ICOMOS (International Council on Monuments and Sites)
    1994 Nara Document on Authenticity. Nara Conference on Authenticity in Relation to the World Heritage Convention, Nara, Japan. www.international.icomos.org/charters/nara_e.htm
    1999 The Burra Charter. The Australia ICOMOS Charter for the Conservation of Places of Cultural Significance. Electronic document, http://www.icomos.org/australia/burra.html, accessed 03/30, 2007.
Johnson, J. S., S. Heald, K. McHugh, E. Brown, and M. Kaminitz
    2005 Practical Aspects of Consultation with Communities. *Journal of the American Institute for Conservation* 44(3):203–215.
Kaufman Doig, Federico
    2005 Un quipu gigante. *Arkinka, Revista de Arquitectura, Diseño y Construcción* 10(114):78–86.

Krzanowski, Andrzej
  1977 Archaeological Investigations in the Upper Huaura Basin (Central Peru), Part I. *Acta Archaeologica Carpathica* 17:121–137.
  1978 Archaeological Investigations in the Upper Huaura Basin (Central Peru), Part II. *Acta Archaeologica Carpathica* 18:201–226.
Lowenthal, David
  1985 *The Past is a Foreign Country*. Cambridge University Press, Cambridge and New York.
Macera, Pablo, Arturo Ruíz Estrada, Luísa Castro, y Rocío Menéndez
  1995(?) *Murales de Rapaz*. Universidad del Pacífico y Banco de Reserva del Perú, Lima.
Necochea, Carlos
  2004 Gigantesco quipu se halla oculto en comunidad ce la serranía de Lima. *El Comercio* (Lima) March 24, 2004:1.
Peru, Instituto Nacional de Estadística e Información, Censo IX Nacional de Población. http://www.inei.gob.pe/BancoCuadros/Bancua20.asp?bco = 14&dep = 15&pro = 09&dis = 01&cat = 06&ccpp = 0005&tit = Departamento:LIMA$Provincia:$Distrito:OYON, accessed 27 March 2007.
Peters, Renata and D. Sully
  2006 Finding the Fallen: Conservation and the First World War. In *IIC Munich Congress. The Object in Context: Crossing Conservation Boundaries*, edited by D. Sauders and J. Townsend, pp. 12–17. James & James, London.
Quilter, Jeffrey and Gary Urton (editors)
  2002 *Narrative Threads. Accounting and Recounting in Andean Khipu*. University of Texas Press, Austin.
Raffo, Cecilia
  2005 Peregrinación por las iglesias de Oyón y Huaura. *Bienvenida* 13(52):28–47.
Ruiz Estrada, Arturo
  1981 *Los Quipus de Rapaz*. Centro de Investigación de Ciencia y Tecnología de Huacho, Huacho.
Salomon, Frank, Carrie Brezine and Víctor Falcón Huayta
  2006 Los Khipus de Rapaz en casa: Un complejo administrativo-ritual centroperuano. *Revista Andina* 43:59–92.
Valentín Montes, Guido Amadeo
  1996 *Rapaz Desde el Fondo de los Siglos*. Librería Gráfica "Miller" S.R.I., Lima.
Viñas, Salvador
  2002 Contemporary Theory of Conservation. *IIC Reviews in Conservation* 3:25–34.

Chapter 7
Geographies of Memory and Identity in Oceania

Janet Dixon Keller

Taking inspiration from my colleague, Martin Manalansan (2003), I would like to open with an excerpt from Salman Rushdie's *Imaginary Homelands*: "The effect of mass migrations has been the creation of radically new types of human being, people who root themselves in ideas rather than place, in memories as much as material things; ... people in whose deepest selves strange fusions occur, unprecedented unions between what they were and where they find themselves" (Rushdie 1991:124–125).

Such transformation is not without crisis and contradiction. The migrant who grapples with the loss of place-based identity may hold dearly to memories rooting the self in cultural topography even as he or she aspires also to "being modern." From the security of a habitus in which practices and spaces cocreate a common sense, intelligible, foreseeable, and, hence, taken-for-granted world (Bourdieu 1977:80), an immigrant is thrust into a new world of conflicting principles and protean possibilities. Positioned by unfamiliar structures, the migrant struggles to navigate among options directed only vaguely toward imagined and desired cosmopolitan ends.

How does intangible heritage fare in such circumstances? And what role, if any, can the tangible and intangible qualities of the past play in guiding mobile subjects?

Rural–Urban Migration: Futuna, Vanuatu to Port Vila

This chapter explores the complex and often divided identity that emerges for rural–urban migrants from an outer island of the Vanuatu archipelago who have taken up residence in the urban capital of Port Vila on the central island of Efate. Vanuatu is an archipelago of roughly 80 islands in Melanesia, southwest Pacific (Figs. 7.1 and 7.2). Somewhat over 200,000 citizens of the relatively

---

J.D. Keller (✉)
Department of Anthropology, University of Illinois at Urbana-Champaign, Urbana, IL 61801, USA
e-mail: jdkeller@illinois.edu

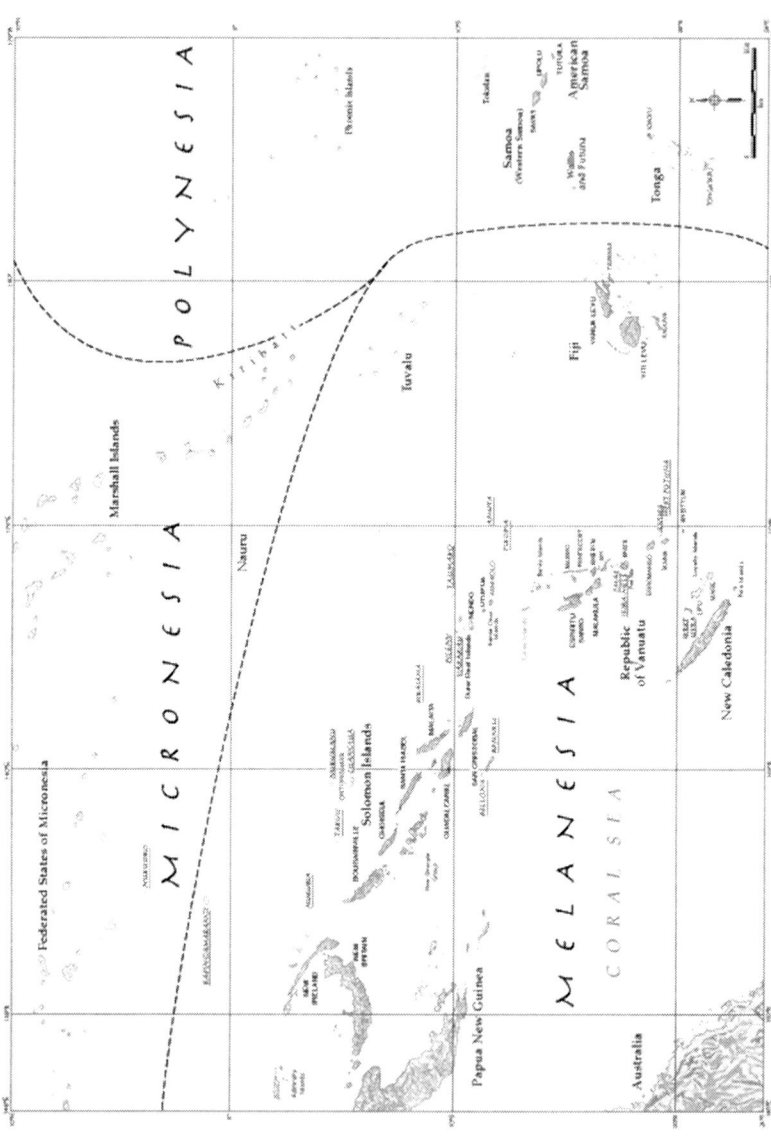

Fig. 7.1 Vanuatu in its larger Pacific setting. Traditional culture areas designated as Polynesia, Melanesia, and Micronesia (©2007 Janet Dixon Keller and Takaronga Kuautonga. Reprinted with permission of Crawford House Publishing Australia)

Fig. 7.2 Republic of Vanuatu locating Futuna at the southern extreme of the archipelago. Adapted from Republic of Vanuatu, Republique de Vanuatu Directorate of Overseas Surveys, Institute National Geographique, 1973. Edition 4 revised by Director of Surveys, Survey Department, Vanuatu, 1995 (©2007 Janet Dixon Keller and Takaronga Kuautonga. Reprinted with permission of Crawford House Publishing Australia)

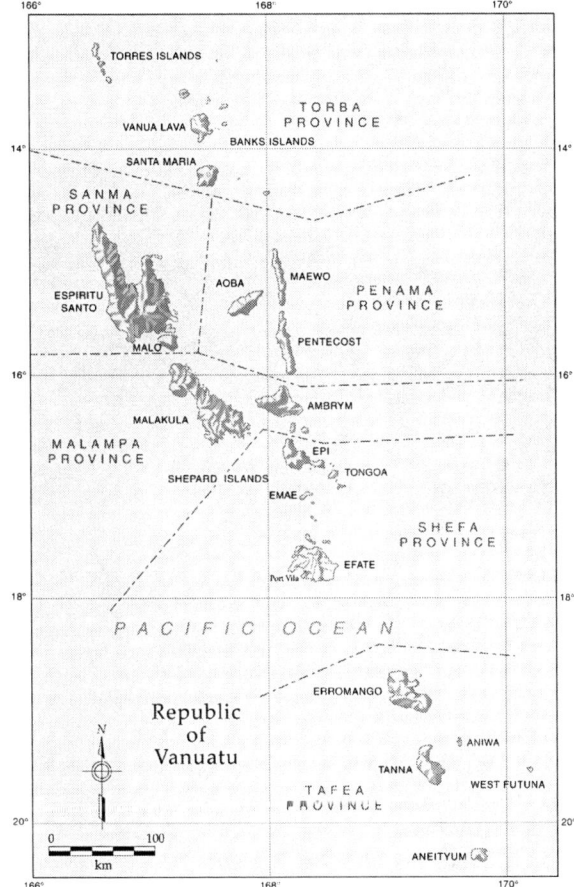

newly independent nation state belong to over 100 distinct ethnic/linguistic communities. The focus here will be on the heritage of one group whose members share ties to the island of Futuna in the southern province of Tafea. The island is often named West Futuna in the scholarly literature in order to distinguish it from the French overseas territory of Wallis-and-Futuna to the east. The very local focus on West Futuna émigrés, initially adopted here, will ultimately broaden to encompass quite general issues of landscape, embodiment, and memory.

Members of the West Futuna (henceforth Futuna) community today reside on their homeland (Fig. 7.3), where people are emplaced by legacies of kinship in rural settings of long standing, or they reside within more urban spaces of the archipelago, most notably the capital city of Port Vila, where a mix of diverse indigenous and foreign peoples buy or rent land that belongs in a profound sense to others (Kling 2006).

Fig. 7.3 Futuna on approach from the west (with permission William R. Dougherty, photographer 1973, and Crawford House Publishing Australia 2007, ©William R. Dougherty)

I first encountered the Futuna community in the 1970s when Vanuatu was the British–French colony of the New Hebrides. I have continued to work with these islanders periodically over 35 years during which time the archipelago attained independence (1980) and a majority of the island population emigrated, leaving elders and young children, but few middle-aged adults, on rural homelands, while those living (often born) in urban settings throughout Vanuatu and the southwest Pacific increased significantly. The community of Futuna now is a virtual one—blurred at the boundaries of belonging by residence, intermarriage, linguistic practices, educational and occupational differences, and social allegiances. The identities of individuals as modern, ni-Vanuatu ("of the republic") citizens compete with and augment their past senses of identity as members of more local communities, neighborhoods, and families.

How are people making this transition? Is there a role for heritage among neoliberal forces for mobility or nationalist forces for a unified Vanuatu identity? How might conditions of modernity and neoliberalism coexist with diversified identities rooted in distinct rural island communities?[1] More specifically, can subjects transform and shape ideological and perhaps even material conditions of migration through recourse to the past?[2]

A Cosmological Order in the Homeland

It is important to recognize the symbolic foundations of rural island lifeways on Futuna in order to investigate the power of memories of past practices in present circumstances. Figure 7.4 illustrates features of a spatialized cosmology

Fig. 7.4 A depiction of the Futuna cosmology (©2007 Janet Dixon Keller and Takaronga Kuautonga. Reprinted with permission of Crawford House Publishing Australia)

that are evidenced in interpretations of oral literatures and musical lyrics of the islanders. This cosmology is one among many of the cultural resources for informing and integrating aspects of rural life on this island (Keller and Kuautonga 2007).[3] People occupy the land, pursuing subsistence and an orderly community life. Their narrative heritage suggests that their activities are guided and encompassed by the supernatural, both original creators and more recent ancestors, who are sources of and protectors for the proper order of life. These supernatural beings may also be participants in everyday lived experience as they seek to influence human affairs. They typically inhabit the highest cliffs, cloudy regions above the land, and the waters beneath the realm of mortal humans and thereby constitute a sphere of protection and influence for those on the land; an enduring, even if sometimes fickle, element of cultural continuity amidst the greater complexities of everyday interactions.

Beyond the cloudy supernatural sphere, the island is surrounded on its horizon by other lands that conceptually and actually constitute a circuit of foreign, human Others (Fig. 7.4). From this perspective the island of Futuna is a sacred center of valued lifeways within a circuit of Others whose beliefs and practices may violate local standards. Flows of peoples among different islands with differing traditions and fashions of living are complicated but long standing. As expressed in oral literatures (Keller and Kuautonga 2007) and recorded in nineteenth-century mission archives (e.g., Steel 1880; Inglis 1860, 1890), contacts among islanders are valued as means for invigorating both individual and community life, but these connections among strangers are also fraught with danger. In addition to the significant perils of sea travel, journeying islanders in the nineteenth century found themselves beyond their insular sphere of supernatural protection and therefore vulnerable in the face of foreign ideas and practices. In order to ameliorate risks of conversion by foreign influence or sanctions for inadvertent transgression of a host's lifeways, inter-island travel in the past was, and is still to some extent today, facilitated by designated receiving communities. These well-known points of entrée for travelers are gateways where local residents (sometimes homeland emigrants, at other times members of the host community) shelter and guide guests in their interactions within the sphere of an Other local community.

The same values are evidenced in village design and communications on Futuna itself. Each village was organized during much of the late nineteenth and twentieth centuries as one or more circuits or horizons of neighborhoods surrounding one or more sacred centers.[4] Reflections of this organization are apparent today. A diagram shows one village plan as instantiated on the ground in 1998 on the island of Futuna (Fig. 7.5), and a photograph of a second village from a path along the steep cliffs above shows the central commons around which homes are located under the protection of tree cover (Fig. 7.6). Each residential center serves as a commons for ritual observances, feasting, and group activities. Diverse individuals and families reside around the centers and are spiritually connected to them. Village life is constructed through convening at the center in various activities where coming together is prescribed and

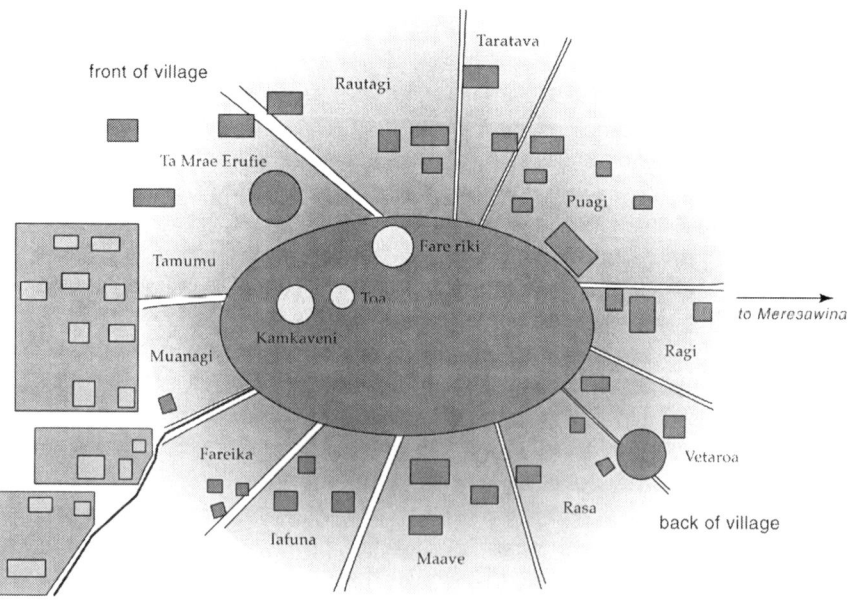

Fig. 7.5 Homesites around the central *marae* in Pau (©2007 Janet Dixon Keller and Takaronga Kuautonga. Reprinted with permission of Crawford House Publishing Australia)

Fig. 7.6 Nakiroa, Futuna. Janet Dixon, Keller 1998 (©2007 Janet Dixon Keller and Takaronga Kuautonga. Reprinted with permission of Crawford House Publishing Australia)

positively sanctioned. But the fiber of community is also constructed in reciprocal interactions on the residential perimeter where the borders of private spaces and persons are crossed continually in social exchange. Interpersonal and social tensions infuse the crossings of even these most local of borders. Social etiquette emphasizes reserve and requires the announcement of a visitor from the edges of a homestead, while prestations, when so desired, can be deposited at a distance from primary residential sites on the commons to be discretely retrieved and shared out. These and other conventions, which functioned in the past, still serve to preserve privacy and imbue residents of each neighborhood with the authority to accept or limit engagements with consociates.

The larger cultural geography of the island as a whole is similarly constructed. Villages encircle the central plateau, the latter considered a core of supernatural presence. Residents of each village are connected to the plateau, the spiritual center of the land, and yet each village also stands uniquely as a node in a circuit of contrasting others. Crossing village boundaries to interact and exchange—a practice essential to survival—was and still is carefully monitored by social prescriptions and subject to a politics of movement and connection. This political etiquette fixes interactional partners across village lines; contacts that allow a guest to communicate information or deposit goods to be held are selectively disseminated from that point to others. The etiquette, the breach of which once incurred the penalty of death, mandated not only with whom one should communicate and exchange resources but even the direction in which one traveled to do so (Keller and Kuautonga 2007). To insure an auspicious encounter, one moved along the pathways at the perimeter of the island from left to right facing the interior, all the time surrounded by that supernatural protective sphere sanctioning the very modes of practice being enacted.

In this concentrically ordered landscape, the cultural structures infused into the world are internalized as a system of lasting dispositions: a matrix of perceptions, apprehensions, and actions that constitute culturally valued modes of living (Bourdieu 1977:82–83; Connerton 1989). The spatialized mnemonics on the ground reflect and inform articulate, tacit, and embodied principles that mutually construct intangible heritage. Continually reproducing and reading the landscape in terms of circuits of neighborhoods, villages, and surrounding foreign lands; repeated journeying among homesites, communities, and islands in prescribed fashion; walking the paths of proper direction over and over again between villages—these modes of acting become incorporated as elements of typically unreflected, taken-for-granted, visual–spatial–kinesthetic representations of right living (Ingold n.d.; Keller and Keller 1996; Hutchins 1995). The spatial orders and the spatial logics of praxis constitute a felt framework for being and a foundation for individual and collective memories (Bourdieu 1977:91).

A Cosmological Order in Homeland Narratives

While ritual and everyday life are informed by spatial logics, oral literature and musical lyrics also constitute a primary resource of collective memory wherein principles of environmentally based order, right living, and embodied heritage constitute structures for making meaning. As islanders explain, the words of their verbal arts are a surface veneer or reflection of deeper wisdom. The spoken words provide clues that enable inferencing in a process that simultaneously recalls and reconstructs intangible heritage.[5] Connecting the said of discursive passages with the enduring unsaid to be gleaned from narrative is a process linking fantastic but superficial events with the profound order of life's experience through recognizing the relevance of the same principles for right living to both.

Two narratives illustrate the mutual constitution of oral literature, musical lyrics, and the generative dispositions of habitus: one is a founding myth and the other a song composed in the nineteenth century (Keller and Kuautonga 2007). Together they demonstrate the continuing relevance of intangible and embodied heritage for contemporary migrants in Vanuatu. To begin, landscape and narrative are integrated in the founding myth of society's endurance; a story that pits culture hero against monster. The monster's power is manifest as he circles the island in violation of the proper direction for movement, annihilating

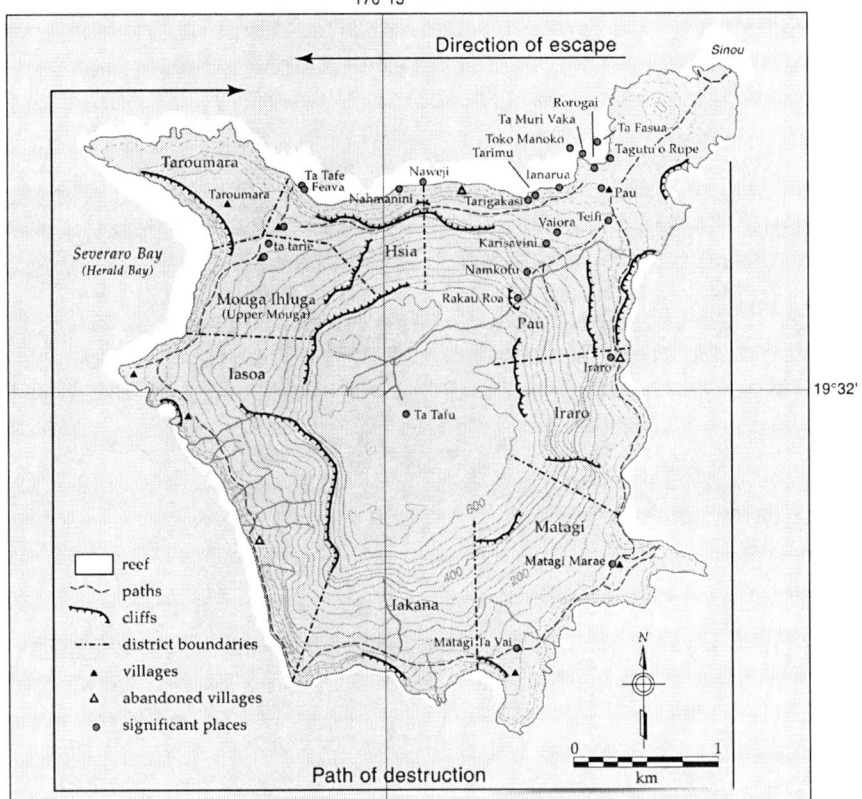

Fig. 7.7 Cultural geography and significance of direction for *Ta Pasiesi and Majihjiki* (©2007 Janet Dixon Keller and Takaronga Kuautonga. Reprinted with permission of Crawford House Publishing Australia)

villagers as he usurps their lands. But the story turns for the better when children escape his grasp and flee in the reverse, auspicious direction (Fig. 7.7). As the children move propitiously, with the culture hero's help, they are able to tease the monster into following their lead and ultimately to effect his demise. The children then resettle the original circuit of villages, creating emplaced and bounded village sites again around the perimeter of the land. With the circuit of villages renewed, the possibilities are recreated for reciprocal connections around the island ensuring the continuity of community integrity through reciprocity.

The interpretation of this tale as summarized here is possible only if the audience understands the profound significance of directional orientations for movement around the island. Likewise the audience must read into the denouement the role that a circuit of similar but distinctive nodes, in this case villages, plays in enabling the reciprocal exchange that constitutes the larger community. These principles of geographic order allow the audience to directly associate with their everyday lives those mythical episodes that appear at first fantastical and irrelevant from the perspective of the everyday world. Making this kind of sense of the story is possible only if one has the intangible cultural tools to work with. Interpreting narrative by applying those tools—tools distilled from experience lived in an ordered landscape that prescribes and engenders particular cultural modes of perceiving and acting—one reproduces their value.

In contrast to timeless myth, songs are composed by the people of Futuna, Vanuatu in historical moments to deal with specific perturbations in the order of life. One nineteenth-century song of lasting relevance was composed with lyrics that refer to lobster trapping and outsider poaching. As "turned words" of metaphor, the lyrics refer to ideological traps set by foreign evangelists aiming to poach local residents via conversion (Feld 1990; Keller and Kuautonga 2007). It is through cultural geography that the tropes can be unpacked and then folded back upon themselves to connect embodied principle with ideological value in song lyrics as in daily life. The lobster trap itself is a particularly apt source for metaphor as its contours mimic those of the land, a material reflection of the topography (Fig. 7.8).

The first line of the song calls listeners to the everyday order of life emplaced:

I was just going out in this land of ours...[6]

As the verse continues, the first person narrator is interrupted in his meanderings to hear a villager's concern with transgression. The complainant reports speech he would like to utter to recently arrived evangelists. These foreigners from a neighboring island have entered Futuna at a distant village site, yet left this original safe point of entrée to wander and preach in violation of the travelers' etiquette. "Go back," the complainant wishes to say to the foreigners in his midst, "return to your host community on Futuna. Preach there where the villagers accepted responsibility for you."

But the villager presumes the visitors are deaf to such chastisement and as the verses continue, lyrics figuratively recount the deplorable strategies of the

Fig. 7.8 Nahjeji. A Futuna lobster trap. (Janet Dixon Keller 1998, (©2007 Janet Dixon Keller and Takaronga Kuautonga. Reprinted with permission of Crawford House Publishing Australia)

guests. In the song, evangelists, referred to as "fruits" (converts), set their traps and seek their prize. The prize is the sea creature in the literal text but metaphorically, as one islander puts it, "We are the lobsters, we fear the traps."
Eventually the lyrics acknowledge the evangelists' defeat:

The lobsters were afraid (of the trap), you (evangelists) return (from reef to village) discouraged.

The lobsters, local people wary of the evangelists' traps, shy away from entrapment; the interlopers have captured no one. Still, the song continues to lament the presence of the outsiders with their lack of respect for the ways of Futuna. Such transgressions of local practice remain an ongoing threat.

Then, as the song ends, the voice shifts from that of the wary villager back to that of the first person narrator whose wanderings were initially interrupted and who now, having heard the complaint, proposes an imagined solution: "Why be discouraged" he asks in verse of the evangelists. This voice, presumably a chiefly authority figure, calls the missionizing converts to step into his canoe (a metaphor for community belonging). He will go with them back into the sea, then reverse direction to return to enter Futuna now arriving at his own village site. From this new point of entrée the outsiders can be properly welcomed by their host. However, this second coming has its prescriptions. The outsiders will be taken to Namtamarou, a spring, font of local knowledge, near the spiritual plateau, where the evangelists will recover awareness of interisland etiquette and the values of Futuna lifeways. They will find themselves newly welcomed as appropriate visitors who respect principles for right living in the hosting land.

The lyrics have great significance, but extracting their meaning requires knowledge of cultural geography and etiquette redundantly embedded in the landscape of the homeland. The song outlines a violation of the local order, the traveler's etiquette of entrée, emplacement and respect, and goes on to provide a plan for domesticating these Others through enacting the spatial mnemonics for proper journeying. This renewed adherence to the proper order of things provides the possibility for transforming outsiders into respectful guests by ending their transgressions and reminding them of the need for respect. The threat of foreign entrapment is nullified by the proposed plan for engendering a resurgence of geographically entrenched principles of right living.

Such redundancies among narrative heritage, lifeways, and cultural landscape are the product of a generative *rationale* that underlay rural habitus of the nineteenth and twentieth centuries on Futuna (Bourdieu 1977: 88). Narratives, such as the song of unsuccessful lobster trapping or the tale of the struggle of a culture hero and his nemesis, have a locally intelligible, common sense quality that rests on cultural topography and the principles for properly negotiating this landscape. The narratives have multiple relevancies (Sperber and Wilson 1986) that establish a synchronous fit between narrative discourse, even as mythically fantastical or metaphorically encoded, and lived experience. The resettlement myth confirms the enduring order of the land, while the affront presented by ancient evangelists provides an opportunity for song to reconstitute valued principles of engagement with the Other. Despite the novelty of the lobster-trapping metaphor and the supernatural events of the myth, both devices return to mortal insiders the power of intangible modes of right living through narrative-based inference (Bourdieu 1977; Bakhtin 1981).

Urban Landscapes, Practices, and Ideologies

A more challenging situation than evangelism or the desires of a greed-driven monster faces the urban populace of Vanuatu and more specifically urban migrants from Futuna today. Gaps between past and present; rural and urban; politics, etiquette, and ideology are seldom formulated within heritage modes. Once redundantly motivated in the land, narrative, and actions of islanders, the self-defining habitus is rent asunder by cosmopolitan conjunctures of alterities. In the new urban settings, heritage has been set aside for progressive expressions and ideals of globalization such as new forms of scientific, financial, religious, and political discourses that appear to mandate mutual exclusivity between past and present. Central to emerging urban lifeways are new values of individual autonomy and competition, freedom of movement and residence, and Western heralded "virtues" of a democratic pastiche of potentially equal but unmoored citizens whose fates depend upon individual efforts in a competitive milieu. Despite this modernizing ideology, values from the rural past, cast out by some in the face of the onslaught of foreign ideas and practices, are yet reintroduced by others in forms of Melanesian socialism and other emerging Pacific orientations that might guide the Republic of Vanuatu. Such political platforms often place value on cosmological encompassment, community, reciprocity, and the order of the land. These, it is argued, can return a deeply desired humanism to development in Vanuatu by taming an individualism gone awry that sunders the spirit of local lifeways (Miles 1998; see also Narokobi 1983 [1980]).

This clash of ideologies is evidenced in reactions to the new forms of emplacement of peoples in cityscapes such as Port Vila. Migration to the city has created overcrowded plots, ghetto-like concentrations, receiving communities but sites where individuals and families lack bounded spaces of their own and reside temporarily (one hopes). The alternative is residential neighborhoods where islanders from diverse communities are interspersed with one another and with outsiders but in the absence of circular order, customary etiquettes, or proper points of entrée. The ghettoized islander is so compactly merged with consociates that the spatial independence on which proper forms of mutual exchange rely cannot be established. Meanwhile, the isolated resident in more suburban surrounds lacks proximity to well-known neighbors with whom a shared etiquette might promote regularized boundary crossings in exchange activities. In both cases the human mosaic of individual and village nodes encircling sacred, ritual centers as well as kin-based access to surrounding subsistence plots are largely absent, preventing the practices that create community through reciprocity in the concentrically organized rural landscape.

In these contexts, the children of Port Vila attend schools that are Western-based autonomous institutions such that learning is no longer distributed throughout the activities of daily life but is concentrated within an exclusive setting. The habitual modus operandi of life becomes Other in the pedagogy of the classroom. Likewise in the urban contexts, adults either find professional employment or roam the streets underemployed; few have access to the resources enabling traditional activities for producing subsistence. In these settings the obvious trappings of the past such as ritual, etiquette, and narrative heritage may be transformed into commodities. Narrative performances in particular are sold to tourists as emblems of Vanuatu national identity and as souvenir experiences of exotic travel. In such performances, the existence of a homeland community is "verified" but only in the participatory ethos of performing or hearing "our" traditions. Although the stories themselves are preserved, the substance of past community values and connections to lifeways that originally informed the music or stories goes unrecognized (Thomas 1992). The significance of these performances is now primarily their cash exchange value or the emblematic heritage contribution of each ethnic group to the nation state. Performances no longer promote dialogue, resolve conflict, create humor in the same ways, or resituate a resident in familiar ideological and physical topography. For many, especially city-born performers, the words of the narratives are unmoored and no longer understood (Thomas 1992:236; see also Rossen 1998:852).

The irony is that as narrative heritage is reaccentuated to become a market commodity or nationalist symbol and as it fails to be recognized as a substantive cultural resource (Bakhtin 1981:421), the very intangible elements of right living that grounded narrative interpretation in the past still persist, perhaps consciously unrecognized, but evident in peoples' expectations for life in the present. This heritage cannot help but persist for it is the distillation of prior experience, life as lived before migration, that has become an ingrained common sense for those who grew up or have intermittently lived on Futuna. This is the component of the contemporary person constituted by yesterday (Bourdieu 1977:79) and by the bodily practices of rural living (Connerton 1989).

Intangible Heritage in Transforming Contexts

Persistent heritage principles, however, no longer function to generate the unreflected habitus of the homeland because the urban context fails to provide the necessary scaffolding in the landscape and in the mosaic patterns of social exchange. Instead, heritage principles surface in both articulate and embodied forms of resistance to the new modes of living encountered in urban spaces that violate yesterday's expectations. Such resistance may range from carefully thought out arguments for land reform to unbidden emotional manifestations directed at the disarray of contemporary life (see also Cole 2006). This evidence of heritage dispositions in the present is not just nostalgia for yesterday's order but constitutes deeply felt reactions to the failure of present urban lifeways to represent specific anticipated and valued redundancies. Residents of urban settings repeatedly express desire for the experience of interconnections among persons emplaced within ordered communities, for landscape patterns that ground a mosaic to which each individual equally belongs in a profound sense, and equally, if differently, contributes (e.g., Rakau n.d.).

Bourdieu (1977:79) has argued that individuals fail to recognize their constitution in the past, for heritage dispositions are taken-for-granted bases of present vantage points. It is, rather, recent developments in their midst that people consciously take stock of. Recent additions to one's lifeways have not yet had time to settle into habitus and may carry the taint of otherness still in need of reconciling with right living. This is indeed the case for many urban migrants, even for long-term residents who have moved from Futuna to Port Vila. The violation of that redundant habitus where place, word, and action were once integrated is received as an affront to one's very being. This affront produces reactions manifest in arguments for reconstructing the urban landscape as community spaces, but for many people it also generates a viscerally experienced and observable rage—an embodied and less articulate reaction evoked in regard to the crowding experienced in urban ghettos or to the isolation enforced by suburban residence. Rage surfaces in resistance to the dissolution of community life that follows from adhering to ideals of Western individualism. "It's all politics," loudly shouts one Futuna migrant evincing despair at the self-interest motivating current interpersonal disputes that tear the original community apart in a dialogue of bitterness and acquisitive desire. Others remark upon the pain of families torn asunder or angrily lament the cost of life's simplest necessities in the city where water and food, once part of the freely accessed riches of island homelands, are now commodities. An existential angst surfaces as many begin to perceive themselves or their co-community members as foreigners in their own land.

These conditions of the ni-Vanuatu diaspora create for the Futuna migrant precisely the kind of crisis that Cornell West (1999:119–139) finds immanent elsewhere in the postcolonial world. It is a crisis, he argues, that calls for revising identities and structures of power through bricoleurmanship and multiperspectivalism (see also Gardner 2007) offering the possibility of new relevancies and a complexly reintegrated yet innovative habitus. Such possibilities are demonstrated in some contemporary practices in Vanuatu.

Let us return for a moment to the human being Rushdie recognized in the opening quotation: one who roots him or herself in ideas rather than place, in memories as much as material things. How might the Futuna subject today engage in revisionist practices and ideologies rooted in memories of intangible heritage? How might memories, both articulate and embodied, of the localized and spatialized cosmology of a rural island survive the loss of place and the loss of significance for figurative modes of expression to offer renewed influence in emerging neoliberal settings?

7 Geographies of Memory and Identity in Oceania 141

Three brief examples will have to suffice. The first derives from the strategies of one Western-trained theologian from Futuna who now lives in Port Vila. His work gives voice to the modern crisis and proposes steps toward resolution (Rakau n.d.). Modernity, he argues, encourages self-interest and gluttony, isolates individuals, ghettoizes segments of the populace; all in disregard for first principles of right living. In desperate appeal to change the chaotic circumstances of contemporary lifeways, he calls on the indigenous wisdom of spatialized practice as a resource to reconstruct local urban lives and domesticate both foreigner and native gone foreign on local shores (Rakau n.d.). His proposal to the government envisions land grants that would offer migrant communities the opportunity to recreate integral neighborhood spaces encircling a *marae* but within the urban landscape. Such designs would reproduce the social structures of support that have traditionally derived therefrom.

The ideology that underlies the mythical Majihjiki's rebuilding of community in the face of the destruction wrought by his nemesis (the monster as community killer) is mirrored in this more contemporary vision for reshaping the urban landscape. Figure 7.9 marks some of the parallels. Embodied and articulate ideals for reinscribing community in the landscape take shape in the calls of Rakau and others for grants or purchase of segments of land where islanders can reestablish residential circuits and grounded practices of reciprocity (Rakau n.d.:90). Rakau turns to the government for assistance in manifesting values and ideals that are best suited, as he remarks, to local lifeways. He demands redistribution of lands in an effort to reshape the urban setting as a confluence of village circuits. As this emplaced heritage would emerge in his vision, residents on the land would be (re)indigenized into reciprocal social interactions inherent in the concentric spatial relations of neighborhood and village design much as the composer of the lobster trapping song imagined domesticating the nineteenth-century evangelists by properly bringing them into his community and emplacing them (Rakau n.d.:91). This is not a misguided turn to the past, but an articulate process of present improvisation and bricoleurmanship in community planning inspired by structures of the past conjoined with contingencies of the present.

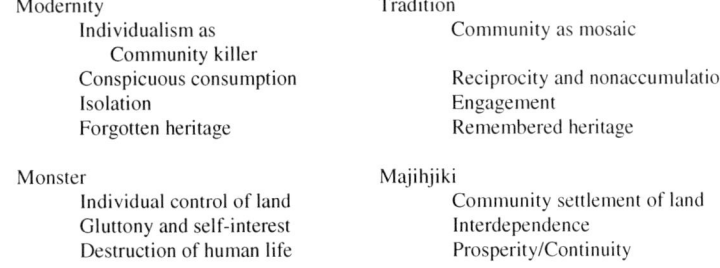

Fig. 7.9 Narrative parallels to modernity-community contrasts

In another recent example, Edward Nipakhe Natape (Prime Minister of Vanuatu 2001–2004), a Fijian educated immigrant to Port Vila from Futuna, placed on his government website (www.vanuatugovernment.gov.vu/ primeminister.html) in 2002 an appeal to attract foreigners to activities that would support sustainable development and investment in Vanuatu: "Vanuatu is one of the few places on earth where you can enter into a very ancient culture and contact your deepest roots and connections with the natural world and feel safe and comfortable at the same time."

Vanuatu has been proposed as a sacred center here. This plea draws implicitly on an analogy of Vanuatu as centered within an international periphery just as the Futuna homeland was originally conceived of within its circuit of foreign Others. In both cases, foreigners are invited to bring new means for sustainable development within the sphere of island exchange. Now, however, Vanuatu has become that centered, paragon of virtue that Futuna once was, offering outsiders safety and ancient roots in exchange for their domestication by and contributions to the nation state. Vanuatu is the *marae* of the global village.

Finally, although the situation is very different today than in the 1850s, the metaphor of lobster trapping remains current with regard to its caution that foreign ideas might entrap. This wariness is apparent as Vanuatu negotiates an international presence that aims to insure local autonomy and authority over ni-Vanuatu affairs. Citizens of the republic envision Vanuatu as one of a circuit of coequal international neighbors as depicted in Fig. 7.10. Any concept of the

Fig. 7.10 A depiction of the political geography of independent Vanuatu in its international landscape (originally published as independent worldview by William F. S. Miles 1998. ©University of Hawai'i Press. Reprinted with permission of the author and University of Hawai'i Press)

7 Geographies of Memory and Identity in Oceania

Pacific or of Vanuatu as peripheral to Western or Eastern metropoles is denied by this imagery. Vanuatu's place in multinational politics is envisioned instead as one in a circuit of nations that, like the original circuit of villages on Futuna, will sponsor reciprocal engagement and mutual respect around the Pacific and the globe.

In this imagery, Vanuatu is positioned as part of a circuit of equally and mutually engaged countries in an international arena that mimics an idealized circuit of villages or neighborhoods. CirumPacific lands as envisioned here are not those of the geographical Pacific rim but those with whom political and economic ties are significant. The geography is literally a political geography. As depicted by Miles (1998), the world is drawn in the minds and utterances of ni-Vanuatu in the image of a reciprocating community of village partners or engaged neighborhoods where each contributes to the other, yet each has control over the flow of ideas and goods within its borders. Collectively a mosaic of the whole emerges.[7]

Conclusions

As these examples demonstrate, the heritage principles derived from emplaced community life of rural landscapes and traditional narratives are clearly still relevant—not by speaking to the past alone as emblematic of identity nor as present commodities in a tourist market but as generative principles embodied in memories subject to transformation and relevant to forming new dispositions and principles of habitus. The memories constitute an intangible heritage that still pervades the present in processes for envisioning a future for Vanuatu. The combination of old and new has spawned an inferencing process (Sperber and Wilson 1986:48) impossible within any one framework alone. The reasoning and planning in the visions of urban or international landscapes instantiate the bricoleurmanship called for by Cornell West to invert the hierarchies of colonial power and restore the power of self-formation to citizens of Vanuatu. The conjunctures are evidence of Bakhtin's reaccentuation of old forms in new ages, and they constitute a radical mode of Bourdieuian improvisation wherein the novel production of lifeways and ideologies is undergirded by the reproduction of heritage. Such "mental bridging" (Miles 1998) promises Vanuatu, including its Futuna migrants, a unique and enduring strength immanent in processes of revisioning modes of right living, domesticating the inexorable global flows of the present and recreating the wisdom of the past.

These processes have three vital features:

(1) Redundancy in geography, narrative, and bodily social practices promotes habitus—transposable dispositions for particular ways of acting governed by common principles and emergent in a range of situations. This is something we know well from Bourdieu.

(2) Embodied and articulate principles constituting intangible heritage endure beyond settings and products that scaffold them originally such as yesterday's narratives and landscape ideals of rural Futuna. The largely taken-for-granted dispositions persist as memory in new situations; their rupture in surface conditions is perceived as an affront. Such heritage dispositions can become the fodder for bricoleurs of postcolonial contexts whose revisioning of the present constitutes a conjuncture of local and foreign ideologies in the creation of multidimensional alternatives to either one or the other.

(3) In these constructive mergers, heritage principles of "right living," although no longer enacted on the ground, remain immanent in improvised strategies for domesticating the foreign, innovatively manifesting the formerly local in the global, and constructing novel ideologies that bridge memories with present conditions. Such steps create a powerful continuity with the intangible past and are simultaneously manifest as moves toward the future.

Notes

1. See Lindstrom (1998) and Iamo and Simet (1998) for a discussion of this question in the context of Papua New Guinea.
2. See Lerner et al. (2007) and Roberman (2007) for related research on transformations accompanying immigration to Israel among Russian Jews.
3. This symbolic resource is increasingly challenged by novel values and principles encountered in contemporary lifeways. Nonetheless as will be argued here, this heritage is still evidenced in the expectations many islanders carry with them as they emigrate.
4. The topography of the land can influence village design significantly, sometimes making it difficult to reproduce the circle of neighborhoods described here. But even where the physical locations of village homesites violate the circular ideal, residential patterns are conceived as neighborhoods surrounding a common center. Sometimes remnants of an older pattern of two centers per village are also reflected in contemporary village design.
5. In Keller and Lehman (1991) a similar project is described. In that case we explored the cosmological principles underlying the logics of *hkano* "essence" and *ata* "image" to argue for the pervasive relevance of this taken-for-granted conceptual structure in the everyday semantics of language.
6. All translations are my own.
7. The conversations from which Miles has derived this vision of global politics involved islanders of many rural and urban locations in Vanuatu (Miles personal communication). Still the imagery of circuits of interacting partners clearly mimics the spatial designs of Futuna neighborhoods and villages. Such designs have a broader relevance throughout the archipelago. Future research might focus on these ties between community living and perceptions of international relations.

References

Bakhtin, Mikhail M.
    1981 *The Dialogic Imagination: Four Essays by M. M.Bakhtin*. Edited by Carl Emerson and translated by Michael Holquist. University of Texas, Austin.
Bourdieu, Pierre
    1977 *Outline of a Theory of Practice*. Cambridge University Press, Cambridge.

Cole, Jennifer
  2006 Malagasy and Western Conceptions of Memory: Implications for Postcolonial Politics and the Study of Memory. In *The Immanent Past*, edited by Kevin Birth. Special issue of *Ethos* 34(2):211–243.
Connerton, Paul
  1989 *How Societies Remember*. Cambridge University Press, Cambridge.
Feld, Steven
  1990 *Songs and Sentiment: Birds, Weeping, Poetics and Song in Kaluli Expression*. Second Edition. University of Pennsylvania Press, Philadelphia.
Gardner, Howard
  2006 *Five Minds for the Future*. Harvard Business School Press, Boston.
Hutchins, Edwin
  1995 *Cognition in the Wild*. M.I.T. Press, Cambridge, Mass.
Iamo, Wari, and Jacob Simet
  1998 Cultural Diversity and Identity in Papua New Guinea: A Second Look. In *From Beijing to Port Moresby: The Politics of National Identity in Cultural Policies*, edited by Virginia Dominguez and David Y. H. Wu, pp. 189–204. Gordon and Breach, The Netherlands.
Inglis, John
  1860 (Sep. 17, 1858) Visit of the *John Knox* to Fotuna. Entry from Rev. Inglis' Journal. In *The Missionary Register of the Presbyterian Church of Nova Scotia*. April, pp. 57–58.
Inglis, John
  1890 *Bible Illustrations from the New Hebrides*. Thomas Nelson and Sons, London.
Ingold, Tim
  N.d. The Anthropology of the Line. Paper presented at Excavating the Mind. Aarhus, Denmark, 2005.
Keller, Janet Dixon and Charles M. Keller
  1996 *Cognition and Tool Use: The Blacksmith at Work*. Cambridge University Press, Cambridge.
Keller, Janet Dixon and Takaronga Kuautonga
  2007 *Nokonofo Kitea: We Keep on Living This Way. Myth and Music of Futuna, Vanuatu*. Crawford House Publishing Ltd, Belair, Australia, and University of Hawai'i Press, Honolulu.
Keller, Janet Dixon and F. K. Lehman
  1991 Complex Concepts. *Cognitive Science* 15(2):271–292.
Kling, Kevin
  2006 Australia. *Alive*. A CD collection of stories written and performed by Kevin Kling. Recorded live at Minnesota Public Radio's UBS Forum on August 15, 2006. East Side Digital, Inc., Minneapolis.
Lerner, Julia, Tamar Rapoport, and Edna Lomsky-Feder
  2007 The Ethnic Script in Action: The Regrounding of Russian Jewish Immigrants in Israel. *Ethos* 35/2:168–195.
Lindstrom, Lamont
  1998 Cultural Diversity and Identity in Papua New Guinea. In *From Beijing to Port Moresby: The Politics of National Identity in Cultural Policies*, edited by Virginia Dominguez and David Y. H. Wu, pp. 141–188. Gordon and Breach, The Netherlands.
Manalansan, Martin F.
  2003 *Global Divas: Filipino Gay Men in the Diaspora*. Duke University Press, Durham.
Miles, William F. S.
  1998 *Bridging Mental Boundaries in a Postcolonial Microcosm: Identity and Development in Vanuatu*. University of Hawai'i Press, Honolulu.

Narokobi, Bernard
  1983 [1980] *The Melanesian Way*. Institute of Papua New Guinea, Boroko, and Institute of Pacific Studies, Suva, Fiji.
Rakau, Fiama
  N.d. (circa 1997) Background Paper IV. In *The Cross and the Tanoa: Gospel and Culture in the Pacific*, pp. 80–98. South Pacific Association of Theological Schools, Suva, Fiji.
Roberman, Sveta
  2007 Fighting to Belong: WWII Veterans in Israel. *Ethos* 35/4:447–477.
Rossen, Jane
  1998 Bellona. In *Garland Encyclopedia of World Music*, edited by A. Kaeppler and J. Love. Volume 9, pp. 848–852. Garland Publishing Co., New York.
Rushdie, Salman
  1991 *Imaginary Homelands: Essays and Criticism 1981–1991*. Granta Books, London.
Sperber, Dan and Deirdre Wilson
  1986 *Relevance: Communication and Cognition*. Harvard University Press, Cambridge, Mass.
Steel, Robert
  1880 *The New Hebrides and Christian Missions with a Sketch of the Labour Traffic and Notes of a Cruise through the Group in the Mission Vessel in 1874*. James Nisbet and Co., London.
Thomas, Alan
  1992 Songs as History. *Journal of Pacific History* 27(2):29–36.
West, Cornell
  1999 The New Cultural Politics of Difference. In *The Cornell West Reader*, pp. 119–139. Basic *Civitas* Books, New York.

Chapter 8
Combating Attempts of Elision: African American Accomplishments at New Philadelphia, Illinois

Christopher Fennell

This chapter examines the ways in which individuals negotiated the complex terrain of past landscapes that were impacted by the institution of slavery and racial ideologies. Present perspectives on such past dynamics are shaped by related concepts of heritage and history. A particular social group's construction of their cultural heritage often entails a selective emphasis on specific subjects within their history. This selective process of heritage construction includes instances of elision and omission as well as those of remembrance and commemoration. In particular, within their histories, some social groups have undertaken efforts to effect an erasure of the accomplishments and self-determination of others in the context of racial strife and deployment of racial ideologies.

These dynamics are manifest in the accomplishments of Frank McWorter, an individual born into slavery in the United States in 1777, who succeeded in attaining freedom for himself and his family (Walker 1983). In 1836, McWorter also founded New Philadelphia, Illinois, the first U.S. town planned and legally registered by an African American. As this town grew as an interracial community in a region shaped by racial strife, the McWorter family also assisted other African Americans to escape bondage. New Philadelphia faced decline, however, after it was bypassed by a railroad in 1869 as a result of the impacts of structural and systemic racism.

Facets of the histories of the McWorters and New Philadelphia are examined here in relation to varying structures of heritage commemoration, including efforts in the United States to memorialize and celebrate the accomplishments of the "Underground Railroad" of persons escaping bondage in the nineteenth century. The United Nations Educational, Scientific, and Cultural Organization (UNESCO) has also engaged in efforts to address the legacies of slavery and the need for safeguarding the tangible and intangible aspects of cultural heritage. But when examined in relation to one another, these various efforts present as much paradox as promise. The problematic characteristics of the

---

C. Fennell (✉)
Department of Anthropology, University of Illinois at Urbana-Champaign, Urbana, IL 61801, USA
e-mail: cfennell@illinois.edu

concepts of culture and intangible heritage utilized by UNESCO are highlighted when comparing them to facets of African American history in the United States.

Aspects of Globalization and Attempted Erasure

From the fifteenth century onward, European colonial regimes created a transAtlantic institution of enslavement that particularly targeted a number of societies in western regions of Africa. The trans-Atlantic slave trade had extensive, brutal impacts upon the many societies caught in its grasp and left a lasting legacy of oppression and pain. UNESCO established the "Slave Route Project" in 1993 to facilitate greater understanding of the contours, causes, and impacts of slavery's destructive legacies (UNESCO 1993). The slave trade is viewed within this perspective as a form of globalization that caused profound economic, social, and cultural disruptions impacting numerous African societies and individuals.

The UNESCO Slave Route Project works to promote greater memory, knowledge, and dialogue concerning the history and continuing impacts of that colonial institution (UNESCO 2006a). This UNESCO project thus works to overcome the "silence that has shrouded" the history of slavery (UNESCO 2006a:3). It further seeks to commemorate the intangible and tangible cultural heritage of the individuals and societies that confronted the adversities of that system of bondage (UNESCO 2006a:7). Focusing on the significance of intangible cultural heritage underscores the importance to today's communities of the histories of their predecessors' strivings to overcome such challenges and prejudices.

UNESCO undertook additional steps in 2003 to conserve and protect the diversity of cultural traditions across the globe by issuing the "Convention for the Safeguarding of the Intangible Cultural Heritage" (UNESCO 2003), which took effect in 2006 (UNESCO 2006b:24). Earlier efforts to protect the cultural heritage of diverse peoples worldwide had focused primarily on "tangible" expressions, such as artworks, architecture, monuments, and the built environment (Ahmad 2006; UNESCO 2003:1–2). While 84 state parties have ratified and joined in a commitment to implement this 2003 Convention, the United States has not done so (UNESCO 2007a). However, Richard Kurin (2007:10), director of the Smithsonian Center for Folklife and Cultural Heritage and an active participant in UNESCO conferences and heritage deliberations, reported recently that U.S. officials may be considering the possibility of moving forward with ratification.

Participating members of UNESCO considered a number of factors in designing a formalized method for addressing the potential dangers facing the intangible cultural heritage of social groups around the world. A primary concern focused on the realization that nationalist movements and the global impacts of free-market economies have often eroded and destroyed such heritage within more "traditional" cultural communities (UNESCO 2003:1). Similar clashes occurred with comparable frequency in the history of European colonial expansions in the past.

The concept of "cultural heritage" can involve destructive manifestations—not just of globalization but also of the actions of particular cultures. Nationalist movements and established nation states have often rationalized their existence and exercise of power by deploying ideologies and cultural traditions that legitimize their actions. For example, numerous decisions of the U.S. Supreme Court emphasize that ours is a nation of Judeo-Christian heritage—not Buddhist, Islamic, Cherokee, Yoruba, or otherwise (e.g., U.S. Supreme Court 1892). Similarly, the institution of slavery in the United States was explained by lawmakers in the eighteenth and nineteenth centuries as a necessary undertaking to fulfill a Judeo-Christian duty of civilizing non-Christian populations of captive Amerindians and Africans (Raboteau 1980). Thus, human bondage was justified as a religious imperative and a sign of social enlightenment. In blunt terms, globalization alone does not kill cultures—dominant cultures kill other cultures.

Another line of development in UNESCO's conventions and declarations has addressed the way that the cultural heritage of a particular group can be deployed for malevolent and intolerant social action. UNESCO has emphasized the importance of fundamental human rights as a baseline that will at times override the heritage claims of individual cultures. For example, Article 4 of the Universal Declaration on Cultural Diversity, which was adopted in 2001, states that the "defense of cultural diversity is an ethical imperative, inseparable from respect for human dignity. It implies a commitment to human rights and fundamental freedoms, in particular the rights of persons belonging to minorities and those indigenous peoples. No one may invoke cultural diversity to infringe upon human rights guaranteed by international law, nor to limit their scope."

Similarly, the 2003 Convention recognizes as intangible cultural heritage "only those forms of cultural expression consistent with human rights" (Kurin 2007:10). Debates concerning the scope and extent of cultural relativism are also inherent in this tension between claims of human rights and cultural heritage. Anthropologists long ago established that one needs to understand a particular culture holistically, with all elements viewed relative to the other facets of that culture. But should cultural relativism be taken to mean that one cannot judge another culture from the perspective of some baseline of fundamental human rights? UNESCO's answer is a resounding "no."

I focus on such tensions because I wish to consider the intangible heritage of the descendants of individuals who lived their lives in nineteenth-century America as persons whom a dominant culture and legal structure sought to oppress. In doing so, should I invoke the basic terms of the 2003 Convention? UNESCO defines intangible cultural heritage as "the practices, representations, expressions, knowledge, skills ... that communities, groups and ... individuals recognize as part of their cultural heritage" (UNESCO 2003:art. 2.1). But we should not read the 2003 Convention as asserting that all instances of "intangible cultural heritage" are unproblematic, benevolent, and to be applauded. For many members of minority groups in American history, their own cultural heritage includes their tireless fight for freedom and basic human rights in opposing the culture of those who sought to subjugate them. This merits celebration; but it also entails commemoration within a context of degraded living conditions, denial of freedom, and even sexual enslavement. Members of some communities may find their intangible cultural heritage is less defined by particular bodies of folklore and ritual than it is by commemoration of their fight for freedom against the tyrannies of another culture.

Histories of Adversity and Success

The history and intangible cultural heritage of New Philadelphia, Illinois, involves such struggles for freedom. Frank McWorter's mother, Juda, was born around 1755 in one of the societies of West Africa targeted by the trans-Atlantic slave trade (Walker 1983:179). Abducted into slavery, Juda survived the horrors of the "middle passage" and was transported to a slave auction in South Carolina. George McWhorter, a plantation owner of Scots-Irish heritage, purchased Juda as an enslaved laborer and took her to his farming operation in the uplands region of South Carolina. Frank was born to Juda in 1777 on that plantation, with George McWhorter as father and owner. When Frank was a young man, George McWhorter moved his plantation operations to new land in Kentucky. In 1799, Frank married Lucy, an enslaved laborer on a neighboring plantation in Kentucky, and they started raising a family together (Walker 1983) (see below concerning Frank's change of spelling in his last name).

Frank McWorter's life history is defined by remarkable industry, sagacity, and skill in overcoming the adversities of enslavement and racism that confronted him. He accumulated funds as an enslaved laborer by renting out his time and skills after satisfying the production demands of his owner. He also later engaged in entrepreneurial projects such as starting a saltpeter mining operation in Kentucky in a period of growing demand for this valuable ingredient for the production of gunpowder. In 1817, he purchased his wife's freedom and then in 1819 his own manumission from slavery (Matteson 1964:1; Walker 1983:28–48). Manumission involved a procedure, either through a purchase contract or provisions in the last will and testament of a slave owner, to grant emancipation to a particular person. In the course of his life, Frank continually worked to accumulate funds and credits with which he purchased the freedom of his family members, obtaining manumission for no less than 16 persons with a cash expenditure that exceeded $350,000 in today's cash values.

In 1830, he took advantage of a new opportunity in the form of land sales in the western portion of Illinois referred to as the "Military Bounty Lands" located between the Illinois and Mississippi Rivers. He purchased a parcel of 160 acres situated in Hadley Township, Pike County, Illinois, and moved his wife and those of his children who were then free to that location on the expanding Midwestern frontier (Matteson 1964; Walker 1983, 1985). Establishing a farmstead on this parcel in western Illinois in the early 1830s, Frank, Lucy, and their family developed social and working relationships with the other landowners and farmers around them, many of whom were of European American heritage (Chapman 1880:739; Simpson 1981:1; Walker 1983:106–107).

A number of Frank and Lucy's children and grandchildren remained in bondage, because the federal and state laws provided that children born to enslaved individuals would remain in bondage themselves until manumitted. Purchase of the parents' freedom did not retroactively free their children. In turn, manumission provided only limited rights and legal capacities to a free African American (Walker 1983).

The federal and state census lists in the nineteenth century worked to deploy the racial ideologies written in law by categorizing each person in a household as "white," "black," or "mulatto" (King 2006). Federal and state laws accorded different legal rights to those who qualified as white versus those who did not. As a free, manumitted African American, Frank still lacked the legal rights in Illinois to give testimony in court against a white person or to engage in sophisticated property transactions with confidence in their enforceability if challenged in court. However, he overcame these limitations in a dramatic way. He petitioned for and obtained an act of the state legislature to legally register his name as Frank McWorter (purposefully changing the spelling of his surname) and to grant him full legal rights. The public record of this 1837 legislation indicates that Frank received support from his neighbors in this petition and that he planned to found a town named Philadelphia (later called New Philadelphia) on undeveloped land that he had acquired just to the south of his farm (Illinois State Archives 1837). He wished to create this planned town so that he could sell the blocks and lots within it to obtain additional funds with which to purchase more of his family members out of bondage. It was also publicly known that he intended for this town to be a welcoming community for other free African Americans (Walker 1983:107). McWorter's strong character, industriousness, and his hopes for the development of this new town were sufficiently well known in the region to be featured in public ceremony speeches and local historical accounts in the 1870s and 1880s (Ensign 1872:54, 100; Chapman 1880:739; Grimshaw 1876:31). It was a daring and courageous undertaking in a region shaped by racial strife in this period.

New Philadelphia was planned as a community of 42 acres in size, with 20 blocks, 144 lots, and a grid pattern of streets and alleyways. The town grew from its founding in 1836 until its decline in the 1880s, with a peak population recorded in the 1865 census of 160 residents in 29 households (King 2006; Shackel et al. 2006). Over the decades of its existence, its residents were recorded in federal and state census lists, with approximately one-third classified as black or mulatto and two-thirds classified as white. During its existence, New Philadelphia had several business operations, including a grocery, blacksmith, carpenter, wheelwright, wainwright, shoemaker, cabinetmaker, and a physician, and the town served as an agricultural service center to the surrounding farmsteads. A well-trafficked road ran along its northern edge, in an east to west path leading to the Illinois and Mississippi Rivers in either direction (Shackel et al. 2006:2–12; Walker 1983:167; Walker 1985:55–56).

The McWorters' farming operations and the town they founded were located within a region buffeted by racial tensions (Davis 1998:18; Shackel et al. 2006:2–4; Walker 1983:110–111). In the antebellum period, Hannibal, Missouri, located along the Mississippi River just 25 miles to the west of New Philadelphia, was part of a slave state and hosted an auction market for the sale of enslaved laborers. The Illinois River was just 15 miles to the east of New Philadelphia. While these two water arteries aided the value of lands in the region, providing transport modes for moving agricultural products to market, they also provided transport for bounty hunters who were known to kidnap free African American into slavery during the antebellum period (Davis 1998:289; Putnam 1909:414; Savage 1943). Illinois law recognized the rights of slave owners in other jurisdictions to seek to recapture those who escaped from bondage, and the harsh "Black Codes" of Illinois belied the state's status as a truly "free" state (Davis 1998:413; Savage 1943:312; Simeone 2000:157).

In addition to the dangers of nearby Missouri, free African Americans in this region saw abolitionist Elijah Lovejoy shot dead and his office and printing press burned in 1837 by a proslavery mob in Alton, Illinois, not far to the south (Simon 1994). The following year abolitionist and pro-slavery factions clashed in Griggsville, Illinois, just 13 miles to the east (Chapman 1880:516). African Americans and European Americans in nearby Quincy and Jacksonville worked to help abolitionist causes and to aid those escaping slavery as they traversed Illinois on their way to Canada (Savage 1943; Turner 2001). Members of the McWorter family, who owned parcels surrounding and within New Philadelphia, were also reported in oral histories to have aided African Americans escaping from bondage (Turner 2001:vii; Walker 1983:149).

Local newspapers in communities surrounding New Philadelphia published reports of the daily economic and social events that occurred within that community, but neither they nor historical studies of New Philadelphia and its residents reveal any overt racial violence within the town in these antebellum and postwar decades of the nineteenth century. Likewise, archaeological investigations to date show no evidence of physical destruction in the town that might be attributed to racial action.

Archaeological studies seek to determine whether the town was developed as planned in the 1836 plat filed by Frank McWorter in the local courthouse (Shackel et al. 2006). The town may have developed in a way that did not fully utilize all of the 42 acres of planned blocks and lots, and those areas that were developed may have been constructed in ways that departed from the original drawn plan. Newspaper reports from the period of the town's existence indicate that residents likely did not follow that design in detail but built residential parcels and businesses in a way that crossed the planned lot lines recorded in the original plat (*Barry Adage* 1876:3). Surveys and excavations have thus far shown that the house and business sites associated with European Americans and African Americans were interspersed with one another, rather than being spatially segregated into different areas within the town, a notable indication of peaceful coexistence (Hargrave 2006; Shackel et al. 2006). The archaeological remains of objects used in daily life within households, such as the ceramic housewares obtained and used by each family, are also similar across households of both African Americans and European Americans within the town (Shackel et al. 2006).

The impact of racial categories and social difference can be seen in other aspects of the town's history, however. The community was served by two separate cemeteries, each close to the town, with one used primarily by African American families, including the McWorters, and the other mostly by European American families. Until at least 1874, the children of town residents were educated in segregated schools located within the community. They were educated in a new, integrated schoolhouse after 1874 when a new building was erected close to the town and then continued in operation through the early 1900s. Preliminary archaeological studies also indicate that there may have been different dietary and culinary traditions across the households of town residents. These patterns may have been correlated with differences in the regional and ethnic backgrounds from which town residents had emigrated when coming to New Philadelphia (Shackel et al. 2006).

While no overt acts of racial violence were reported within New Philadelphia during the town's existence, that community was impacted in a profound way by structural and systemic influences of racial ideologies. Such structural forms of racism have been characterized by analysts as forms of "aversive" racism, in which members of a dominant social group channel economic opportunities and social resources away from individuals targeted by their racial prejudices (Gaertner and Dovidio 1986; Kleinpenning and Hagendoorn 1993; Kovel 1970). Such aversive racism can be seen in events that started in the late 1850s and culminated in the 1869 construction of a railroad that bypassed New Philadelphia.

The effect of the bypass was dramatic. Businesses and residents moved out of the town in the following years, with the town's population dropping steadily (Simpson 1981:1; Walker 1983:165–167; Walker 1985:56). By 1885, an order was entered in the courthouse records that vacated a large portion of New Philadelphia's land from holding the status of a town, with public rights of way, streets, and lots lines, and converted that land into large parcels for agricultural use. Local history publications in 1872 and 1880 reported on the town's demise, with observations that the "railroad did not run through the town, which has greatly ruined its trade" (Ensign 1872:10) and the fact that "the railroad passing it a mile distant, and other towns springing up, has killed it" (Chapman 1880:740–741).

In the many varied histories of railroads constructed across segments of the United States, there have been a multitude of reasons why one town became a depot and expanded, while others were bypassed and often withered away (Conger 1932:285; Davis 1998:368–370; Jenks 1944:14). As one historian of railroad histories observed: "Every enterprising hamlet had visions of becoming an important commercial city if at least one railroad could be built through the community" (Carlson 1951:103). A disturbing pattern also emerges from these histories: towns and settlements that were known to be the communities of African American families and businesses were typically bypassed by new railways of the Midwest in the nineteenth century (Cha-Jua 2000:42).

Any of a number of rational business reasons often led to a railroad being built along a route that bypassed or avoided the location of a particular town. If a town was located next to significant topographic features, such as deep ravines, broad river crossings, or high ridges, it would often be more cost-effective to route the railroad so as to avoid those areas (Cootner 1963:484; Vose 1857:32). A town might be bypassed because other nearby towns successfully lobbied the railroad company to move the route in their direction so that they could enjoy the economic benefits of becoming depot towns. In turn, the residents of some towns might prefer to avoid the social and aesthetic impacts of a railroad being built through their community, no matter what future economic losses might be predicted as a result of such avoidance.

I have not found any *direct, documentary* evidence of an overtly expressed decision to bypass New Philadelphia due to racial bias. However, after a thorough study of the corporate records of the railroad companies involved in building the railway that bypassed the town, and critical examination of numerous reports in regional newspapers concerning the railroad planning and construction, it is clear that New Philadelphia was bypassed because of the impacts of aversive racism. A large body of contextual evidence points to no rational business reason for the railroad company to have bypassed the town. In fact, the arc of the railroad route running to the north, around New Philadelphia, followed a path that was distinctly *not* optimal for rational business reasons. Of the extensive body of evidence, analysis, and pursuit of alternative hypotheses undertaken in evaluating the reasons for this event, a summary of the principal evidence and findings is provided here. In view of such contextual evidence, and the absence of proof for a rational business reason for bypassing the town, the most persuasive explanation of this incident focuses on the structural and systemic impacts of racial ideologies and biases.

Planning for the construction of a railroad to link Hannibal, Missouri, with Naples, Illinois, began by the 1850s and gained momentum with the formation of the Pike County Railroad Company (PCRC) in 1857 (Grant 2004:22; PCRC Records 1857–1863; *Pittsfield Union*, 18 May 1853:3). This new railway across Pike County would link up two existing railroad routes that had been constructed earlier with federal and state subsidies (Fishlow 1971:190–191). One subsidized rail project had connected Hannibal with the city of St. Joseph on the Missouri River to the west, thus linking Hannibal by rail to an expanding western frontier of settlement and agricultural production (*Alton Telegraph & Democratic Review* 1849:3; Cochran 1950:55–57). Another subsidized project had linked the towns of Springfield, Jacksonville, and Meredosia in Illinois, and that rail was then extended to a terminus at Naples, along the Illinois River just opposite the border of Pike County (Grant 2004:7–12; Corliss 1934:19). Government subsidization of such railroad construction had lost popularity after those first projects were completed with extensive cost overruns (Carlson 1951:100; Davis 1998:230). Later construction of railroads in various segments and regions would have to be undertaken through private holding companies that received very basic state charters and obtained funding subscriptions through stockholders and investors (Dobbin 1994:23–24; Fishlow 1971:190–191; Riegel 1923:154–156). The PCRC was formed for just that purpose.

Although called the Pike County Railroad Company, this commercial entity was dominated by the business interests of enterprises centered in Hannibal (Chapman 1880:904–905; PCRC Records, 14 February 1857, 4 June 1860, 4 June 1862). In 1857, that city was situated within a slave state and hosted a local marketplace in which African Americans were sold as laborers in lifelong bondage. Construction of the Pike County Railroad would make Hannibal an interregional hub linking the Missouri River valley to the west with central Illinois and other transport connections to Chicago, Buffalo, Toledo, and market centers in the east (Grant 2004:22; *Hannibal Daily Courier*, 15 January 1878:1). The city of Hannibal owned the largest share of stock in the PCRC and the company's board of directors was dominated by entrepreneurs based in that city. After initial efforts toward planning, designing, and surveying the railroad route over a few years, the PCRC was reorganized in 1863 as the Hannibal and Naples Railroad Company (HNRC), which was again dominated by business interests in Hannibal (Chapman 1880:904–905; HNRC Records, 12 February 1863, 4 August 1863).

The route of the railroad was largely planned and surveyed in 1857 and that route was described in a final surveyor's report submitted to the PCRC at the end of that year (PCRC Records, 21 August 1857, 29 December 1857). Progress on the project was interrupted by economic difficulties in 1857 and then by the onset of the Civil War (Cootner 1963:499; Grant 2004:22; PCRC Records 1857–1863). Construction efforts were taken up after conclusion of the Civil War, in 1868 and 1869, using the original survey plans (HNRC Records 1868–69). Route planning for railroads generally followed fairly predictable guidelines for keeping costs to a minimum. The greatest expense items in railroad construction involved the linear feet of roadbed to be graded and built up and the linear feet of iron rails to traverse the designated route (Grant 2004:21; HNRC Records, 21 August 1868). It is important to note that wherever possible, railroad engineers sought to take a straight route from one terminus point to the next, while avoiding topographic features that would require climbing to higher elevations or descending into ravines (Cleeman 1880:12–13; Jervis 1861:48; Webb 1917:3–5). The expense, for example, of crossing small streams with culverts was very minor compared to the primary expense of the linear distance of iron rails and roadbed (Cleeman 1880:29–31, 44–60).

The route planned for the railroad across Pike County generally followed these guidelines, until it reached the vicinity of New Philadelphia. An 1897 map of Pike County shows the railroad route that runs east to west from Naples, on the Illinois River, to Hannibal, on the Mississippi River (Fig. 8.1). The name of New Philadelphia did not appear on this map, because it no longer existed as a town at the time of this 1897 publication. New Philadelphia was located where the letters "de" in the name "Arden" appear on this map, approximately midway on an east-to-west line between the towns of New Salem and Barry. The depot communities and stations of Baylis, Cool Bank, and Arden that are shown on the map did not exist until after the railroad was constructed in 1869. What was first constructed as the "Hannibal and Naples Railroad" bears the name of the "Wabash" line on this map, for the company that operated trains along the line at that time. Although Pittsfield was a commercial center and the county seat in the 1850s and 1860s, that town had been unable to lobby the PCRC and HNRC to direct the main route from Naples to Hannibal

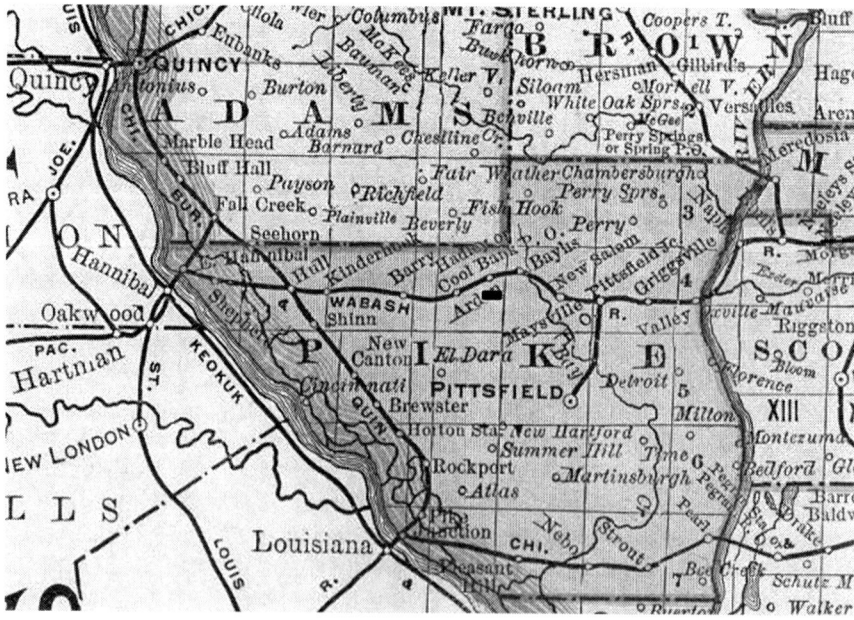

Fig. 8.1 This excerpt from "Rand, McNally & Company's New Business Atlas Map of Illinois," published in 1897 (Chicago, Illinois), shows the route of the Hannibal and Naples Railroad, labeled as the Wabash line on this map, across Pike County Illinois. The town of New Philadelphia was located between the towns of New Salem and Barry, in the area marked by a black rectangle on this map

through their community. Instead, a small connecting rail was built to link Pittsfield to the main railway line crossing Pike County (Ensign 1872:7; Grant 2004: 22; HNRC Records, 2 June 1870).

The PCRC and HNRC plans for the rail route took a sensible, low-cost approach by running along the level ground of the Illinois River valley from Naples down south to a point of relatively low topography, where it crossed the river and proceeded due west toward the existing town of Griggsville (PCRC Records, 29 December 1857). The overall surveyor's plan was to then proceed east to west along flat topography from Griggsville, to New Salem, to Barry, and then on to a point opposite Hannibal on the Mississippi River (PCRC Records, 29 December 1857). Yet, the map shows that between New Salem and Barry the route circled to the north and bypassed the existing town of New Philadelphia, which would have otherwise fallen directly along that east-to-west line.

Was there a significant topographic feature at or near New Philadelphia that prompted this bypass? The answer is "no." The topography runs fairly level in a gradual line from New Salem (at 784 feet elevation above average sea level) to New Philadelphia (732 feet elevation) to Barry (712 feet elevation) (U.S.G.S. 2007). A shallow stream bed existed just to the west of New Philadelphia, called Kiser Creek. Yet, this creek would have been crossed easily and without significant expense by building small-scale culverts. The company records of PCRC and HNRC, as well as newspaper reports about the construction and later operation of the railroad, do not indicate that Kiser Creek was prone to flooding or otherwise presented a topographic challenge (PCRC Records 1857–63; HNRC Records 1863–70).

The expense of building a culvert over a streambed near New Philadelphia would have been minimal compared to the significant increase in costs incurred by the railroad company in extending the route in a several mile arc to the north, only to turn back to the south for several miles to continue on to Barry and the east-to-west line to Hannibal. Those extra linear feet of iron rail and roadbed were increased even more by a significant rise and fall in elevation along that detour of the route (Cootner 1963:484; Vose 1857:32). At the location where a depot town named Baylis appears at the northernmost point on that arc, the elevation increases to 863 feet, a rise of over 150 feet from the elevation of Barry (Fig. 8.1) (*Barry Adage* 1876:2; U.S.G.S. 2007). In addition to significantly inflating the construction costs in linear feet of iron and roadbed, this elevation later required the companies operating the freight trains on this route to maintain a helper locomotive near Hannibal that would assist in pulling trains over the high point of Baylis (*Barry Adage* 1876:3; *Barry Adage* 1877:1). Such helper locomotives were very expensive to operate, as they were detached after getting the freight train over the summit of Baylis, then returned to wait near Hannibal for the next freight train (*Barry Adage* 1876:3; *Barry Adage* 1877:1; Cootner 1963:484; Wellington 1901:601–604). This happened frequently, as the traffic flow was principally from west to east, moving agricultural and livestock products to market centers farther to the east.

Did the railroad line detour to the north because other towns along that route lobbied the railroad to become depot stations and perhaps plied the company with funds to compensate for the construction expense? The answer is "no." There were no towns in existence along that route when the railroad was built. Baylis and other towns along that stretch were created as depots *after* the rail was constructed.

Was there a large-scale landowner who held land along that northern arc and lobbied the railroad to divert the route for his own profit? The answer, again, is "no." That arc of railroad route traversed the land holdings of over a dozen smaller scale landowners, none of whom appear in the histories of this region to have operated as a local real-estate baron (*Barry Adage* 1876: 3; Chapman 1880:641–642; Ensign 1872:10; Pike County Deed Records 1865: 247–248). Nor is there any evidence that the railroad company received any payments from those landowners for conveyance of the railroad's right-of-way across their parcels. The strips of land for the railroad to cross those parcels were conveyed through simple, contingent deeds that would become null and void if the railroad was never constructed (Pike County Deed Records 1865:247–248).

One might ask whether members of the McWorter family or other prominent African American families living in or near New Philadelphia attempted to lobby the railroad company to make that town a depot along the planned rail route. Frank McWorter died in 1854, but his wife, adult sons, and other prominent African American residents could have undertaken such lobbying efforts (Chapman 1880:752; Ensign 1872: 23, 54, 58). For example, Frank's son, Solomon, was a prominent entrepreneur, profiled in a local history published in 1872 as owning over 500 acres of farm lands and working successfully in raising crops and livestock for sale (Ensign 1872: 54). Yet no evidence has been uncovered to date to show that such lobbying efforts were undertaken. The same concept of aversive racism that explains how a Hannibal-dominated railroad company could be motivated to bypass New Philadelphia also provides a sense of why African American residents of that locality would not have much reason to try to lobby and negotiate with that company.

Several central lessons can be learned from these histories of the McWorters and New Philadelphia. One lesson focuses on the histories of oppression, racism, and attempted erasures undertaken by European Americans in the past and the continuing impacts of those legacies in the present (Leone et al. 2005; Shackel 2003). In renewed efforts to look unflinchingly at such instances of malevolent conduct by European Americans, one can demand that these acts of racism and attempted destruction of communities and lives not be forgotten but enter into the preserved heritage of that place and those communities (now dispersed). Efforts today to combat the continuing influences and distortions of racial ideologies and structures of oppression are enhanced by focusing on and condemning the reprehensible acts of earlier generations. Yet, within this perspective, one primarily focuses on the acts and determinations of European Americans. The lives and communities of African Americans are seen largely as victims at the hands of others.

Another perspective focuses on the struggles for freedom and successes of African Americans in combating racism, expropriation, and oppression (Leone et al. 2005; Shackel 2003). Frank McWorter's life story is exemplary of such successes in overcoming adversities through incredible acts of industry, skill, and determination. As another example, after the railroad bypassed New Philadelphia and the town's population began to wane, Solomon McWorter adapted to the new economic conditions by driving 100 head of his cattle several miles to the depot at Barry to ship them out by rail (*Barry Adage* 1873: 4). The other African American families who departed from New Philadelphia similarly pursued new opportunities through their own acts of self-determination (Walker 1983: 169).

While the impact of the railroad detour brought New Philadelphia to an end as a town, the legacies of that community and the McWorter family were not forgotten. Numerous descendants of those families, as well as historians working at the local, regional, and national scales, have contributed to recording, maintaining, and celebrating the heritage of those past lives and community. These efforts have included publications such as those of Ensign (1872), Grimshaw (1876), Chapman (1880), Matteson (1964), Simpson (1981), and Walker (1983, 1985). In 1988, Juliet Walker, an historian and McWorter descendant, succeeded in placing Frank McWorter's grave site, located within the African American cemetery close to New Philadelphia, on the National Register of Historic Places (Shackel et al. 2006: 2–24). In doing so, Walker achieved a remarkable success. Only two other grave sites in Illinois have been recognized by the National Register of Historic Places: those of Abraham Lincoln and Stephen Douglas. Moreover, in 2005, the New Philadelphia collaborative archaeology project that I codirect with Paul Shackel and Terry Martin succeeded in placing the entire town site of New Philadelphia on the National Register of Historic Places (Shackel et al. 2006: 2–25). Thus, the past acts of overt and aversive racism that sought to erase the accomplishments of Frank McWorter and the residents of New Philadelphia did not succeed in attaining such an elision of those vital facets of American history.

Concepts of Heritage and the Paradox of Culture

When comparing frameworks for recognizing histories and heritage in the United States with the approaches taken by UNESCO projects, one finds points of divergence and a number of paradoxical operational mechanisms. For example, UNESCO's 2003 Convention for the Safeguarding of the Intangible Cultural Heritage privileges oral histories and related oratory performances over the tangible resources of documentary records and material culture that embody the same subjects and expressions. In contrast, the National Park Service (NPS) of the federal government in the United States views oral histories as only a tentative, first step toward the compilation of evidence that would support historical recognition of a particular location's role in aiding individuals escaping slavery in the antebellum years (NPS 2007: pt. F). In doing so, the NPS follows the federal legislation that sponsored that agency's investment in such heritage sources (Public Law 105–203). The NPS and this enabling legislation emphasize the importance of tangible, documentary evidence of such activities as a proper basis for historical recognition of a particular location and its built environment.

The heritage of the McWorters includes long-established oral testimony that Frank and his family aided individuals who were escaping slavery in the antebellum years. Western Illinois was traversed by many persons escaping bondage, as they traveled from more southern locations up through Illinois to points along the Great Lakes and transit into Canada where they could be free of the fear of bounty hunters. Juliet Walker's excellent study of the history of the McWorter family provides persuasive details of the oral history reports that the McWorters aided escapees in their home, which served as a "safe house" (Turner 2001:vii; Walker 1983:149). Yet, the house in which Frank McWorter lived no longer survives above ground, and no documentary evidence from his day has yet been revealed to corroborate these oral histories. Using the guidelines of evidentiary emphasis provided by the NPS, should one disregard this history of aid to escaping slaves and of resistance against an immoral institution of bondage?

The NPS is sensitive to many issues concerning the history of African American resistance to slavery. For example, NPS guidelines for those exploring local histories of the Underground Railroad recognize that "the majority of assistance to runaways came from slaves and free blacks, and the greatest responsibility for providing shelter, financial support and direction to successful runaways came from the organized efforts of northern free blacks" (NPS 2007: pt. E). Those guidelines further observe that, by definition, the escape routes and the activities of the Underground Railroad were "clandestine so information about sites and routes was kept secret or not widely distributed" (NPS 1998:1). Nonetheless, when addressing proposals to commemorate particular instances of these past endeavors, the NPS focuses on anchoring such events to particular "sites" and "properties" supported by tangible, documentary evidence (NPS 2007: pt. F), and not upon the oral histories that may speak more to networks of people and their moral commitments.

With such a focus on extensive documentary evidence and surviving buildings related to past safe house operations of the Underground Railroad, the NPS programs tend to place greater emphasis on the heritage of abolitionist operations conducted by European Americans. Many historical houses and properties recognized today within the United States are related to the history of such abolitionist societies and prominent European Americans, rather than being the stories of free African Americans and fellows in bondage who assisted individuals in their escape to freedom. In the region of New Philadelphia, one sees analogous elision and biased emphasis in the histories of Hannibal, Missouri. Historical exhibits in Hannibal today speak hardly at all of the city's past role in slavery, its deployment of racial ideologies, and past resistance by African

Americans. Instead, one is confronted at every turn with the story of Samuel Clemens, who, in his literary efforts as the author Mark Twain, spoke out against slavery (Dempsey 2003).

Ideally, one might look at the provisions of the 2003 Convention for the Safeguarding of the Intangible Cultural Heritage as a better vehicle for commemorating facets of the heritage and oral histories of the McWorter family and New Philadelphia. But there is an impediment to the fact that the United States, like the United Kingdom, has rarely ratified such UNESCO conventions in the past 12 years (Alleyne 2003:25; Jones and Coleman 2005:36). Such conventions, declarations, and resolutions of UNESCO only have effect to the extent that they are ratified, explicitly adopted, and implemented by member states (Jones and Coleman 2005:76). Yet, over the past two decades, nations such as the United States have advocated significant restraint in the scope of UNESCO undertakings, while other countries have pushed for progressive programs like the 2003 Convention on intangible heritage. The result has been that the United States and the United Kingdom have chosen not to ratify conventions put forward by UNESCO and have thereby made those conventions inapplicable within their own territories. As Phillip Jones and David Coleman (2005:73) observe, this has become a "permanent reality of UNESCO at work, an organisation unable to afford its view of itself."

The 2003 Convention for the Safeguarding of the Intangible Cultural Heritage provides that member states ratifying and implementing its provisions should compile an inventory of instances of intangible cultural heritage to be recognized, commemorated, and safeguarded within their territories (UNESCO 2007b). As a start for this process, the 2003 Convention incorporated by reference the intangible cultural heritage entities listed as qualifying under the "Proclamation of Masterpieces of the Oral and Intangible Heritage of Humanity" that was initiated in 1998 (Bouchenaki 2007:107; UNESCO 2007b). Member states of UNESCO were free to submit candidates to this list of masterpieces and an international jury was created to review and approve such proposals (UNESCO 2007c). Within the framework of this inventory of masterpieces, "nineteen forms of cultural spaces or expression were proclaimed 'Masterpieces of Oral and Intangible Heritage' by the Director-General of UNESCO in May 2001, another set of twenty-eight 'Masterpieces' gained international recognition in November 2003, and forty-three in 2005" (Bouchenaki 2007:107). Given the 2003 Convention's incorporation of this inventory of masterpieces, one would assume that those proclaimed examples "provide a useful indication of the types of intangible heritage that different Member States wish to safeguard" under the Convention (Bounchenaki 2007:107). If nothing else, the representatives of the United States have been consistent: they chose not to participate in this "Proclamation of Masterpieces," and that inventory includes no instances of "Oral or Intangible Heritage of Humanity" within the United States (UNESCO 2007c).

The consistent refusal by the United States and the United Kingdom since the 1980s to participate in the activities of UNESCO may have some limited, rhetorical benefits for that international organization. UNESCO was created in 1945 with the mission of disseminating information and educational efforts to communicate the goals, perspectives, and principles of the United Nations (UN) worldwide to combat intolerance, prejudice, and racial ideologies (Alleyne 2003). UNESCO's operations were constrained, however, by the power given to member states of the UN, many of which could choose not to ratify proposed undertakings of UNESCO. The influence of member states of the UN over the operations of UNESCO led to a series of criticisms of the latter organization, with some analysts condemning it as a mechanism for "recolonization" and global exercises of white supremacy in the late twentieth century (Jones and Coleman 2005:15; Mills 1997:36–37, 73–75). Such criticisms lose persuasiveness, however, when one sees numerous UNESCO conventions ratified and implemented by many countries in South America, Europe, Asia, and Africa, while the United States and the United Kingdom abstain from participation.

Such abstention by influential and wealthy industrialized nations contradicts accusations that a global conspiracy exists that employs UNESCO as a tool of white, capitalist supremacy in the manner proposed by critics such as Charles Mills (1997). However, by withholding participation and the contribution of resources, these wealthy member states severely constrain the success of UNESCO's programs. "The typical interplay between western governments calling for program restraint and governments from the south advocating program expansion assumed ritualised status long ago, the low points of the organisation's effectiveness and credibility being reached when commitments were wide and resources severely constrained" (Jones and Coleman 2005:73). Thus, one paradox facing UNESCO is the contrast of program aspirations with resource deficits. Another dilemma arises from the concepts of agency and culture frequently incorporated in UNESCO's conventions and proclamations.

Since its creation in 1945, UNESCO has worked to combat concepts of race and racial ideologies (Alleyne 2003). In related efforts, UNESCO has advocated proper regard for individual cultures worldwide and has promoted multicultural tolerance by emphasizing that diverse "cultures" and "ethnicities" should be treated with respect (Lentin 2004:76). Yet, in doing so, UNESCO conventions and resolutions have often incorporated a concept of culture in which individuals are passive actors shaped by their cultural traditions. As Barbara Kirshenblatt-Gimblett (2004:58) has observed, the concepts of cultural traditions incorporated in the 2003 Convention on intangible heritage view individual practitioners as "carriers, transmitters, and bearers of traditions, terms which connote a passive medium, conduit, or vessel, without volition, intention, or subjectivity." This is a fairly outdated view of the basic character of cultural belief systems and traditions, in which such traditions are viewed as static and unchanging, all-encompassing, and as shaping and directing the conduct of individuals to such a degree that actors lack personal agency or capacities for innovation and self-determination. Such a static concept of culture is particularly ill-suited to addressing the heritage of individuals who undertook, through their own initiative and ingenuity, to combat the oppressive conduct of a dominant culture that sought to subjugate them.

Rather than viewing individual agency as part of the internal engine of cultural traditions, UNESCO conventions and declarations largely cast individual rights as a counterpoint to the sanctity and respect to be afforded to particular cultures. In this vein, the 2001 Universal Declaration on Cultural Diversity includes a specific provision emphasizing the importance of "a commitment to human rights and fundamental freedoms, in particular the rights of persons belonging to minorities," with the caveat that particular cultural traditions and heritage should be overridden in specific cases where those traditions violate the basic human rights of individuals (UNESCO 2001:art. 4). When one views the 2001 Declaration and the 2003 Convention together, condemnation of a culture's past practice of enslavement and commemoration of individual acts of resistance against bondage would be addressed in an abstract manner at best. The 2003 Convention does not provide a vehicle for commemorating the self-initiative of individuals resisting a dominant culture's attempts to violate basic human rights. At best, the 2001 Declaration would operate to disallow any attempt by an interest group in the United States that sought a UNESCO imprimatur for their desire to commemorate, rather than condemn, the institution of slavery in America's past.

The potential for cultural heritage claims within the United States remains hypothetical, because the United States has not yet ratified and participated in such UNESCO conventions and declarations. However, the same tensions will be present for minority social groups within other nations that have ratified the 2003 Convention and are now seeking to implement its provisions. As Richard Kurin (2007:13) observes, it will be unfortunate if nations participating in the 2003 Convention on intangible heritage simply appoint a government agency within their territory to inventory and safeguard those cultural traditions that the *state* deems worthy of attention. UNESCO and participating nations can best fulfill the goal of respecting such traditions of intangible cultural heritage by providing *citizens* an active voice in the process of implementing the 2003 Convention. This is particularly important because "[i]n many countries around the world, minority cultural communities do not see government as representing their interests—particularly when it comes to their living cultural traditions and their vitality as living, dynamic communities" (Kurin 2007:13).

Conclusion

Recognition of the significance of intangible cultural heritage raises the importance to today's communities of understanding the histories of how their predecessors strove to overcome past challenges and prejudices and the ways in which past actors confronted obstacles, failures, opportunities, and successes. The 2003 Convention emphasizes the importance of safeguarding particular facets of heritage to ensure that they do not disappear from the consciousness of current and future generations. For some aspects of the history and heritage of African Americans, their legacies of self-determination and resistance against racism will be subverted if the subjects of past and present racism in America are elided from national discourse. Yet, attempts to effect such an erasure are currently underway in national political debates in the United States. Those commentators who advocate a "color-blind" society in which race is no longer a consideration often seek a cessation of debates about the continuing impacts of past institutions of bondage and racism in America. Countervailing currents of commemoration and elision clash once again, with implications for both yesterday's heritage and the vitality of living communities.

Acknowledgments Some of the research results presented here are based on work supported by the National Science Foundation under grant numbers 0353550 and 0752834. Any opinions, findings, conclusions, or recommendations expressed here are those of the author and do not necessarily reflect the views of the National Science Foundation. I am also very grateful for generous funding support of the University of Illinois Research Board.

References

Alleyne, Mark D.
    2003 *Global Lies? Propaganda, the UN and World Order*. Palgrave Macmillan, New York.
Alton Telegraph & Democratic Review [Alton, Illinois]
    1849 30 November: 3.
Ahmad, Y.
    2006 The Scope and Definitions of Heritage: From Tangible to Intangible. *International Journal of Heritage Studies* 12(3):292–300.
Barry Adage [Barry, Illinois]
    1873 18 January: 4; 7 June: 4.
    1876 22 January: 3; 26 February: 3; 10 June: 3; 17 June: 2.
    1877 20 October: 1.
Bouchenaki, Mounir
    2007 A Major Advance towards a Holistic Approach to Heritage Conservation: The 2003 Intangible Heritage Convention. *International Journal of Intangible Heritage* 2:106–109.
Carlson, Theodore L.
    1951 *The Illinois Military Tract: A Study of Land Occupation, Utilization, and Tenure*. University of Illinois Press, Urbana.
Cha-Jua, Sundiata Keita
    2000 *America's First Black Town, Brooklyn, Illinois, 1830–1915*. University of Illinois Press, Urbana.
Chapman, Charles C.
    1880 *History of Pike County, Illinois*. C.C. Chapman, Chicago.
Cleeman, Thomas M.
    1880 *The Railroad Engineer's Practice*. G. H. Frost, New York.

Cochran, Thomas C.
  1950 North American Railroads: Land Grants and Railroad Entrepreneurship. *Journal of Economic History* 10 (supp.): 53–67.
Conger, John L.
  1932 *History of the Illinois River Valley*. S. J. Clarke, Chicago.
Cootner, Paul H.
  1963 The Role of the Railroads in United States Economic Growth. *Journal of Economic History* 23 (4):477–521.
Corliss, Carlton J.
  1934 *Trails to Rails: A Story of Transportation Progress in Illinois*. Illinois Central System, Springfield.
Davis, James E.
  1998 *Frontier Illinois*. Indiana University Press, Bloomington.
Dempsey, Terrell
  2003 *Searching for Jim: Slavery in Sam Clemens's World*. University of Missouri Press, Columbia.
Dobbin, Frank
  1994 *Forging Industrial Policy: The United States, Britain, and France in the Railway Age*. Cambridge University Press, Cambridge.
Ensign, D. W.
  1872 *Atlas Map of Pike County, Illinois*. Andreas, Lyter & Co., Davenport, Iowa.
Fishlow, Albert
  1971 *American Railroads and the Transformation of the Ante-Bellum Economy*. Harvard University Press, Cambridge.
Gaertner, Samuel L., and John F. Dovidio
  1986 The Aversive Form of Racism. In *Prejudice, Discrimination, and Racism*, edited by John F. Dovidio and Samuel L. Gaertner, pp. 61–89. Academic Press, Orlando.
Grant, H. Roger
  2004 *"Follow the Flag": A History of the Wabash Railroad Company*. Northern Illinois University Press, DeKalb.
Grimshaw, Hon. William A.
  1876 History of Pike County: A Centennial Address Delivered by Hon. William A. Grimshaw at Pittsfield, Pike County, Illinois, July 4, 1876. Illinois State Historical Society, Springfield.
Hannibal and Naples Railroad Company
  1863–1876 HNRC Records, Norfolk and Western Railway Archives, Ms90-096.
Hannibal Daily Courier [Hannibal, Missouri]
  1878 15 January: 1.
Hargrave, Michael L.
  2006 Geophysical Investigations at the New Philadelphia Site, Pike County, Illinois, 2004–2006 U.S Army Engineer Research and Development Center, Construction Engineering Research Laboratory, Champaign, Illinois. http://www.anthro.uiuc.edu/faculty/cfennell/NP/Geophys/geophysics.html
Illinois State Archives
  1837 An Act to Change the Name of Frank McWorter. General Assembly Records, Illinois State Archives Enrolled Laws No. 2031, HR No. 18, Box 48. On file, Illinois State Archives, Springfield.
Jenks, Leland H.
  1944 Railroads as an Economic Force in American Development. *Journal of Economic History* 4 (1):1–20.
Jervis, John B.
  1861 *Railway Property: A Treatise on the Construction and Management of Railways*. Phinney, Blakeman and Mason, New York.

Jones, Phillip W., and David Coleman
: 2005 *The United Nations and Education: Multilateralism, Development and Globalisation*. RoutledgeFalmer, London and New York.

King, Charlotte
: 2006 *Census Data for New Philadelphia*. University of Maryland, College Park, MD. http://www.heritage.umd.edu.

Kirshenblatt-Gimblett, Barbara
: 2004 Intangible Heritage as Metacultural Production. *Museum International* 56 (1–2):52–76.

Kleinpenning, Gerald, and Louk Hagendoorn
: 1993 Forms of Racism and the Cumulative Dimension of Ethnic Attitudes. *Social Psychology Quarterly* 56 (1):21–26.

Kovel, Joel
: 1970 *White Racism: A Psychohistory*. Pantheon Books, New York.

Kurin, Richard
: 2007 Safeguarding Intangible Cultural Heritage: Key Factors in Implementing the 2003 Convention. *International Journal of Intangible Heritage* 2:10–20.

Lentin, Alana
: 2004 *Racism and Anti-Racism in Europe*. Pluto Press, London.

Leone, Mark P., Cheryl J. LaRoche, and Jennifer J. Barbiarz
: 2005 The Archaeology of Black Americans in Recent Times. *Annual Review of Anthropology* 34:575–598.

Matteson, Grace
: 1964 "Free Frank" McWorter and the "Ghost Town" of New Philadelphia, Pike County, Illinois. Pike County Historical Society, Pittsfield.

Mills, Charles W.
: 1997 *The Racial Contract*. Cornell University Press, Ithaca.

National Park Service
: 1998 The Underground Railroad: A Special Resource Study. National Park Service, United States Department of the Interior, Washington, D.C. http://www.nps.gov.

National Park Service
: 2007 Underground Railroad Resources in the United States: A Theme Study. National Park Service, Washington, D.C. http://www.nps.gov.

Pike County Deed Records
: 1865 Pike County Courthouse, Pittsfield, Illinois.

Pike County Railroad Company Records
: 1857–1865 PCRC Records, Norfolk and Western Railway Archives, Ms90-121.

Pittsfield Union [Pittsfield, Illinois]
: 1853 18 May: 3.

Public Law 105-203
: 1998 National Underground Railroad Network to Freedom Act of 1998.

Putnam, J. W.
: 1909 An Economic History of the Illinois and Michigan Canal: III. *Journal of Political Economy* 17(7):413–433.

Raboteau, Albert J.
: 1980 *Slave Religion: The Invisible Institution in the Antebellum South*. Oxford University Press, Oxford.

Riegel, Robert E.
: 1923 Trans-Mississippi Railroads During the Fifties. *Mississippi Valley Historical Review* 10 (2):153–172.

Savage, W. Sherman
: 1943 The Contest Over Slavery Between Illinois and Missouri. *Journal of Negro History* 28 (3):311–325.

Shackel, Paul A.
  2003 *Memory in Black and White: Race, Commemoration, and the Post-Bellum Landscape*. Altamira Press, Walnut Creek, California.
Shackel, Paul A., with contributions by Alison Azzarello, Megan Bailey, Caitlin Bauchat, Carrie Christman, Kimberly Eppler, Christopher Fennell, Michael Hargrave, Emily Helton, Athena Hsieh, Jason Jacoby, Charlotte King, Hillary Livingston, Terrance Martin, Maria Alejandra Nieves Colon, Eva Pajuelo, Marjorie Schroeder, Erin Smith, Andrea Torvinen, and Christopher Valvano
  2006 *New Philadelphia Archaeology: Race, Community, and the Illinois Frontier*. Report on the 2004–2006 excavations sponsored by the National Science Foundation Research Experiences for Undergraduates (Grant #0353550), http://heritage.umd.edu/chrsweb/New%20Philadelphia/2006report/2006menu.htm.
Simeone, James
  2000 *Democracy and Slavery in Frontier Illinois: The Bottomland Republic*. Northern Illinois University Press, DeKalb.
Simon, Paul
  1994 *Freedom's Champion: Elijah Lovejoy*. Southern Illinois Press, Carbondale, Illinois.
Simpson, Helen McWorter
  1981 *Makers of History*. Laddie B. Warren, Evansville, Indiana.
Turner, Glennette T.
  2001 *The Underground Railroad in Illinois*. Newman Educational Publishing Co., Glen Ellyn, Illinois.
UNESCO [United Nations Educational, Scientific, and Cultural Organization]
  1993 Resolution 27C/3.13 of the General Conference. UNESCO, Paris.
  2001 Universal Declaration on Cultural Diversity. Adopted by the 31st session of the UNESCO General Conference, Paris, 2 November. UNESCO, Paris. http://unesdoc.unesco.org/images/0012/001271/127160m.pdf.
  2003 Convention for the Safeguarding of the Intangible Cultural Heritage. UNESCO, Paris. http://www.unesco.org/culture/ich/index.php?pg=00006.
  2006a The Slave Route Project. UNESCO, Paris.
  2006b Report of Expert Meeting on Community Involvement in Safeguarding Intangible Cultural Heritage: Towards the Implementation of the 2003 Convention. UNESCO and the Asia/Pacific Cultural Centre for UNESCO, Paris.
  2007a The States Parties to the Convention for the Safeguarding of the Intangible Cultural Heritage (2003) (as of Oct. 24, 2007). UNESCO, Paris. http://www.unesco.org/culture/ich/index.php?pg=00024.
  2007b Intergovernmental Committee for the Safeguarding of the Intangible Cultural Heritage, UNESCO, ITH/07/2.COM/CONF.208/14, July 23, 2007. UNESCO, Paris.
  2007c Proclamation of Masterpieces of the Oral and Intangible Heritage of Humanity: Guide for the Presentation of Candidature Files. July 9, 2007. UNESCO, Paris. http://www.unesco.org.
United States Geological Survey [U.S.G.S.]
  2007 *Geographic Names Information System*. U.S. Department of the Interior, Washington, D.C. http://geonames.usgs.gov.
United States Supreme Court
  1892 *Church of the Holy Trinity v. United States*, Case No. 143. 143 U.S. Reports 457.
Vose, George L.
  1857 *Handbook of Railroad Construction; For the Use of American Engineers*. J. Munroe and Co., Boston.
Walker, Juliet E. K.
  1983 *Free Frank: A Black Pioneer on the Antebellum Frontier*. University Press of Kentucky, Lexington.

1985 Entrepreneurial Ventures in the Origin of Nineteenth-Century Agricultural Towns: Pike County, 1823–1880. *Illinois Historical Journal* 78(1):45–64.

Webb, Walter L.

1917 *Railroad Construction: Theory and Practice*. John Wiley and Sons, New York.

Wellington, Arthur M.

1901 *The Economic Theory of the Location of Railways*. John Wiley and Sons, New York.

Chapter 9
Folk Epigraphy at the World Trade Center, Oklahoma City, and Beyond

Joy Sather-Wagstaff

The former sites of the Word Trade Center's twin towers in Manhattan and the Murrah Federal Building in Oklahoma City are today commemorative places of deep symbolic and historical importance. The tragic events of scale that occurred at these sites on September 11, 2001 and April 19, 1995, respectively, are processually signified and resignified by a broad public through performative and embodied practices enacted by both tourists and locals at these sites and beyond. These practices work in the service of socially constructing memoryscapes, engendering the creation and performance of diverse subjectivities, politicized identities, and citizenship in a number of communities of belonging from the local to the global. The complex and ever-changing "heritage that hurts" (Schofield et al. 2002:1) that these sites represent is brought into being through a variety of tangible and ephemeral modes.

In the cases of the events of September 11, 2001 and April 19, 1995, along with other tragedies of scale, ephemeral modes of memory-making and performing commemoration include the creation of commemorative folk assemblages and the performance of vernacular written and oral narratives of individuals' memories of and sentiments about these events and their aftermaths. These modes of expression are understood by both heritage practitioners and the public to be critically important to individual and social processes of memorialization, public participation in historiography, and the making of individual and collective historical consciousness. Yet in order to become a part of any relatively enduring historical record, and broadly shared memories over time, these ephemeral modes of expression must be somehow rendered less intangible.

By addressing folk epigraphical practices within the contexts of commemorative sites and museum and virtual spaces, I present here several processes of and problems with making more durable folk epigraphy as a form of fundamentally intangible heritage. In doing so, I look to how both individuals and organizations are participating in these processes through a shared culture of

---

J. Sather-Wagstaff (✉)
Department of Sociology, Anthropology and Emergency Management, North Dakota State University, Fargo, ND 58108, USA
e-mail: joy.sather-wagstaff@ndsu.edu

collecting and display. This shared culture of collecting and display involves both old and new traditions and technologies for public and personal historiography. The active archiving of textual messages by both individuals and public historians is argued to have indeed rendered these markings somewhat more durable but not truly permanent. The dissemination of these texts also produces a new form of historiography, one that brings together vernacular and professional public history practices in novel ways. And with the inclusion of folk epigraphy into the physical architecture of present and future memorials, a once highly ephemeral mode of expression is becoming more permanently embedded in the material culture of commemorative sites themselves. However, folk epigraphy should continue to be understood primarily as an intangible heritage form.

Folk Assemblages

As a form for expressing sentiments and marking place, contemporary epigraphical practices play a role in the ongoing vernacular sanctification of commemorative sites. Processes of sanctification involve the creation of specific places that represent loss to a broad public rather than single individuals; according to Kenneth Foote (2001:8–15), such places are made distinct by the emplacement and maintenance of a "durable marker" of scale such as a memorial garden or park landscape, monument, or building. While this definition addresses the official establishment of architectural or landscape elements at sites, the various epigraphical practices performed by visitors at such sites—and even prior to their official establishment—constitute a processual, vernacular dimension to the making of commemorative places.

At contemporary sites of tragedy, violence, and death a wide range of popular epigraphical practices are performed, among them graffiti inscribed directly on landscape surfaces and participatory message-making on surfaces that are provided specifically for this purpose. At contemporary commemorative sites in general, both small and large, these modes of folk epigraphy are a means for speaking to and of the dead and expressing individual and collective sentiments and stories regarding the events and their aftermath in current contexts. This practice is a series of embodied acts that literally mark the site as part of the active process of making the site historically salient in individual and collective memory. As part of the folk assemblages (Fig. 9.1) found at the both the World Trade Center site and the Oklahoma City National Memorial and Museum, this particular form of visual and material expression takes numerous forms and serves multiple communicative functions.

In general terms that include both commemorative displays and everyday displays such as seasonal yard decorations, folk assemblages are intentionally arranged formations and displays of material culture that are "created for an undefined public" (Santino 1992:27) by individuals or groups. They are "holistic

9 Folk Epigraphy at the World Trade Center

Fig. 9.1 Anti-graffiti Port Authority of New York and New Jersey sign on the fence around the World Trade Center site, 2003 (photo by Joy Sather-Wagstaff)

entities made up of symbolic elements placed in proximity with one another... the meanings of each element inform the other metonymically; the assemblage itself is a context that frames each symbolic element within" (Santino 1992:27–28). Commemorative folk assemblages emerge at sites of death or other public sites of mourning and include a wide array of material and visual culture, from flowers and toys, candles and balloons to religious objects, photographs, and patriotic items. Not unlike religious shrines, these secular assemblages are a means for publicly paying respects to the dead while producing numerous social effects, both individual and collective, including participation in imagined communities of mourning, belonging, closure, and spiritual or emotional healing. As Sylvia Grider (2001:1) notes, the assemblages that emerged around the world following September 11, 2001 as "spontaneous and communal performances of grief," were also a means for "people to work out a *personal connection* to an otherwise numbing catastrophe" (emphasis added).

Efforts to collect or otherwise document these ephemeral assemblages in some form have emerged as organizations like City Lore in Manhattan, the Oklahoma City National Memorial Museum, and the Smithsonian National Museum of American History have acknowledged their value as historically specific, expressive material culture forms.[1] They are understood to represent collective, ceremonial rituals for apprehending and making sense of a tragedy, rituals that are part of recovery's initial phase but that also endure into the present when displayed in museums. "Ceremony classifies the calamity; simultaneously it launches an interpretation of it, one of numerous 'framings' to come" (Hoffman 1999:43) and these future interpretive framings often take place at a temporal distance from the event and in the case of museum exhibits, a spatial distance. In Albany, New York, the State Museum of New York's *The World Trade Center: Rescue Recovery Response* exhibit features a section of fence originally located in Liberty Plaza (adjacent to the World Trade Center site proper) that displays a commemorative assemblage. Both the physical exhibit and its digital online version form new frames for interpretation that are geographically and temporally distant from the past event and aftermath at the World Trade Center site, engendering new ways for viewers to apprehend and historicize the tragedy of September 11, 2001 over time and in space.[2]

Folk Epigraphy

As one of many components in the commemorative assemblages that continue to endure at the currently semiformal site of the World Trade Center, folk epigraphy takes a number of forms. This includes but is not limited to graffiti, traditionally defined as typically illegal markings made by an individual on a durable surface in the landscape, "pictorial or written inscriptions for which no official provision is made and which are largely unwanted" (Blume 1983:137). Despite signs that forbid such writing (Fig. 9.2), local and non-local visitors write on the fence, construction barriers, and sidewalks surrounding the site, leaving messages to specific victims, a simple "I was here" name and date, sentiments of sympathy, patriotic statements, and political or cultural criticism. In doing so they are engaging in a very old cultural practice of leaving epigraphical evidence of their presence in a place, documenting attitudes and experiences (Lindsay 1960; Stocker et al. 1972), and making "sensible marks that act as a confirmation of a place's sacred [or otherwise culturally important] character" (Plesch 2002:169–70).

Graffiti such as this was commonly seen over the course of my research at the World Trade Center site (2002–2008). While not all visitors produced this type of epigraphy, most did take the time to read the writings of others and these written items were subjects for photographs and videos. Visitors expressed to me a clear understanding that their acts of writing and reading are critically important in the embodied, lived and recalled experience of the tragedy, the visit to sites themselves, and the ways in which they will remember it all. They were engaging in the most fundamental purposes for graffiti: leaving physical traces that represent an individual's voice, to indicate ownership of a place, or to record the moment of physical presence at a place. By doing so, they are literally inscribing themselves into the commemorative landscape as invested

Fig. 9.2 Commemorative assemblage at the World Trade Center site, 2007 (photo by Joy Sather-Wagstaff)

stakeholders and active individual participants in its making through their physical presence.

Graffiti and other epigraphical practices are also a highly dialogic practice, a means for "speaking" to anonymous persons who are not copresent, socially positioning both writers and readers, and contributing to a wider visual, material, and embodied discursive field of meaningfulness accorded to the event, the space in which it occurred as a place for commemoration, and individual and collective memory. In the public spaces of commemoration, these various markings constitute a series of "image acts" (Bakewell 1998:22) where the text, as a public utterance, is understood as a communicative visual image with the capacity for diverse social actions and effects. Such acts of display in general "not only shows and speaks it also does" (Kirshenblatt-Gimblett 1998:128), and graffiti and other forms of folk epigraphy do so by conversationally linking both markers and readers.

As image acts, these temporary markings of grief, empathy, commemoration, anger, cultural criticism, and political sentiment represent both paradigmatic and diverse perspectives in performative public conversation. Contrary to what is often assumed, the World Trade Center site is not wholly dominated by a single political and commemorative narrative of victims, heroism, and fanatical patriotism. There are instead numerous narratives that are processually woven between, among, and against the formal plaques and signs narrating the events of September 11, 2001, visitors' spoken and written conversations, and the visual and material culture that make up the commemorative folk assemblages on display. Anti-war and progressive political sentiments act in conversation with jingoistic patriotic discourse, articulating alternative means for "never forgetting" other than through war, political bigotry, and projections of cultural or religious superiority (Fig. 9.3). These acts of writing and reading are participatory, embodied forms of individual expression that have a number of salient and often powerful social effects.

The first effect is that which results from embodied experience, the act of marking one's physical presence and expressing sentiments, tucking the action away in memory or even photographing it for posterity—one vernacular means of making the epigraphical performance durable. The second is that of viewing and reading, being spoken to by non-copresent fellow visitors who may be nonetheless directing a message (Fig. 9.4) at a specific audience. The act of reading is powerful as one may agree with the content, one may disagree, one may find their subjectivity transformed, one may be moved to tears. Third, taken collectively by a viewer as a conversation, these image acts constitute a collective reflection upon and sometimes contestation over the event itself. The conversational component to the graffiti in Fig. 9.3 represents two different positions that create, at minimum, three distinct statements for viewers to interpret: "God bless USA," "God help USA," and "God bless help USA." Likewise, the ongoing conversation in Fig. 9.5 is representative of this collective reflection, with the

Fig. 9.3 Graffiti on the viewing fence along Church Street, World Trade Center site, 2003 (photo by Joy Sather-Wagstaff)

Fig. 9.4 Graffiti on the Liberty Street wall, World Trade Center site, 2005 (photo by Joy Sather-Wagstaff)

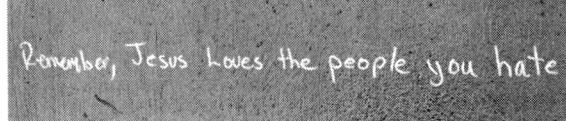

Fig. 9.5 Graffiti on the Liberty Street wall, World Trade Center site, 2003 (photo by Joy Sather-Wagstaff)

patriotic statement that "these colors don't run" flanking "nationalism kills," "mulims [sic] kills," "nationalism kills mulims [sic]," and "nationalism kills provides freedom," depending upon how one reads and interprets the graffiti.

Because graffiti is understood to have real social effects, it is an ephemeral, temporary mode of communication. City and civic organizations will quickly eliminate graffiti as a means to remove "dangerous" or "offensive" image acts as well as keep private and public property free of "unwanted" visual clutter. This is also the case at the World Trade Center site; not only are there signs meant to discourage graffiti but graffiti on fences and other objects is also eliminated regularly by steam blasting and painting. However, at this and other sites of tragedy there are other popular, diverse, and more socially acceptable epigraphical forms that have effects similar to that of the commemorative graffiti discussed thus far.

Handwritten notes were often seen tucked into the fence at the World Trade Center site, inserted into bouquets of flowers, or attached to other material culture items left in the assemblages. These often tended to be messages to specific victims and when often securely folded or rolled up, were clearly not intended for the public. Condolence cards, typed letters, poems, stories, song lyrics, passages from religious texts, and messages collected via email that were more broadly addressed to all victims, the City of New York, the United States, or a more general viewing public were also left as part of the folk assemblages. These written messages ranged from entire narratives of "where I was on September 11, 2001" to condolences to victims' families and patriotic statements. They included sentiments of solidarity from and intended for various communities of belonging spanning the United States and the world, such as religious groups, schools, the brotherhood of firefighters, businesses, and various ethnic organizations.

As another alternative to graffiti and these highly ephemeral paper-based materials and a means to more permanently archive messages, numerous civil organizations and individuals regularly provided temporary materials for marking. They provide banners, posters, flags, and t-shirts along with markers and pens for public, participatory message-making (Figs. 9.6 and 9.7). From homemade foam core "memory boards" and spiral-bound notebooks to elaborately

Fig. 9.6 "Save the Cross" poster with messages on the Church Street viewing fence, World Trade Center site, 2004 (photo by Joy Sather-Wagstaff)

printed banners and stretched canvases, these other surfaces offer a socially sanctioned alternative to the defacement of site property. This wide array of materials provided for marking sentiments is an outgrowth of older traditions of condolence books at funerals and the late twentieth century practice of leaving blank notebooks at commemorative folk assemblages, a custom that emerged widely following the death of Princess Diana in 1997 in tandem with the practice of creating commemorative folk assemblages of scale (Grider 2001:2).

In New York City, the provisioning of these materials was particularly popular during the September 11 anniversaries as well as on weekends and national holidays. Preprinted posters, t-shirts, and banner-sized articles listing victims' names, iconic images, or themes of peace or mourning were frequently displayed throughout the pedestrian accessible areas, sidewalks, and construction barriers around the World Trade Center site during these times. Tourists, victims' family members and friends, locals from all walks of life, survivors, and first responders, rescue, and recovery workers made drawings and wrote messages, poems, stories, and sentiments with the pens, crayons, and markers provided for them. Some of these canvases and posters for marking are provided by non-profit and charity groups such as ArtAid and the Save The Cross

9 Folk Epigraphy at the World Trade Center 177

Fig. 9.7 Peace banner at the World Trade Center site, 2004 (photo by Joy Sather-Wagstaff)

Foundation while others are provided by various activist, peace, religious, and youth groups.[3] Some of these items are collected after being marked on, intended for display in future formal memorial sites and museums or traveling exhibits. Several international youth peace groups have exhibited collectively marked banners from September 11, 2003 and September 11, 2004 in cities throughout the world. Other items are collected when the site is cleaned and will likely never be seen again.

Archiving the Ephemeral

As part of oral history and public memory preservation programs, professional cultural heritage and historical organizations have developed and implemented various methods for officially collecting, archiving, and disseminating individuals' narratives about and responses to both September 11, 2001 and April 19, 1995, historically the two most disastrous acts of terrorism to take place in the United States. This includes those that are made as a part of the assemblages discussed above as well as stand-alone sentiments and narratives collected through other written, oral, or digital means. These sentiments also represent the highly diverse subject positions of what Kai Erikson (2005:354) identifies as the "hinterland" population of the USA and beyond, a broad public that has been typically overlooked because they live beyond the "official [geographic] boundaries" of the disasters of September 11, 2001, but who nonetheless "feel that they were witnesses *to*, victims *of*, even actors *in*" these events.

Perhaps the most simple of these official collection and archiving practices is found at the temporary Flight 93 memorial site in Shanksville, Pennsylvania, already under the auspices of the National Park Service. A chain link fence serves as the temporary memorial and houses a commemorative assemblage whose non-perishable items are removed, catalogued, and archived when becoming too weathered. Blank notebooks, cards, and pens are provided at the site so that visitors can write their sentiments and messages and leave them on display with assurances that, unlike at the World Trade Center, they will be collected each evening and kept for possible use in the future memorial site. This basic system of materials provisioning and collecting is adequate for a site such as this where the number of visitors is a little more than 100,000 a year, compared to the millions that visit the World Trade Center site each year.

Through various web-based and on-site participatory activities such as the September 11 Digital Archive and the Wall of Hope at the Oklahoma City National Memorial Museum, both oral and written narratives have also been documented digitally and photographically and made available to a geographically dispersed public through internet archives and print media. One characteristic that the Oklahoma City museum and various temporary September 11, 2001 museum exhibitions have in common is the opportunity for visitors to physically leave messages, sentiments, and stories and the subsequent collection, archiving, and dissemination of these narratives in various forms.

Visitors to the Oklahoma City National Memorial are explicitly invited to leave messages, stories, drawings, and sentiments in four spaces. The first space is a section of the original chain link fence that surrounded the area after the Murrah Federal Building was bombed. Visitors can attach items or notes to the fence and participate in the ongoing folk assemblage that is an official part of the formal, outdoor Memorial landscape. The second space is a children's area in front of the museum's main entrance, a brick patio surrounded by ceramic tiles made by children from around the world and equipped with sidewalk chalk. Both of these spaces are open to the public 24 hours a day, 7 days a week. Inside the museum is another children's space for visitors of any age to create drawings or writings.

Until 2005 when a computer-based system was introduced, the third space was also inside the Memorial Museum. The Memorial Tile Registry/Wall of

Fig. 9.8 The Wall of Hope in the Oklahoma City National Memorial Museum, 2004 (photo courtesy of the Ferguson-Watkins Collection, Oklahoma City National Memorial Museum. © 2001 Oklahoma City National Memorial Foundation)

Hope was the last section of the exhibit space and visitors used dry-erase markers to leave messages and draw on removable magnetic whiteboard tiles placed on the wall (Fig. 9.8). Archive staff removed the marked tiles, photocopied, and erased each one daily so that the wall contained blank tiles for the new day's visitors. In 2003 the museum published a book, *Shared Voices: 04.19.95–09.11.01*, containing a selection of the messages left on the Wall of Hope in the months after September 11, 2001 juxtaposed with photographs from the aftermaths of both events. In 2005, as a means to better manage the archiving of messages, The Wall of Hope was changed from the manual whiteboard tile system to a digitized one where computer stations are used for leaving messages.[4]

A number of temporary September 11, 2001 exhibits also include spaces for folk epigraphical practices. Some are solely digitally based, like those at the earliest of the New York Historical Society's various September 11, 2001 exhibits. At these exhibits, computer stations linked to the September 11 Digital Archive allowed visitors to contribute their stories and sentiments. Paper-based forms were provided at the endpoint of the Smithsonian's *September 11: Bearing Witness to History* exhibit which had over 1 million visitors during its exhibition period of September 11, 2002 to July 6, 2003. This exhibit included a large room supplied with tables, pens, and forms for leaving comments, drawings, and messages as well as phone booths for calling and recording stories and messages in the digital archive. For both of these activities, visitors were invited to "tell how they had changed" or create any messages they liked. Completed forms could be or dropped in a collection box or pinned to a board at the exit to the exhibit. Like the folk epigraphy at the World Trade Center site, the posted forms created a meaningful conversation between visitors not copresent.

At the close of the exhibit, over 20,000 completed forms were collected. They were scanned and are now available for public viewing online as part of the September 11 Digital Archive.[5] The September 11 Digital Archive was created to collect and archive firsthand accounts along with emails, various images, and other digitally based media related to the events of September 11, 2001. Funded by the Alfred P. Sloane Foundation, it is run by the City of New York Graduate Center American Social History Project and the Center for History and New Media at George Mason University. As of September 2003, the archive became the largest digital collection held by the Library of Congress and it serves as the Smithsonian's officially designated repository for digital objects related to September 11, 2001. There are also means for calling into the Archive and leaving brief stories and messages orally and by TTD.

Inscription and (Im)permanence

The collection, archiving, and dissemination of folk epigraphy through the internet, publications, and museum display do geographically disperse experiences and sentiments that continually construct commemorative site meanings from afar, write histories that may otherwise be completely omitted, and contribute an amazing amount of diverse public memory to these new types of historical archives. However, be they the original paper forms or the digitized versions, these are not materially robust records compared to many other tangible artifacts from tragic events such as collected and archived debris. The contents of the September 11 Digital Archive are still fundamentally ephemeral due to its digital format—we do not yet know how long digitized data can last with current storage technology and even average computer users know well the fragility of electronic data systems: servers unexpectedly crashing, hard drives corrupting, power outages damaging systems and perhaps most the unavoidable of problems, human errors that result in the loss of digital data.

This suggests that despite the present, constructed semi-durability of these presentational forms through acts of collection and dissemination, the written sentiments, stories, and messages themselves essentially remain and thus should be understood primarily as intangible heritage. While digital formats take up less archive space and offer a means to better manage collections of folk epigraphy and other commemorative culture, they are still fragile in both different and similar ways to the ephemeral culture they aim to preserve.

And perhaps even more importantly, while the epigraphical performances themselves—the acts of writing and the finished result—may be recorded photographically or digitally, individual vernacular memories of the performance cannot be physically archived, only recalled through embodied acts of remembering.

However, the recent incorporation of folk epigraphy into memorial architecture is one way in which it is being made more durable. In Madrid, Spain, on March 11, 2006, the M11 Memorial to the 191 victims of the March 11, 2004 train bombings was opened at the Atocha train station. It was designed by the FAM Studio Madrid, a group of five young Spanish architects. The memorial is an 11-meter high glass brick cylinder that acts as a skylight into the station area underneath ground level (Fig. 9.9). Inscribed on the inside of the cylinder are messages that were left at the four bombing sites on notes, cards, and banners as well as collected on computers located near the sites (Fig. 9.10). They are in multiple languages and tell multiple stories, express an array of sentiments, and represent the narratives of many who felt it important to share, through acts of writing, their messages. While this is the first memorial to incorporate folk epigraphy into the formal memorial form, it is not to be the only one to do so.

On September 10, 2007, the Tour for the National September 11 Memorial and Museum began in Columbia, South Carolina. At the time of this writing, the 4-month fundraising tour and memorial exhibit is scheduled to visit a significant part of the United States heartland, stopping in North Carolina, Virginia, Pennsylvania, West Virginia, Ohio, Kentucky, Indiana, Michigan,

Fig. 9.9 Exterior of the M11 Memorial in Madrid, Spain, 2007 (photo courtesy of Maria Angel Alfonseca-Cubero)

Fig. 9.10 Looking up into the interior of the M11 Memorial in Madrid, Spain, 2007 (photo courtesy of Maria Angel Alfonseca-Cubero)

Illinois, Wisconsin, South Dakota, Iowa, Nebraska, Kansas, Missouri, Arkansas, Tennessee, Oklahoma (where it will be adjacent to the Oklahoma City National Memorial), Texas, Louisiana, Mississippi, Alabama, Georgia, and Florida. This traveling exhibit includes September 11, 2001 photographs, artifacts, and videos of firsthand accounts. Of critical interest here is the display of steel beams that will be used in the construction of the National September 11 Memorial at the former site of the World Trade Center towers: the visiting public is invited to write on these beams, leaving messages, names, and sentiments that will become a part of the future memorial's built environment.

Both public memory and history "emerge from the intersection between official [homogenous and authorized] and vernacular [multiple, ambiguous, local, and heterogeneous] cultural expressions" (Bodnar 1992:13). Acknowledging the role of digital media in better enabling this dialogic relationship, Tom Scheinfeldt, assistant director of the Center for History and New Media at George Mason University, said, "History is no longer told by just a select few" but made by many and available to an even broader public than ever before (Collins 2007). The collection, archiving, and display of folk epigraphy as a powerful form of vernacular cultural expression, be it digitally or as literally inscribed upon elements in formal commemorative architecture, indeed represents a significant manifestation of the intersection between official and vernacular cultural expressions. And in the case of both the Madrid memorial and the future September 11 memorial in New York City, the intangible, fleeting, and ephemeral have been and will be rendered as permanent as possible by becoming a part of commemorative site architecture for a "heritage that hurts" (Schofield et al. 2002:1).

Notes

1. This is not a new practice for the Smithsonian. Items left at the Vietnam Veterans Memorial in Washington, DC, have been actively collected and archived since 1984 and numerous items are on permanent display in the National Museum of American History.

2. The exhibit began in 2002 and continues to be an ongoing feature in the museum. As of September 11, 2007, this exhibit can be viewed in online form at http://www.nysm.nysed.gov/wtc/.
3. See http://www.artaid.org/ for more information on ArtAid's artworks and charitable activities for numerous causes.
4. While virtual archives characterize a great deal of the September 11, 2001 collections, it should be noted that the Oklahoma City National Memorial archive proactively planned a digital archive for material and narrative culture during a time when the technology for such was limited and often prohibitively expensive (see Brown 1999).
5. See http://911digitalarchive.org/galleries.php?collection_id = 31 to browse a selection of submitted forms. In addition to these paper forms, the Smithsonian also provided a closed line telephone system for visitors to leave brief spoken messages. These messages are also archived on the September 11 Digital Archive and available for listening online.

References

Bakewell, Liza
    1998 Image Acts. *American Anthropologist*100(1):22–32.
Blume, Regina
    1985 Graffiti. In *Discourse and Literature: New Approaches to the Analysis of Literary Genres*, edited by Teun A. van Dijk, Pp. 137–148. John Benjamins Publishing, Philadelphia.
Bodnar, John
    1992 *Remaking America: Public Memory, Commemoration, and Patriotism in the Twentieth Century*. Princeton University Press, Princeton.
Brown, Carol
    1999 "Out of the Rubble": Building a Contemporary History Archive—The Oklahoma City National Memorial Archives. *Perspectives Online: The Newsletter of the American Historical Association*.October 1999 issue. http://www.theaha.org/Perspectives
Collins, Glenn
    2007 Remembering 9/11, Digitally. New York Times City Room Blogs, Electronic document, http://cityroom.blogs.nytimes.com/2007/09/11/remembering-911-digitally/ (accessed September 22, 2007)
Erikson, Kai
    2005 Epilogue: The Geography of Disaster. In *Wounded City: The Social Impact of 9/11*, edited by Nancy Foner, pp. 351–362. Russell Sage Foundation, New York.
Foote, Kenneth
    2001[1997] Shadowed Ground: America's Landscapes of Violence and Tragedy. University of Texas Press, Austin.
Grider, Sylvia
    2001 Spontaneous Shrines: A Modern Response to Tragedy and Disaster. *New Directions in Folklore* 5, online. http://www.temple.edu/isllc/newfolk/shrines.html
Hoffman, Susanna M.
    1999 The Worst of Times, the Best of Times: Toward a Model of Cultural Response to Disaster. In*The Angry Earth: Disaster in Anthropological Perspective*, edited by Anthony Oliver-Smith and Susanna M. Hoffman, pp. 134–155. Routledge, New York.
Kirshenblatt-Gimblett, Barbara
    1998 *Destination Culture: Tourism, Museums, and Heritage*. University of California Press, Berkeley.
Lindsay, Jack
    1960 *The Writing on the Wall: An Account of Pompeii in its Last Days*. Frederick Muller, London.

Plesch, Veronique
    2002 Memory on the Wall: Graffiti in Religious Wall Paintings. *Journal of Medieval and Early Modern Studies* 32 (1):167–197.

Santino, Jack
    1992 Yellow Ribbons and Seasonal Flags: The Folk Assemblage of War. *The Journal of American Folklore* 105 (415):19–33.

Schofield, John, William Gray Johnson, and Colleen M. Beck
    2002 Introduction: Matériel Culture in the Modern World. In *Matériel Culture: The Archaeology of Twentieth-century Conflict*, edited by John Schofield, William Gray Johnson, and Colleen M. Beck, pp. 1–8. Routledge, London.

Stocker, Terrence Linda Dutcher, Stephen Hargrove and Edwin Cook
    1972 Social Analysis of Graffiti. *Journal of American Folklore* 85 (338):356–366.

Chapter 10
Problematizing Technologies for Documenting Intangible Culture: Some Positive and Negative Consequences

Laura R. Graham

The 2003 UNESCO Convention to "safeguard intangible cultural heritage" raises a number of interesting political questions:

- Who decides what cultural forms are to be recorded, documented, and safeguarded?[1]
- What is the purpose(s) of heritage documentation, in specific instances?
- In practice, whose interests does this safeguarding primarily serve?
- Who is doing the safeguarding and what are the relationships, particularly relationships of power and authority, between various parties involved in safeguarding practices, including institutions such as museums, universities, non-governmental organizations (NGOs), as well as their representatives in interactions with various local-level community organizations, institutions and their individual members?
- Who are the audiences of heritage documentation and how are safeguarding practices and presentations of safeguarded materials accountable to the needs and interests of distinct audiences?
- What practices are appropriate, and not appropriate, to safeguarding intangible expressive forms for specific cultures or social groups?
- How are safeguarded performances made accessible (in culturally appropriate ways) to members of traditional communities whose forms of intangible heritage are being safeguarded?
- How is the Convention's educational mandate carried out with respect to traditional communities,[2] especially indigenous communities, who receive special recognition in the Convention's framing paragraphs (UNESCO 2003)?
- Ultimately, who are the beneficiaries of heritage safeguarding and preservation?

While this is not an exhaustive list, these questions focus attention to some of the political entailments and issues of power and control that pertain to institutional "safeguarding," documentation, management, and display of intangible cultural forms. They are especially relevant to indigenous as well as other

L.R. Graham (✉)
Department of Anthropology, University of Iowa, Iowa City, IA 52242, USA
e-mail: laura-graham@uiowa.edu

subaltern peoples who typically have not been active participants in institutional debates and decisions about efforts to record and document their intangible as well as tangible cultures. Historically, outsiders have been the primary leaders of these initiatives. The extent to which individual and community collaboration in such projects may be influenced by perceptions of outside institutions and their representatives' power and prestige rather than by local understandings of the objectives, uses, and implications of such projects, as well as local motivations or commitments to such projects is, in many cases, an open question.

Ethnographic work is necessary to understand local ideologies of intangible culture in relation to safeguarding, documentation and representational practices. It is also essential to comprehending the precise nature of indigenous conceptions of and participation in such activities. Further, greater ethnographic transparency is needed to identify and understand the nature of outside cultural mediators' involvement in and ways that it affects all aspects of safeguarding practice—from decisions about what intangible cultural forms are selected to be safeguarded, how they are recorded and documented, as well as how they are subsequently managed and represented both within local communities and to outside audiences. As local communities increasingly become involved in intangible heritage representation and management, ethnographic documentation of all aspects of these processes in specific cases will help provide bases for understanding the nature of outside cultural mediators' involvement as well as indigenous attitudes toward participation in and conceptions of this work.

To advance thought along these lines, this chapter has two objectives. The first is to provoke critical reflection about dimensions of power and control that are entailed in documentation and dissemination of forms of indigenous intangible culture, particularly the use of technologies for recording and documenting. To bring attention to the existence of alternative ideologies concerning the use of technology in safeguarding and documenting indigenous languages and intangible cultural forms I begin by discussing some of the ideological assumptions that underpin the UNESCO Convention. Consideration of perspectives articulated by contemporary Yuchi who are working with the last few remaining fluent speakers to revitalize their language raises important questions about some fundamental presuppositions of intangible cultural documentation and preservation. Yuchi language activists are highly skeptical of technology as a means of safeguarding and revitalizing their language. Generally speaking, their experience with past documentary projects makes them leery of such projects. The Yuchi example provokes thought about whose interests "safeguarding" projects ultimately serve and whether documentation and recording as a means of "safeguarding" is really, in all cases, the best way to serve the interests of local communities.

This chapter's second objective is to advocate for greater local control over and involvement with technologies and processes related to the documentation and representation of intangible culture. Using the example of the central

Brazilian Xavante community of Eténhiritipa (also known in Portuguese as Pimentel Barbosa), I argue that increasing indigenous access to and command of technologies creates new possibilities for and engagement in local management of cultural documentation and representational practices. I caution, however, that while taking charge of representational forms and processes may provide means for empowerment and cultural revitalization (see for example, Turner 1991, 1992; Prins 2002), it may also reinforce or create new forms of dependency. Before considering the Xavante, who exhibit tremendous enthusiasm for technology and new forms of cultural documentation and representation (both to themselves and to outsiders), it is useful to first contemplate some assumptions that underlie the UNESCO Convention for the Safeguarding of Intangible Cultural Heritage and heritage management practice in general.

Ideological Presuppositions of UNESCO

Grounded in the discourse of international human rights and recognizing the importance of intangible cultural heritage as a source of cultural diversity, the UNESCO Convention presupposes that intangible cultural forms should be safeguarded. Insofar as safeguarding practice implies recording, documenting, and preserving this documentation, most educated Westerners, especially those schooled in the Liberal Arts tradition, probably would agree (on humanistic as well as scholarly grounds) that these affirm expressive practices as well as the communities and individuals who perform them. Safeguarding practices that record and document intangible performance forms (such as speech, song, dance, and ritual performance) make these accessible to humanity, so that audiences beyond the initial targets may appreciate and enjoy them. Recording also enables them to be further analyzed and studied. Documentation, safeguarding, and various forms of representation open up new possibilities to, as the Convention Text states, enrich and affirm cultural diversity, human creativity, and respect for difference.

The degree to which social groups share the assumption that intangible forms of cultural expression should be "made tangible" via recording and documenting techniques as such is an open question, however. The possibility exists that some peoples and communities may not positively view such recording and documenting endeavors. The degree to which peoples view their intangible culture practices (or some of these practices) as "objects" to be documented, recorded, archived, or managed as tangible forms, particularly by outsiders, is open to ethnographic investigation. The possibility exists for distinct cultural conceptions concerning recording and documentary practices. And furthermore, beyond these considerations, there are questions about who can or should have access to this documentation, an issue that is beyond the scope of this discussion (but see, for example, Michaels 1994 [1986]).

A Western ideology of objectification underlies the notion that documenting and recording are positive means of safeguarding or preserving intangible cultural forms. Western practices of scientific knowing and ways of viewing are steeped in this objectifying tradition (Berger 1972). Western scientific practices of linguistic study offer an excellent example. Linguists traditionally document languages by recording through writing, spoken words, and grammatical forms. The International Phonetic Alphabet (IPA) provides a standardized convention for graphically representing the sounds of human language. Writing using the IPA or any other convention objectifies speech. It makes the intangible sounds of spoken human language tangible.[3] Linguists employ the IPA to transform ephemeral speech forms into objects for subsequent linguistic analysis. Field linguists, for example, traditionally convert spoken discourse—words, morphemes, and sentences—into material form when they use the IPA to write spoken utterances onto little slips of paper. They then categorize and file these, traditionally in boxes. Linguists literally put language into a shoebox. Now, in the digital age, a useful software program available to linguists is appropriately and nostalgically named "shoebox."

With the affordability and accessibility of portable recording devices in the 1960s and 1970s, field linguists began to make uninterrupted recordings of larger stretches of spoken discourse. This enabled them to turn greater attention to oral literatures and facilitated consideration of broader aesthetic patterns and discourse beyond the sentence (for example Tedlock 1977; Sherzer and Woodbury 1987).[4] Audio and later audiovisual field recordings increased scholarly as well as general appreciation of verbal arts, not only of spoken literature, but also as Brenda Farnell (1995) shows, as embodied social practices. Audio and audiovisual recordings enable audiences beyond those present at the moment of actual performance to hear and also see embodied aesthetic patterns of oral traditions in new contexts.

While field recordings enable broader audiences to gain a richer sense of performance, as embodied practice beyond what is apparent in written texts, they nevertheless remove expressive performances from their original contexts. Recording processes, whatever form they take (written, audio, audiovisual) extract or decontextualize instances of performance from the rich and dynamic social situations in which they occur. Decontextualization is an extractive process that inevitably removes elements that, for local participants and audiences, confer meanings. No matter how technologically sophisticated they are, recordings never completely capture performance. Recordings are metonyms, parts of larger wholes that only partially represent the documented event.

Thus, while documentary processes may open up access for new and often remote audiences, they are never complete replicas of original events; elements that are essential to local meanings may be lost. For some, recordings may do injustice to contextually rich forms that derive meaning from the social situations in which they occur. Further, and perhaps more problematic, is that documentary technologies may restrict some peoples' access to the performances they record. This is particularly the case when local populations—for a variety of possible reasons including their location, financial resources, access to or command of technology—do not have means to access or control the media in which their performances are secured and contained.[5] The Yuchi offer a powerful example.

Yuchi: Problematic Technologies in Documenting Living and Dying Language

Scholars assert that language is a living process, one that lives through the discursive exchanges between speakers. For many indigenous peoples, such as the Yuchi (also Euchee) who now reside in Oklahoma, this is not an academic issue. Language is a living process that is profoundly spiritual. It is not a "thing" that can or should technologically objectified or contained. The Yuchi word for language is "breath."

According to Richard Grounds (2007), director of the Yuchi Language Project, no available technology is suitable to their urgent efforts to revitalize their language. Technology appears to hold promise for safeguarding language, but past experience teaches otherwise. Grounds recounts a poignant and anecdote to illustrate how technology can distract rather than support safeguarding and revitalization programs.

Several years ago Grounds, along with three other Yuchi including an elderly fluent speaker, traveled to Philadelphia to recover documentation of their language from the papers of a deceased linguist that had been donated to the archives of the American Philosophical Society (APS). The trip involved a considerable investment of money, effort, and time. Upon arriving in Philadelphia the travelers encountered a number of obstacles: they found the archive open to the public only a few hours a day and further, they were not permitted to photocopy the archived documents, which consisted of volumes of little slips of paper. Given their limited time and resources and so many slips of paper, the Yuchi had to decide how best to proceed. They could either attempt to go through the slips to determine which contained new linguistic information and then record this, or they could attempt to digitally photograph as many slips as possible. The second option seemed to offer the greatest potential to recover the most information. This meant they deferred considerations of content until they returned to Oklahoma.

For the next 3 days they worked in a frenzied assembly line, laying out as many slips as could fit into the screen of their digital camera, snapping a photograph, gathering up the photographed slips, and replacing these with new slips. When they ran out of money and had to return to Oklahoma, they had not completed recording even half of the linguist's data. Once home they faced new technological challenges: uploading the digitized images to a computer and printing them. This accomplished, each word the linguist had recorded then had to be read aloud so that the elders, who do not read, could hear them. At this point, after all their effort, time, and expense, they discovered that only a tiny percentage of what they had recovered was new information. Whatever data that might be useful to them remain on the slips of paper they did not have time to retrieve.

From this, Yuchi learned a hard lesson about technology. Perhaps sophisticated technology, including writing, had made the Yuchi language accessible to others, especially to scholars to use for academic purposes, but the linguist's documents and the archive that housed them were of little use to Yuchi peoples themselves who are desperately trying to save their language. Technology has not proved to be a satisfactory means for safeguarding their language *for them*, and it has not been especially productive in Yuchi's efforts to pass language to future generations.

For Grounds, investing in technology does not make the best use of the precious limited time Yuchi have with the five elderly Yuchi who are the only living fluent speakers. He is skeptical of projects that are heavily invested in technology and even, to some extent, of writing. Even projects like collecting data for archives or writing books are of limited value, for they distract attention from living interactions between those who are fluent speakers and the youth who hold promise for the language's future.

> Every choice ... about how they [the elders] spend their time ... has enormous consequences for the possible future of the language and culture... Our choice is to keep our language alive in the community as a spoken, living thing. We choose not to invest ourselves heavily in a documentation project that would take the time of our elders and leave a record of recordings that ends up on a shelf in a library, or of books in which their words are written [without breath or life].
>
> (Grounds 2007)

Given limited time and resources, the stakes are high for Yuchi (a linguistic isolate; Native Languages of the Americas 1998–2007) and other groups involved in revitalizing. Instead of investing in technologies that *for them* have not proved to be a satisfactory means for safeguarding their language, Yuchi emphasize living interactions. Yuchi Language Project efforts promote direct interactions between the few living Yuchi speakers and members of the younger generation. This is for them immensely more productive and rewarding.

Recordings—of words written on slips of paper in a shoe box, recorded in a dictionary, written in books, or even in an audiovisual platform that will inevitably become outmoded (as the cases of beta, vhs, video-8, and high-8 illustrate)—generate tremendous amounts of work, distract attention from interactions between living speakers and youth and ultimately do little to bring the language to life right now when they need it. At least one Yuchi speaker requested that the notes and archives based on his work as an informant in an academic study be buried with him when he died. For him, if no one speaks the language, if pieces of it are just sitting, inert and moribund on slips of paper in a shoebox, it is better to eliminate the traces altogether. Yuchi honored his request. Now objects of their language are as dead and inaccessible to them as their deceased speaker.

The Yuchi experience serves as a powerful reminder that safeguarding projects may conceal problematic relations of power and control, and these are often complicated by issues of access. Whereas contemporary Yuchi place little value on recording intangible culture, the Xavante, a central Brazilian Ge-speaking people, offer an example of the opposite extreme. Xavante peoples, whose historical circumstances are very distinct from Yuchi, enthusiastically welcome opportunities to use new technologies to document and disseminate their culture and many are actively involving themselves in these processes.

Xavante: Maximizing Opportunities and Technologies to Circulate Culture

Compared to the Yuchi and other native North Americans, Xavante have had sustained contact with non-indigenous peoples for only a brief period. Distinct Xavante groups established peaceful relationships with representatives of Brazilian national society only relatively recently, in processes that took place beginning in the late 1940s and ended in the early 1960s (see Maybury-Lewis 1974; Graham 1995; Garfield 2001; Lopes da Silva 1992). Like the Yuchi, Xavante emphasize the transmission of cultural forms from one generation to the next, through processes that I call "vertical transmission." Contemporary Xavante are also invested in processes that can be thought of as "horizontal transmission." Horizontal transmission extends Xavante culture outward into broader national and international spheres (Graham 2005). For men who live in a community known in Portuguese as Pimentel Barbosa (Eténhiritipa in Xavante), horizontal transmission appears to be a strategy for resisting pressures that are resulting from increased interaction with national and international society. (I am currently examining the gendered aspects of these efforts, see Graham 2007.) By extending their culture outward they pressure non-indigenous Brazilians and others to acknowledge and recognize the cultural practices they value (Graham 2005).

Over the last decade, men from Eténhiritipa have intensified efforts to present "intangible" Xavante culture to broader audiences. (These are the result of community members' ability to take advantage of changes in national indigenous policy that enable Xavante to move more freely outside of their territories and that permit outsiders—representatives of NGOs especially—direct access to communities.) However, reaching out and creatively using available means and opportunities to do this is part of a broader historical pattern. Indeed such endeavors may possibly extend back as far as the contact period itself. The first cultural event staged for a large national audience took place at the National Theatre in São Paulo in 1974 when Mario Juruna staged a cultural performance with members from his community of São Marcos. This performance riveted audiences in the theater and beyond, for the national TV network A Globo featured it in its evening news report (Globo Archives).

Xavante are masterful at creatively shaping local expressive forms and adapting new technologies to increase the circulation and circulability of their culture and knowledge (see Urban 2001). In my own research beginning in the early 1980s, members of Eténhiritipa and certain individuals in particular, perceived opportunities to represent culture—through me—to broader audiences. One male leader, an elder named Warodi, showed extraordinary creativity, resourcefulness, and vision to utilize me and my skills as an ethnographer to disseminate Xavante culture to audiences that otherwise he could not access. Warodi imaginatively modified traditional expressive forms to make the most of my presence, my interest in expressive forms, and the documentation technologies I possessed (writing, a tape recorder, and a still camera) as means of transmitting intangible culture and valued knowledge to wider publics. At that time few outsiders visited the community and those who did—mostly government workers—tended to exhibit little interest in Xavante people or culture. Most community members appreciated my interest in their way of life but Warodi especially understood my presence and documentary skills as valuable instruments for communicating beyond the community's borders to reach audiences "across the sea," as Xavante say. His understanding of my intention to write about my experiences and understanding of Xavante culture inspired him to present events that would attract my attention. Ultimately, via my work, this would amplify his voice, the community's presence and awareness of Xavante culture in larger discursive arenas.

Initially I perceived Warodi's efforts to stage cultural events for my benefit as extremely problematic. They ran counter to my wish to observe, document, and ultimately understand speech and other socially situated performance events within their "naturally occurring" social contexts. Only later did I come to appreciate these as inspired moves designed to transform local expressive forms and knowledge to enable them to travel in new ways and reach new audiences.

During my first visit in 1982, when I spoke and understood little Xavante and no one was available to translate Xavante into Portuguese, the language situation presented Warodi with a unique challenge. He wanted me to know and understand a story known as *Wasi Pi'õ* (Star Woman) that relates the origin of garden produce. But, since this story is communicated exclusively by oral means, that is to say people *tell* it, how to tell the narrative without speaking it?

Warodi came up with a brilliant and highly creative way to "show" the narrative. He and the members of his family improvised a theatrical performance, even though dramatic enactment of myth is not a part of Xavante tradition. Warodi directed an extraordinary performance in which the members of his extended family played the parts of the principal protagonists. His brother's wife, decorated with the body paint designs used in the women's naming ceremony (*pi'õ ñisi*), played Star Woman. One of his nephews, a boy about 9 or 10 years old, played the part of the boy who sings as he taps a palm tree (*wa'a wede*) thus charming it to carry him to the sky where he meets the Star Woman. At this point in the dramatization, one of Warodi's adult brothers replaced the boy and assumed the role of the male protagonist who later, as an adult married man, returns to earth with the Star Woman, now his wife, bearing gifts of garden produce that become staples in the Xavante diet.

Warodi designed this ingenious performance so as to convey the story horizontally, across cultural and linguistic borders, to me and, he hoped, through me to people abroad. Simultaneously, he directed this experience vertically, across generations, in a powerful and embodied way. Rather than simply telling the tale and conforming to traditional patterns of narrative transmission, Warodi brought the narrative to life, transforming the story into a powerful and unforgettable experience, especially for the boy and also for me. Even years later, whenever I visit, the young boy and members of his family remember and talk fondly about this extraordinary performance. If Warodi's goal in staging this innovative and powerful dramatization was indeed to promote greater circulation of the Star Woman tale, he achieved his objective. Writing this chapter, as well as my master's thesis that focused on this event, provide testament to this (Graham 1983).

In 1984, when I next returned to the community on a brief reconnaissance trip before committing to doctoral research in Eténhiritipa, Warodi again led the community in staging another extraordinary theatrical performance. This time in a dramatic reenactment of a dream he involved the entire community (representatives of all families in the community except some members who were trekking at the time) (Graham 1995). In staging this performance, Warodi and other male members of the community were clearly reaching out to broader audiences and seeking to achieve broader circulation and recognition. They explicitly designed this event so that I would document it, both with my camera and my tape recorder. One man made the men's intentions clear during the rehearsal. He explained to the youth, "if she understands what you say, it is to be published" (Graham 1995:172). Warodi exhorted the women to "sing loudly for the tape recorder" (Graham 1995:174). These statements illustrate that men perceived me and my recording technologies as means by which to disseminate Xavante culture and knowledge to outside publics that, at that time, they could not otherwise directly access.

Warodi and others brilliantly understood that they could harness my interest in Xavante expressive culture as a means to reach a broader audience, to amplify their voices, and circulate their culture within wider public spaces (Graham 1995). These examples show that as far back as the 1980s, and probably before,[6] members of this community took immensely creative steps and made concerted efforts to use new opportunities (ethnographers' presence) and new technologies (writing, ethnographers' cameras, and tape recorders) to document and extend their intangible culture outward across cultural space.

Beginning in the 1990s, I introduced video recording and playback equipment to Eténhiritipa (Graham 1995: 230). The idea for this project stemmed from my understanding of Warodi and other elders' interest in documenting and disseminating Xavante culture, Warodi's efforts to achieve this, as well as conversations we shared about "cultural projects." I envisioned this technology, together with the linkage I helped establish between Video in the Villages (*Video nas Aldeias*, a non-governmental organization that supports indigenous film, then based in São Paulo) and Caimi Waiassé (the young man designated as the community's filmmaker), as steps toward greater local control of means to document local culture and possibilities to represent it to outside publics. I also imagined that leaders might actively use this technology to advance political struggles, as have other indigenous groups such as the neighboring Kayapo (see, for example, Turner 1992; Ginsburg 1997). Yet, while I thought of the community's ability to control means of documentation and viewing as inherently political, I avoided introducing this equipment as part of any explicit political or activist agenda; I hoped that leaders would apply this technology to achieve community goals rather than those defined by me or any other outside intermediary.

Local understandings of audiovisual media, the ends it may serve, and the collaborations involved, are constantly evolving. From the beginning this technology was gendered, even though people had seen me filming as part of my research for several years. Many women are curious about the camera, wanting to look through the viewfinder to "see" and know it at a basic level, yet they shy away from greater participation. My attempts to involve women in the use of media technologies still have not met with success. New media, like most domains associated with outsiders, tends to be viewed as "male."

From the outset, elder men and male leaders—those who are involved in this technology—saw and used video as a means to document local activities (ceremonial as well as everyday events) and reflect on these (see for example, Turner 1992, 2002; Ginsburg 1993, 1995, 2002; Michaels 1994). They also enjoy it as entertainment. Community members delight in seeing their images on the television screen. Further, via recordings that Waiassé has made of his travels—to meetings with other indigenous filmmakers, festivals, and workshops—people also see and hear images of people, places, and events beyond the borders of the Pimentel Barbosa indigenous territory.[7]

During the first years that video was in the community, leaders exhibited no motivation and made no active attempts, as perhaps Warodi (who was no longer living) might have, to use video to project Xavante culture outward to reach new audiences. Residents of Eténhiritipa were happy to document and view themselves and to use the technology for purely internal purposes. It was Video in the Villages, then São Paulo-based NGO, that took the initiative to produce the first "product" which makes Waiassé's filming accessible to outside audiences. Tutu Nunes (personal communication, 1999), who worked with Waiassé to produce *One Must Be Curious* (Waiassé 1996), explained:

> Caimi had had the camera for several years and was accumulating a lot of footage. He was filming, filming, filming but didn't have the slightest idea what to do with all of the images. We [Video in the Villages] decided that it was time for him to do something.

Tutu positioned Waiassé in front of a camera, clipped on a microphone, and interviewed him about the images Waiassé had filmed as they watched them on a screen. Waiassé's explanations from this interview provide the narrative backbone for *One Must be Curious* which Tutu edited with Waiassé at his side (Tutu Nunes, personal communication, 1999).

The process by which *One Must Be Curious* came into being illustrates one way that indigenous video is a highly mediated collaborative endeavor. Early experiences with audiovisual products, edited films and videos intended for external consumption, are inevitably collaborative and highly mediated (see Michaels 1994; Ruby 1991, 1995; Elder 1995; Turner 1995; Prins 2002).

"One Must Be Curious" transformed Waiassé's work into a form that is accessible to outsiders. It made portions of Waiassé's narrative and footage into a tangible product that could be shown in a variety of contexts, including festivals and classrooms. Further, it could be shown to donors and potential donors, for Tutu's and Waiassé's cooperation must also be understood within the context of demands placed on institutions that support indigenous media, such as Video in the Villages. These products are essential for the institution's ability to solicit or justify donor support as maintaining equipment, facilities (for editing, archiving, work-shopping), and providing ongoing technical support involve considerable costs (see Carelli 1995, cited in Aufderheide 1995: 84; also Aufderheide 1995).

The most recent work to emerge from Eténhiritipa illustrates ways that community elders are employing this technology to document local expressive practices to transmit culture across generations (vertical transmission) as well as project it to new audiences (horizontal transmission). In 2005 in collaboration with Nosso Tribu, another São Paulo-based NGO, Waiassé and his colleague Jorge Protodi, a second filmmaker, released *Darini: the spiritual initiation of Xavante children*. This film documents a ceremonial that men perform once every 15 years or so. According to Waiassé (personal communication, February 2005), the idea for this project came entirely from the elders who, recognizing the likelihood that they will no longer be living when a *Darini* is next performed, requested that it be filmed. These elders wanted to leave a record for future generations, so that their descendants could know how they perform and understand this important ceremony.

The ceremonial that Waiassé and Protodi filmed to make *Darini* took place more than 10 years after the community had its first experience with filming. In this ceremony men interacted with and responded to the camera completely differently than they have behaved during previously filmed events. In previous filmed events, for example, in events that were filmed to make *One Must Be Curious* or in my earlier field recordings,[8] men attempted to ignore the camera; typically they tried to avoid eye contact with the camera and its operator and maintain a focus on the event in which they were participants.

In "*Darini*," on the other hand, numerous elders (and several youth) intentionally approach the camera and speak directly to it. Hipru, Serebu'rã, and Paulo, for example, step out of their roles within the *Darini* ceremonial and speak to the camera. They do so to provide explanations of the events that are being filmed. These individuals break the frame (Goffman 1974) of the ceremonial to step into a new frame. This new frame is psychologically but not physically distinct from the ceremonial that they are participating in and about which they speak.⁹ Within this new frame they do not speak to Waiassé or Protodi, who hold the camera but instead address a remote audience. Their intended viewers are the members of a future audience who will eventually watch the anticipated film; their explanations provide a metanarrative intended to help future viewers make sense of the filmed events.

Waiassé and Protodi needed assistance to transform their footage into an edited film for future generations according to the elders' wish. Nosso Tribu supported this and, after a year of fundraising and having identified an institution that offered facilities and editing expertise, sufficient funds had been raised to move the project forward.

During the editing process, which took place at a university in São Paulo, Waiassé and Protodi returned to the community several times to get elders' input and feedback on successive rough-cut versions. Within this process, the elders expanded their initial vision and decided that a version of *Darini* suitable for non-Xavante audiences should also be edited. This version is now available to outside audiences with subtitles in Portuguese, English, French, and Japanese (Waiassé and Protodi 2005). As a result of this collaboration, the elders who conceived of this project now have the potential to transmit their knowledge and vision of this ceremonial not only to future generations of Xavante, but also to national and international audiences.

For well over 25 years and possibly longer, men from Eténhiritipa have been conceptualizing creative projects and working with outsiders to document and imaginatively represent Xavante culture both to themselves and to others. To the extent that these collaborations promote pride, enable them to project positive images of Xavante culture to themselves and to broader publics, as well as to take greater control of means and forms of representation to outside publics, they are potent means of empowerment.

Yet, insofar as documentation and externally directed representational projects depend on outsiders' participation, power differentials persist (see Prins 2002; Halkin 2009). When documentation projects involve differences in knowledge, skill, and access to resources or representational venues, no matter how well intentioned participants may be, the potential exists for the creation or perpetuation of dependency relations. This potential exists even when less technologically sophisticated technologies (such as writing) are involved, as the Yuchi case and Warodi's reliance on my ability to write and publish make clear. Sophisticated and expensive technology magnifies this possibility. Managing equipment, storing data, keeping up with advances in technology, not to mention editing (in the case of film and video) or having access to archived material, demand financial resources, technical expertise, and knowledge that many indigenous peoples do not have. Social inequities, unequal access to resources and knowledge mean that most indigenous groups must depend on outsiders to supply some, or most of these resources. This is true even of projects, such as the Xavante video example, that are conceptualized to give indigenous peoples greater access to means of documenting and managing external representation. Thus, to Faye Ginsburg's keen cautionary observation that new media technology offers indigenous users a "double set of possibilities"— providing tools for a response "to and through the categories that have been created to contain" indigenous peoples but simultaneously threatening to "impos[e] the values and language of the dominant culture" (2002:51, also 1991)—I would add a further caveat: the possibility that these technologies may reinforce or even create new forms of dependency.

Conclusion

In this chapter, I set out to provoke thought about some of the problems entailed in projects, especially technologically oriented projects, designed to document and record intangible culture. The Yuchi case suggests that not all peoples value technology as the best means to document or "safeguard" intangible culture. Yuchi place a high value on direct processes of cultural transmission that do not involve technological mediation. For them, recording and documenting that does not immediately advance their goal to form a new generation of Yuchi speaker is a distraction. Their work has to be focused on efforts that are internal to the community. Taking care to promote face-to-face interactions between elders and future Yuchi speakers and focusing on making sure that youth learn as much from the elders as possible is, for them, the best way to safeguard the language.

When indigenous peoples value technology as part of their efforts to insure the vitality of their expressive practices, I advocate for as much local control of and participation in all aspects of its use as possible. The men of Eténhiritipa highly value technology and its use in recording, documenting, and disseminating intangible cultural practices. They have a tradition of creatively devising ways to utilize new technologies to transmit culture both to future generations and to reach broader publics; these interacting processes appear to reinforce each other and actually increase cultural vitality. While technologies and collaborations may create new forms of dependency, the benefits these bring to advancing their culture's circulation so far, at least for the men of Eténhiritipa, appear to outweigh any negative consequences. They continue to enthusiastically participate in and embrace new opportunities to document and show their intangible culture to outside audiences.

The Yuchi and Xavante examples challenge us to think critically about the potential imperialist entailments of using technology in specific cases. They remind us that the social and historical circumstances, as well as ideologies of documenting and representing intangible culture are unique. Hopefully, awareness of the individual particularities specific to each case will lead to greater sensitivity to some of the problems with using technology as well as its potential for empowerment in discussions and practices related to documenting and safeguarding intangible cultural forms.

Notes

1. "Safeguarding" means measures aimed at ensuring the viability of the intangible cultural heritage, including the identification, documentation, research, preservation, protection, promotion, enhancement, transmission, particularly through formal and non-formal education, as well as the revitalization of the various aspects of such heritage.
2. The Convention recognizes that communities, in particular indigenous communities, groups and, in some cases, individuals, play an important role in the production, safeguarding, maintenance, and re-creation of the intangible cultural heritage, thus helping to enrich cultural diversity and human creativity.
3. The movements of human visual languages, such as American Sign Language, can be made tangible using other representational forms such as Laban notation (see Farnell 1995).
4. Prior to their use of tape recorders, linguists such as Edward Sapir did, of course, record larger stretches of discourse. To enable linguists to transcribe their narratives informants were forced to pause in their speech and this inevitably influenced narrative flow. Dell Hymes's analyses of textual representations of Native American narrative brought awareness to aesthetics and performance aspects of these as literatures (for example Hymes 1981). Portable recording devices greatly improved the ability to record texts as they are actually spoken.
5. Recordings may also allow access to individuals who are members of social categories or groups who, according to the original performance contexts, should not be able permitted to see or hear them (for example, Eric Michel's 1986[1994] discussion of the ethical complications of video recording among Australian Aboriginals).
6. The Xavante word for tape recorder literally translates to "speech holder" (*da-mreme-tete-ze*; impersonal possessive-hold-instrumental). Nancy Flowers, an anthropologist who worked in Pimentel Barbosa in the late 1970s, reports that the community's leader, Warodi's father, sometimes requested her to record his narratives (personal communication, 1989). The same leader appears to have done the same with David Maybury-Lewis (1974), the first anthropologist to work with the Xavante in the late 1950s.
7. These opportunities were initially provided by Video in the Villages or myself and later through collaborations with other non-governmental organizations (see Graham 2005).
8. The first time most people in Eténhiritipa experienced a video camera was during my doctoral field research when, in 1986, I used it briefly. Members of this community previously, however, had been filmed and had seen edited films of themselves and other Xavante.
9. This frame breaking is exactly the inverse of the "breakthrough into performance" that Dell Hymes (1975) describes, where linguistic consultants began to perform the narratives that they were talking about with the anthropologist. Instead, this is breaking out of performance and *into* a metanarrative frame.

References

Aufderheide, Patricia
    1995 The Video in the Villages Project: Videomaking With and By Brazilian Indians. *Visual Anthropology Review* 11(2):83–93.
Berger, John
    1972 *Ways of Seeing*. British Broadcasting Corporation, London; Penguin, New York.
Carelli, Vincent
    1995 The Project and The Documentaries: Two Distinct and Complementary Dimensions of the "Video in the Villages" Project. Unpublished Ms., New York University, Center for Media, Culture and History, New York.
Elder, Sarah
    1995 Collaborative Filmmaking: An Open Space for Making Meaning, A Moral Ground for Ethnographic Film. *Visual Anthropology Review* 11(2):94–101.

Farnell, Brenda
  1995 *Do You See What I Mean? Plains Indian Sign Talk and the Embodiment of Action.* University of Texas Press, Austin.
Ginsburg, Faye
  1991 Indigenous Media: Faustian Contract or Global Village. *Cultural Anthropology* 6(1):92–112.
  1993 Aboriginal Media and the Aboriginal Imaginary. *Public Culture* 5(3):557–578.
  1995 The Parallax Effect. *Visual Anthropology Review* 6:92–112.
  1997 "From Little Things, Big Things Grow": Indigenous Media and Cultural Activism. In *Between Resistance and Revolution: Cultural Politics and Social Protest*, edited by Richard G. Fox and Orin Starn, pp. 118–144. Rutgers University Press, New Brunswick.
  2002 Screen Memories: Resignifying the Traditional in Indigenous Media. In *Media Worlds: Anthropology on New Terrain*, edited by Faye D. Ginsburg, Lila Abu-Lughod, and Brian Larkin, pp. 39–57. University of California Press, Berkeley.
Garfield, Seth
  2001 *Indigenous Struggle at the Heart of Brazil: State Policy, Frontier Expansion, and the Xavante Indians, 1937–1988.* Duke University Press, Durham.
Graham, Laura R.
  1983 Performance Dynamics and Social Dimensions in Xavante Narrative: *Höimana'u'ö Wasu'u*. Unpublished master's thesis, Department of Anthropology, University of Texas at Austin.
  1995 *Performing Dreams: Discourses of Immortality Among the Xavante of Central Brazil.* University of Texas Press, Austin.
  2005 Image and Instrumentality in a Xavante Politics of Existential Recognition: The Public Outreach Work of *Eténhiritipa* Pimentel Barbosa. *American Ethnologist* 32(4):622–641.
  2007 Gender and the circulation of Xavante public culture. Paper presented at the annual meeting of the American Anthropological Association, November 2007, Washington, D.C.
Goffman, Irving
  1975 *Frame Analysis.* Harper and Row, New York
Grounds, Richard
  2007 *shadjwanE dathlandA* (Rabbit and Wolf): Feeding Technology and Passing Forward Indigenous Languages. Closing Keynote, Indigenous Peoples in Digital Cultures: Communications Technologies and the Impacts on Indigenous Languages and Cultural Identity in the Americas. The University of Florida, Center for Latin American Studies. Gainesville, Florida, February 14–16.
Halkin, Alexandra
  2009 Outside the Indigenous Lens: Zapatistas and autonomous video making. In *Global Indigenous Media: Cultures, Poetics, and Politics*, edited by Pamela Wilson and Michelle Stewart, pp. 160–180. Duke University Press, Durham.
Hymes, Dell
  1975 Breakthrough into Performance. In *Folklore: Performance and Communication*, edited by Dan Ben-Amos and Kenneth Goldstein, pp. 11–74. Mouton, The Hague.
  1981 *"In Vain I Tried to Tell You": Essays in Native American Ethnopoetics.* University of Pennsylvania Press, Philadelphia.
Lopes da Silva, Aracy
  1992 Dois Séculos e Meio de História Xavante. In *História dos índios no Brasil*, edited by Manuela Carneiro da Cunha, pp. 357–378. Editora Schwarcz, Ltda., São Paulo.
Maybury-Lewis, David
  1974 *Akwẽ-Shavante Society*, second edition. Oxford University Press, New York.
Michaels, Eric
  1994 *Bad Aboriginal Art: Tradition, Media, and Technological Horizons.* University of Minnesota Press, Minneapolis.

1994 [1986] A Primer of Restrictions on Picture-Taking in Traditional Areas of Aboriginal Australia. Reprinted in *Bad Aboriginal Art: Tradition, Media, and Technological Horizons*, pp. 1–18. University of Minnesota Press, Minneapolis.

Native Languages of the Americas website
1998–2007 www.native-languages.org/yuchi.htm (accessed 13 November 2007).

Prins, Harald E.
2002 Visual Media and the Primitivist Perplex: Colonial Fantasies, Indigenous Imagination, and Advocacy in North America. In *Media Worlds: Anthropology on New Terrain*, edited by Faye D. Ginsburg, Lila Abu-Lughod and Brian Larkin, pp. 58–74. University of California Press, Berkeley.

Ruby, Jay
1991 Speaking For, Speaking About, Speaking With, or Speaking Alongside: An Anthropological and Documentary Dilemma. *Visual Anthropology Review* 7(2):50–67.
1995 The Moral Burden of Authorship in Ethnographic Film. *Visual Anthropology Review* 11(2):77–82.

Sherzer, Joel and Anthony C. Woodbury (editors)
1987 *Native American Discourse: Poetics and Rhetoric*. Cambridge University Press, Cambridge and New York.

Tedlock, Dennis
1977 Toward Oral Poetics. *New Literary History* 8(3):507–519.

Turner, Terence
1991 Representing, Resisting, Rethinking: Historical Transformations of Kayapo Culture and Anthropological Consciousness. In *Colonial Situations: Essays on the Contextualization of Ethnographic Knowledge*, edited by George Stocking, pp. 285–313. University of Wisconsin Press, Madison.
1992 Defiant Images: The Kayapó Appropriation of Video. *Anthropology Today* 8(6):5–16.
1995 Representation, Collaboration and Mediation in Contemporary Ethnographic and Indigenous Media. *Visual Anthropology Review* 11(2):102–106.
2002 Representation, Politics, and Cultural Imagination in Indigenous Video: General Points and Kayapo Examples. In *Media Worlds: Anthropology on New Terrain*, edited by Faye D. Ginsburg, Lila Abu-Lughod, and Brian Larkin, pp. 75–89. University of California Press. Berkeley.

Urban, Greg
2001 *Metaculture: How Culture Moves through the World*. University of Minnesota Press, Minneapolis.

UNESCO
2003 Convention for the Safeguarding of Intangible Cultural Heritage. http://www.unesco.org/culture/ich/index.php?lg=EN&pg=00022 (accessed 29 March 2007).

Waiassé, Caimi
1996 *One Must Be Curious* (video, 16 min). Video nas Aldeias, Centro de Trabalho Indigenista, São Paulo.

Waiassé, Caimi and Jorge Protodi
2005 *Darini: Iniciação Espiritual das Crianças Xavante* (video, 46 min). Department of Communications, Methodist University and Nossa Tribo, São Paulo.

Index

Note: The letters 'f' and 'n' following the locators refer to figures and notes respectively

A
A-bomb memorial dome, 71–73
Africa, 148, 150, 162
African American accomplishments at New Philadelphia, Illinois
  concepts of heritage and paradox of culture, 159–163
    heritage of McWorters, 159–163
    race/racial ideologies, 159–163
  globalization and erasure, 148–150
    state parties, 148
  histories of adversity/success, 150–159, 156f
    archaeological studies, 152–153
    'aversive' racism, 153
    building culvert, 157
    lessons, to be learnt, 158
    manumission, 150
    "Military Bounty Lands", 151
    Pike County Railroad Company, 155–156, 156f
    planning for construction of railroad, 154–155
Aggarwal, Indra, 50
A Globo (national TV network), 191
Ahmad, Nizam al-Din, 83
Ahmad, Y., 148
Ahmadabad (India), 79, 83
Aitchison Chiefs' College (Lahore), 45
Akhtar, Altaf Hussain, 49
Alabama, 182
Albany, 172
Albro, Robert, 11
Alfonseca-Cubero, Maria Angel, 181, 182
Alfred P. Sloane Foundation, 180

Al fresco (singing gathering), 33
Alizé (wind), 61
Allauca, 103
Alleyne, Mark D., 161, 162
Alliance for Struggle Against Poverty and Memorial *Khipu* of the Fallen, 119
Alton, 152
Alton Telegraph & Democratic Review, 155
Alva Salinas, José, 103
American Philosophical Society (APS), 189
American Sign Language, 198 n3
Amerindians, 149
Amir's Manzil, 92
  See also Water intelligence, Champaner
Amritsar, 39, 45, 49
Ancient jetties, proposed re-creation of (Ottagawa), 70f
Andrews, Walter, 58
Antebellum period, 152
Anthropologists, 1, 10, 61, 101, 149, 198 n6, n9
Anti-graffiti Port Authority of New York/New Jersey sign on fence around the World Trade Center, 171f
Anwar, Ali, 46
APS, *see* American Philosophical Society (APS)
Archaeological Survey of India (ASI), 83, 88, 96, 98 n3
Architectural forms and ornamentation, Champaner, 89–91
  garbha griha (womb house), 89
  Jami Masjid's dome and second-story terrace, 90f
  shikhar (mountain crest), 89

See also Champaner, past/present
Archiving ephemeral, World Trade Center, 177–180
  Memorial Tile Registry/Wall of Hope, 178–179
  September 11 Digital Archive, 180, 183 n5
  web-based/on-site participatory activities, 178
    See also World Trade Center, Oklahoma City and beyond
Arden, 156
Arkansas, 182
ArtAid (non-profit/charity group), 176
Asanapatta, 90
Asano Nagaakira (Daimyo of Hiroshima), 75
Asher, Catherine, 91
Ashikaga family/park, 65
Ashrams, 84, 96
Ashwatthama (character in Indian epic), 37, 38
ASI, *see* Archaeological Survey of India (ASI)
Atak Fort (Champaner), excavations in, 95
Atasoy, Nurhan, 57
1932 Athens Charter for the Restoration of Historic Monuments, 3, 4
Atlantic slave trade, 148, 150
Aufderheide, Patricia, 195
Aukin/Awkin (ritualist), 105, 114–115, 121–122
'Aversive' racism, 153
Avrami, Erica, 110
Awan, Mohammed Saeed, 41–42

B
Baddi Nali (railway station), 41–42
Bakewell, Liza, 173
Bakhtin, Mikhail M., 139, 143
Balochistan, 44–45
Barry Adage, 153, 157–159
Barry (town), 156–157, 159
Bayley, Edward C., 83
Baylis, 156–158
Beas (river), 37
Begara dynasty, 80–81
Beijing, 15, 17, 28, 29, 30, 31, 32, 33
Beijing- *Kunqu* Company, 29
Benoît, Yet Catherine, 61
Berger, John, 188
Bhadrakali plateau, 84, 94
Bhadrakali Temple, 84
Bhasin, Kamla, 39
Bhatti, P.S., 49
Bhausaheb Hiray College of Architecture, 97 n1
Biji (anecdotal notebook), 21

Birmingham, 62
Black Codes, 152
  See also Gardens and landscapes, tangible/intangible heritage
Blume, Regina, 172
Bodnar, John, 182
Bouchenaki, Mounir, 161
Bourdain, Anthony, 1
Bourdieu, Pierre, 127, 134, 137, 139, 143
Braj region (India), 58, 59–60
  pilgrim itinerary and principle of circumambulation, 60 *f*
  See also Gardens and landscapes, tangible/intangible heritage
Brezine, Carrie, 101, 108
Bristol, 62
Brosseau, Sylvie, 63, 64, 65, 73, 76
Brown, Carol, 183 n4
Brown, Michael F., 10
Brown, Percy, 81
Budhiya Darwaza, 83
  See also Champaner-Pavagadh (Gujarat, India)
Buffalo, 155
Bureaus of Culture of Jiangsu, 30
Burra Charter (ICOMOS 1999), 110
Bu Yuan (Garden), 23

C
Cai Zhengren, 32–33
Cambridge University, 11
Canada, 9, 54, 152, 160
Cang Lang Ting pavilion (garden in Suzhou), 54, 55*f*
  interior view of pavilion, 56*f*
Capurro, Hugo Ramón, 103
Carelli, Vincent, 195
Carlson, Theodore L., 155
CCTV, *see* Chinese Central Television (CCTV)
Centeno Farfán, Edgar (architect), 108
Center for History and New Media, George Mason University, 180, 182
Chador or *burqa* (social practices in Muslim countries), 2, 44, 45
Chahar bagh (four-part garden), 98 n2
Cha-Jua, Sundiata Keita, 154
Champakdurga (city in 8th century), 80
Champaner, past/present, 79–87
  as hindu sacred site, 84
  Jains, sacred region, 84
  Jami Masjid, entry pavilion, 82*f*
  Kalika (Goddesss), 87
  Pavagadh Hill

Index

Chassiya Talao and Lakulish Temple, 85*f*
Kalika Mata Temple, 81*f*, 85*f*
royal enclosure, 82*f*
Sadhu dressed as monkey god Hanuman, 86*f*
Shiva Temples, 84
topography, 80
See also Champaner-Pavagadh (Gujarat, India)
Champaner-Pavagadh (Gujarat, India)
architectural forms/ornamentation, 89–91
garbha griha (womb house)/shikhar (mountain crest), 89
Jami Masjid's dome and second-story terrace, 90*f*
conservation approaches, 95–97
cultural landscape, 87–89
change, human inhabitants, 88
human values/belief systems, 88
opportunity to study interrelationship, 88
water management, talaos (ponds)/kunds (tanks)/vavs (stepwells), 89
past/present, 79–87
as hindu sacred site, 84
Jains, sacred region, 84
Jami Masjid, entry pavilion, 82*f*
Kalika (Goddess), 87
Chassiya Talao, and eleventh-century Lakulish Temple, 85*f*
Kalika Mata Temple with domes Muslim shrine on top, 85*f*
with Kalika Temple at crest, 81*f*
royal enclosure, 82*f*
sadhu dressed as monkey god Hanuman, 86*f*
Shiva Temples, 84
topography, 80
site plan of, 80
vision and movement, 93–95
excavations in Atak Fort, 95
"goddess ecology", 97
Shehri Masjid (late 15th century) with enclosure fence installed by ASI, 96*f*
temples, 93–94
water intelligence, 91–93
Chandigarh, 40, 48
Chang sheng Dian (palace), 22–23
Chapman, Charles C., 151, 152, 153, 155, 158, 159

Charters/Conventions/Declarations Cited (list), 12–13
Checras (river), 102, 118
Chenab (river), 37
Chernela, Janet, 11
Chhatris (open-sided cupolas), 81
Chicago, 155–156
China, 15–34, 16, 19, 21, 24, 25, 26, 27, 28, 30, 31, 34 n2, 53–57, 63
Chinese Central Television (CCTV), 31
Chinese Communist Party, 27
Chinese Ministry of Culture, 16
Chopra, Bimla, 45
Chopra, Narinder Nath, 45
Chuan (actor), 20, 26–27, 28–29, 30, 31, 32, 34
Chuanqi (drama), 19, 20
Chuanqi libretto, 19–20
See also Kunqu
Church Street, (World Trade Center site), 174
CirumPacific lands, 143
"Citizen's life in the park", 66
City Lore, Manhattan, 171
City of New York Graduate Center American Social History Project, 180
"City of thousand wells" (Champaner), 92
Clavir, Miriam, 109, 110
Cleeman, Thomas M., 155, 156
Clemens, Samuel, 161
Cochran, Thomas C., 155
Cole, Jennifer, 139
Coleman, David, 161, 162
Collins, Glenn, 182
Commemorative assemblage at World Trade Center site, 171, 173*f*
Communism and *Kunqu*, 27–31
Great Leap Forward campaign, 29
Hundred Flowers Movement (Mao Zedong), 29
"walk with both legs" (tolerant policy), 28
See also Kunqu
Comunidad campesina (peasant community), 102, 103
Confucius, 22
Conger, John L., 154
Connerton, Paul, 134, 139
Conservation approaches, Champaner, 95–97
Convention for the Safeguarding of the Intangible Cultural Heritage, 1, 53, 148
Convention Text (UNESCO), 187
Cootner, Paul H., 154, 155, 157
Corliss, Carlton J., 155

Cosmological order in homeland, Oceania, 130–134
 depiction of Futuna cosmology, 131*f*
 homesites around central *marae* in Pau, 132*f*
 sacred centers, topography, 131, 144 n4
 supernatural beings, 131
 villages, 133
 visual/spatial/kinesthetic representations of right living, 134
 See also Oceania, memory and identity
Costumbrista, 103
Crawford House Publishing, Australia, 128–130, 132, 135, 136
"Creative water intelligence", 92
Creswell, K. A. C., 89
Cultural heritage, intangible
 categories of (UNESCO), 2
 definition (Logan, William), 1
Cultural Heritage and Human Rights, 11
Cultural Heritage and Human Rights (Silverman and Ruggles 2007), 11
Cultural landscape, Champaner, 87–89
 change with respect to human inhabitants, 88
 human values and belief systems, 88
 opportunity to study the interrelationship, 88
 water management (talaos (ponds)/kunds (tanks)/vavs (stepwells)), 89
Cultural Revolution, 16, 30, 31–32, 56

D

Daimyo gardens, 69, 75
Damascus, 57
*Dan*role (young female), 28
Darini: the spiritual initiation of Xavante children (film), 195–196
Das, Rajinder, 49
Das, Seth Hemal, 45
Dattathreya (character in Indian epic), 84
Davis, James E., 152, 154, 155
Da xi (gestures), 26
D.C. Patel School of Architecture, 97 n1
Declaration of Amsterdam (1975), 7, 12
Defence Housing Area (Lahore), 40, 42–43
de las Casas, Gino, 108, 111
de la Torre, Marta, 110
Demography, 31
Dempsey, Terrell, 161
Deng Xiaoping, 30
Department of Landscape Architecture, University of Illinois, Urbana-Champaign, 97 n1

Diana, the Princess, 176
Dobbin, Frank, 155
Dougherty, William R., 130
Drona (character in Indian epic), 37

E

East China Academy of Dramatic Arts, 28
Edinburgh Drama Festival, 32
Edo's cherry blossom, 63–65
Edward Nipakhe Natape (Prime Minister of Vanuatu 2001–2004), 142
Elder, Sarah, 195
Elephant valley, 84
Emery, Elizabeth, 4
England, 62
Ensign, D. W., 159, 151, 153, 157, 158, 159
Erikson, Kai, 178
Estabridis Cárdenas, Ricardo, 103
Eténhiritipa, 187, 191–197, 198 n8
Ethnographic work, necessity of, 186
Euchee, *see* Yuchi
Evliya Çelebi (Ottoman traveler), 57

F

Falcón, Elisa, 122
Falcón, Melanio, 113
FAM Studio Madrid, 181
Farfán, Edgar Centeno, 108
Farnell, Brenda, 188, 198 n3
Faustino, Nelly, 111
Feld, Steven, 136
Fishlow, Albert, 154, 155
Flight 93 memorial site, 178
Floating paper lantern ceremony (Buddhist event), 77, n3
Florence Charter, 6, 8, 53, 57, 76
Florida, 182
Flowers, Nancy, 198, 198 n6
Folk assemblages, World Trade Center, 170–172
 commemorative, 171, 173*f*
Folk epigraphy, World Trade Center, 172–177
 alternatives to graffiti, 175–176
 handwritten notes, 175
 social effects of, 174
 See also World Trade Center, Oklahoma City and beyond
Foote, Kenneth, 170
Forestry Department, 96
Formas Aplicadas (firm), 110
Fuller, C. J., 93
Futuna, 127–130, 131–132, 133, 136–137, 139, 140–144
Futuna community, 129

Index

approach from West, 130f
Republic of Vanuatu locating Futuna, 129f
See also Oceania, memory and identity

G

Gaben Shah tank, 92
Gaertner, Samuel L., 153
Galla, Amareswar, 10
Ganga (river), 92
Garba (Indian folk dance/song), 87, 97
Garbha griha (shrine, Indian temple), 89
Gardens and landscapes, tangible/intangible heritage
    culture in Japan, 63–65
    garden conservation in China, 53–57
    garden groves of Braj, 59–60
    gardens of slave descendants in Guadeloupe, 60–62
    historic garden, definition, 57–59
    municipal parks, British cities, 62
    Otagawa Embankment Project in Hiroshima, 69–73
    re-creation of a garden at Koga, 65–69
Gardens of the Great Mughal, 54
Gardner, Howard, 140
Garfield, Seth, 191
Genoa, 57
Georgia, 182
Ghats, 97
"giant *khipu*", 106
Gino de las Casas (architect), 108, 111
Ginsburg, Faye, 194, 197
Glasgow, 62
Globalization and attempted erasure, New Philadelphia, Illinois, 148–150
    "state parties", 148
Globo Archives, 191
Goetz, H., 81
Goffman, Irving, 195
Gonzales, Rosalía Choque, 108, 111
Goshonuma pond, 69
Graffiti, alternatives to, 175–176
Graham, Laura R., 185
Granada, 57
Grant, H. Roger, 154, 155, 157
Great Lakes, 160
Great Leap Forward campaign, 29
Grider, Sylvia, 171, 176
Griggsville, 152, 157
Grimshaw, Hon. William A., 151, 159
Grover, Karan, 97 n1
Gu, Duhuang, 24, 33
Guadeloupe, gardens of slave descendants

Benoît, Catherine (2007), 61
    garden in front of cabin, 61f
Guillet, David, 103
Gujarat/Gujrat, 42–44, 79–98
Guo Feng (theatrical troupe), 27, 29
    See also Kunqu
Guying, Liang, 16

H

Hague Convention (Convention for the Protection of Cultural Property in the Event of Armed Conflict), 4
Hajji al-Dabir, Abdullah Muhammad al-Makki al-Asafi al-Ulughkhani, 80, 83
Hakim (traditional doctor), 44
Hanami (ancient practice of rural villagers, Japan), 58, 63–65, 77
    in evening in Ueno Park, Tokyo, 64f
    leisure activity, 63
    in Tokyo, practice of (mourning for the dead in Hiroshima), 77
    See also Gardens and landscapes, tangible/intangible heritage
Hangzhou, 15–16, 27, 29, 31, 57, 75
Hankou, 25
Hannibal, 152, 154–158, 160, 182
Hannibal and Naples Railroad Company (HNRC), 155–157
Hannibal Daily Courier, 155
Hargrave, Michael L., 153
Harvest Moon Festival, 17–18, 33
Havell, E.B., 81
Heian-Ko, city of, 63
Helical Stepwell, 92
Heritage
    and paradox of culture, New Philadelphia, Illinois, 159–163
        combat concepts of race/racial ideologies, 159–163
        heritage of McWorters, 159–163
        See also African American accomplishments at New Philadelphia, Illinois
    from tangible to intangible
        development of intangibility as concept, 3–11
        focus of heritage preservation, 7
"Heritage that hurts", 182
Heritage Trust of Baroda, 80, 96, 97 n1
Hervé, Dominique, 103
"Hill of hundred pools" (Pavagadh), 92
Hiroshima, 63, 65, 69–77
HNRC, *see* Hannibal and Naples Railroad Company (HNRC)

Hoffman, Susanna M., 172
Homeland narratives, cosmological order in Oceania, 134–138
   cultural geography/significance of direction for Ta Pasiesi and Majihjiki, 135*f*
   metaphor (lobster trapping/outsider poaching), 136
   Nahjeji, Futuna lobster trap, 136*f*
   oral literature/musical lyrics, 134
   redundancies, 137, 143
   See also Oceania, memory and identity
Hong Kong, 16, 30, 33–34
Huang Zuolin (Chinese Shakespearean scholar and stage director), 32
Huan Sha Ji (Cleaning the Silk Garment), 19
Huaura (river), 102, 119
Huayta, Víctor Falcón, 101, 108
Hu, Ji, 17, 25
Humble Administrator's Garden, 23
Hundred Flowers Movement (Mao Zedong), 29
Hung Sheng, 22–23
Hutchins, Edwin, 134
Hymes, Dell, 198

I

Iamo, Wari, 144 n1
Ibaraki prefecture, 63
ICOMOS, *see* ICOMOS (International Charter for the Conservation and Restoration of Monuments and Sites)
ICOMOS (International Charter for the Conservation and Restoration of Monuments and Sites), 3, 4, 5, 6, 7, 8, 53, 110
ICOMOS International Cultural Tourism Charter, 7
ICOMOS 1994 Nara Document, 5
Illinois (river), 151–152, 155, 157
Illinois State Archives, 151
Imaginary Homelands (Rushdie, Salman), 127
Impressions of a Forgotten City: Architectural Documentation of Champaner Pavagadh, 98
Incas, 101
India, 10, 38–41, 43–50, 61, 79–98
Indiana, 181
Indus (river), 37
Inglis, John, 131
Ingold, Tim, 134
Insaniyat, 51
"*Insaniyat amidst insanity*" (article in the tribune), 48

Inscription and (im)permanence, 180–182
   M11 Memorial, 181
   tour for National September 11 Memorial and Museum, 181–182
   See also World Trade Center, Oklahoma City and beyond
Instituto Nacional de Cultura, Peru, 111, 120
Instituto Nacional de Estadística e Información (1993), 102
Intangible cultural heritage, definition (UNESCO), 149
Intangible Heritage Convention, 2
Intangible Heritage Embodied, 1
Intangible heritage in transforming contexts, Oceania, 139–143
   narrative parallels to modernity-community contrasts, 141*f*
   ni-Vanuatu diaspora, 140
   political geography of independent Vanuatu in its international landscape, 142*f*
   Rushdie, on, 140
   See also Oceania, memory and identity
International Journal of Intangible Heritage, 11
International Phonetic Alphabet (IPA), 188
"Inventive analysis method", 71
Iowa, 182
Islamabad, 37
Israel, 144 n2
Iwahori, Y, 66

J

Jacksonville, 152, 155
Jami Masjid, Champaneer, 81, 82, 90, 90*f*, 91, 91*f*, 92, 93, 95
   stepwell, 93*f*
   stone relief with pot-and-vine motif, 91
Jang (newspaper), 39, 42
Japan, 6, 26, 54, 58, 63–65, 67–69, 74, 75, 77
Japan, culture of gardens/landscapes
   Edo's cherry blossom festival, 63
Jenks, Leland H., 154
Jerusalem, 8
Jervis, John B., 155
Jhelum (river), 37
Jiajei (scenery), 58
   See also Gardens and landscapes, tangible/intangible heritage
Jiang Qing (1914-1991), 16, 29, 30
Ji chang yuan wen ge ji (song), 22
Jingju (theater), 15
John F. Dovidio, 153
Johnson, J. S., 110

Index 207

Jones, Phillip W., 161, 162
Joshi, Ghanshyam, 97 n1
Judeo-Christian heritage, 149
Junta's conservation of Buddhist religious monuments, Myanmar, 10
Juruna, Mario, 191

K

Kaha Wayi, 104–107, 109, 110, 111, 113–119, 121
  See also Patrimonial buildings and contents
Kakasana, 90
Kali, 81, 84, 87, 93
Kalika Temple, 81, 84, 94
Kalpavalli, 91
Kansas, 182
Karen hill tribes, Thailand, 2
Kaufman Doig, Federico, 103
Keller, Janet Dixon, 10, 133
Kentucky, 150, 181
Kesler, Gary, 97
Kevada Mosques, 90
Khan, Inayat, 91
Khosla, Gopal Das, 38
King, Charlotte, 151
Kirshenblatt-Gimblett, Barbara, 10, 162, 173
Kiser Creek, 157
Kleinpenning, Gerald, 153
Kling, Kevin, 129
Koga, 63, 65–73
  and Hiroshima projects, 73
  re-creation of garden
    aspects, projects, 66
    children replanting rice, 68*f*
    citizen associations, 68
    entrance to redesigned park, 66
    garden at Jelateria with European and contemporary landscape features, 67*f*
    "The Meadow of Spring Grass," place name along Goshonuma pond, 69*f*
Koga Park, family rest area in, 74*f*
Kovel, Joel, 153
Krishna (Indian god), 59, 84
Krzanowski, Andresz (Polish archaeologist), 103
Kshatriya (race), 37
Kuitert, Wybe, 63
Kunqu, 15–34, 54
  after UNESCO, 31–34
    Shanghai, 32
    in Suzhou, 33
  association with theater, 18–21

  chuanqi drama, 18
  chuanqi libretti, 19, 20
  under communism, 27–31
    Great Leap Forward campaign, 29
    Hundred Flowers Movement (Mao Zedong), 29
    "walk with both legs" (tolerant policy), 28
  instruments used in, 17
  patron/garden and, 21–24, 34 n2
    biji (anecdotal notebook), 21
    families of Suzhou, 23–24
    Humble Administrator's Garden, 23
    lyrics, 22
    Suzhou, 21–22
  Taiping uprising and modern *Kunqu* actors school, 24–27
    OpiumWar, 25
    "The School for the Perpetuation of *Kunqu*", 26
    Yu Zhengfei, 25
  as vocal art, 17–18
    dizi (bamboo transverse flute), 17
    instruments used, 17
    new *kunqu* vocal style in Hu Qiu, 17
    qing chang lineage in *kunqu*, 18
    Wei Liangfu, codified vocal style, 17
Kunqu Chuan Xi Suo (training school), 26
"*Kunqu* goes to the globe" (UNESCO slogan), 31, 33
Kunqu play *Pipa Ji,* scene from, 16*f*
Kun-yi theater, 31–32
Kurin, Richard, 000, 6, 8, 9, 10, 11, 148, 149, 163
Kurukshetra (town), 37
Kwun-chu, *see Kunqu*
Kyoto, 63

L

Laban notation, 198 n2
Lady Li (play), 29
Lahore, 38
Lambert, David, 62
Lassus, Bernard (artist), 71
Lehman, F. K., 144 n5
Lentin, Alana, 158, 159, 162
Lerner, Julia, 144 n2
Liberal Arts tradition, 187
Liberty Plaza (adjacent to the World Trade Center), 172
Liberty Street (World Trade Center site), 175
Lindsay, Jack, 172
Lindstrom, Lamont, 144 n1

Logan, William, 1, 2, 9, 10
London, 40, 57, 62
London's Old Vic, 32
Lopes da Silva, Aracy, 191
Los Angeles, 54
Louisiana, 182
Lovejoy, Elijah, 152
Lowenthal, David, 110
Lu, Gu, 57
Lu, O-ting, 21
Luo, Song, 55, 71 n1

M
Macera, Pablo, 103
Machi Plateau, 84
McWorter, Frank, 147–164, 150–153, 158–161
McWorter, Juda, 150
McWorter, Lucy, 150
McWorters, heritage of, 159–163
McWorter, Solomon, 158–159
Madrid, 3, 4, 181, 182
    Conference (1904), 4
Mahabharata (epic), 37
Maharaja Sayajorao University of Baroda, 97 n1
Majihjiki, 135*f*, 141
    See also Oceania, memory and identity
Malik, Abdur Rab, 44–45
Manabe-Katahira, Miyuki, 54
Manalansan, Martin F., 127
Manchu dynasty, 15
Mandapa seats (asanapatta), 90
Manumission, 150–151
Marae, 132*f*, 141–142
Marrakech, 58
Martin, Terrance, 152, 159
Maru-Gurjara (architectural style in Gujarat and Rajasthan), 89
Mason, Randall, 110
Mathur, Prabha, 49
Matteson, Grace, 150, 151, 159
Mauliya Plateau, 84, 92, 94
Max van Berchem Foundation of Geneva, Switzerland, 97 n1
Maybury-Lewis, David, 191, 198 n6
Mehta, R. N., 87
Meiji period, 64
Mei Lanfang (actress), 28
Meishos (Japan), 58, 64
Memorial Tile Registry/Wall of Hope, 178–179
Menon, Ritu, 39
Mesa calzada (invocation, oracle, and sacrifice), 111

Michaels, Eric, 187, 194, 195
Michell, George, 89
Michigan, 181
Micronesia, 128
Mihrabs, Jami Masjid, 90
Miles, William F. S., 138, 142, 143, 144 n7
"Military Bounty Lands", 151
Mills, Charles W., 162
Ming dynasty, 15, 17, 19, 20, 21, 23, 29, 54
Ministry of Culture, 16–17, 28, 30, 31–32, 33
Mir Ahmed Sher Garh (village), 40
Mississippi, 182
Mississippi (river), 151–152, 156–157
Missouri (river), 154–155
Mithais (sweets), 45
M11 Memorial in Madrid (Spain), 181*f*, 182*f*
Model Town (Lahore), 44, 49
Modi, Sonal, 89, 92, 93, 97
Modi, Sumesh, 89, 97, 98
Monokhipu, 106
    figurine KR08, 106*f*
    See also Rapaz *Khipu* Patrimony, governance and conservation of
Montreal, 54
Mo Ouchu, 25–26
Morality tales, Buddhist/Daoist, 19
Mount Fuji, 67
Mulatto, 151–152
Mumbai University, 97 n1
Murrah Federal Building, 169, 178
Museum International (2004), 11
Muslim Punjabis, 38, 50
Myanmar junta's conservation of Buddhist religious monuments, 10

N
Nagaakira, Asano, 75
NAGPRA (1990), the Nara Document on Authenticity (ICOMOS 1994), 110
Nahjeji, Futuna lobster trap, 136*f*
Naji, Nazir (*Jang*, columnist), 39
Nakamura, Prof. Yoshio, 66, 68, 70, 71
Nanxi (Southern Theater), 17, 19
Nara Document, 5–6, 6, 8, 110
Narokobi, Bernard, 138
Nasuh Matrakç, 57
Nath, Kedar, 45–46
National Geographic Channel, 1
National Park Service (NPS), 159–160, 178
National Register of Historic Places, 159
National Theatre, São Paulo, 191
Native Languages of the Americas, 190
Nebraska, 182

Index

Necochea, Carlos, 103
New Delhi (India), 37–40, 45, 48, 49
New Hebrides, 130
New Media at George Mason University, 180
New Philadelphia (Illinois), 11, 147–164, 156*f*
   archaeological studies, 152–153
   "aversive" racism, 153
   building culvert, 157
   lessons, to be learnt, 158
   manumission, 150
   "Military Bounty Lands", 151
   Pike County Railroad Company, 155–156, 156*f*
   planning for construction of railroad, 154–155
   See also African American accomplishments at New Philadelphia, Illinois
New Salem, 156–157
New York, 8, 54, 171, 172, 175, 176, 179, 180, 182
New York Historical Society, 179
Nila Gumbad Mosque (India), 90
ni-Vanuatu diaspora, 140
Nizam al-Din Ahmad, 83
Non-governmental organizations (NGOs), 119, 185, 191, 194, 195
Nora, Pierre, 8
"No Reservations" (television program), 1
North Carolina, 181
NPS, *see* National Park Service (NPS)
Nunes, Tutu, 194–195

O

Oceania, memory and identity
   cosmological order in homeland, 130–134
      depiction of Futuna cosmology, 131*f*
      homesites around central *marae* in Pau, 132*f*
      sacred centers, topography, 132, 144 n4
      supernatural beings, 131
      villages, 133
      visual/spatial/kinesthetic representations of right living, 134
   homeland narratives, cosmological order in, 134–138
      cultural geography/significance of direction for Ta Pasiesi and Majihjiki., 135*f*
      metaphor (lobster trapping/outsider poaching), 136
      Nahjeji, Futuna lobster trap, 136*f*
      oral literature and musical lyrics, 134
      redundancies, 137, 143
   intangible heritage in transforming contexts, 139–143
      narrative parallels to modernity-community contrasts, 141*f*
      ni-Vanuatu diaspora, 140
      political geography of independent Vanuatu, 142*f*
      Rushdie, on, 140
      rural–urban migration, Futuna, Vanuatu to Port Vila, 127–130
   urban landscapes/practices/ideologies, 138–139
      Melanesian socialism/Pacific orientations, 138
      schools, 139
Oceanic people of Vanuatu (Keller, Janet), 10
Ohio, 181
Oklahoma, 169–183, 189
Oklahoma City National Memorial Museum, 170, 171, 178, 179
One Must Be Curious (video), 194–195
Open-door policy, 16, 30
Opium War, The, 25
Oral or Intangible Heritage of Humanity, 161
Otagawa Embankment Project in Hiroshima flood-control authorities
   A-bomb memorial dome, 71
   project by Yoshio Nakamura, 71*f*
   project with single tree/lawn used by associations with cherry trees, 72*f*
   project by Yoshio Nakamura, 71*f*
   proposed re-creation of ancient jetties, 70*f*
Otagawa river bank conservation, 74
Ottoman world, characteristics of gardens, 58
   See also Gardens and landscapes, tangible/intangible heritage
Oxford English Dictionary, 101

P

Painting (Indian), themes, 59
Parikrama yatra (pilgrimage), 96
Paris, 57
"Parkmaster", 66
Partition memories
   from myth to history to remembering to healing (project), 38–39
   power of stories, 48–50
   stories selected from *The tribune*
      Chaudhry Muhammad Hayat of Gujrat tehsil, 42–45
      Prem Pandhi, "Tennis Star", 45–47
      Sughra Rasheed About Jalandhar (Jullundur), 47–48

unpublished stories
    Ahmed Hayat Kalyar About Sargodha, 40
    Dawood Pervaiz "From He Knows Not Where", 42
    Maqbool Elahi of Ropar, East Punjab, 40–41
    Mohammed Saeed Awan of Hoshiarpur, East Punjab, 41–42
Patel, Alka, 90
Patrimonial buildings and contents
    Kaha Wayi, 104
    Pasa Qullqa (storehouse), 105*f*, 107
    precinct's *Kaha Wayi* or "*khipu* house" before restoration, 105*f*
    See also Rapaz *Khipu* Patrimony, governance and conservation of
Pau, central *marae* in, 132*f*
Pavagadh Hill, (abode of a Hindu goddess), 79, 81, 83, 84, 85, 90, 93, 94, 97
    fortifications, Budhiya Gate with steps cut into bedrock, 83*f*
    with pilgrim path winding up steep incline, 94, 94*f*
PCRC, *see* Pike County Railroad Company (PCRC)
PCRC Records, 154–155, 157
Peace banner at World Trade Center site, 177*f*
Peking Opera, 15, 19, 20, 25, 26–27, 27, 28, 31–32, 32
Penalties for offenders, municipal gardens, 62
Pennsylvania, 178, 181
Pentecostal, religious sector, 114
People's Republic of China, 16, 27
Peru, 101, 111, 123
Pervaiz, Dawood, 42
Pervaiz, Nayla, 42
Piésizé, 61
Pike County Deed Records, 158
Pike County Railroad Company (PCRC), 154–157, 156*f*
Pimentel Barbosa, 187, 191, 194, 198 n6
    See also Technologies for documenting intangible culture, values of
Pipa Ji (*kunqu* play), 16
Pir, Sadan Shah, 84
Pittsfield Union, 154
Plesch, Veronique, 172
Polylepis racemosa, 106
Polynesia, 128
Portland, 54
Port Vila, 127–130, 138–141
Pot motif (purnaghata), 91

Pre-Hispanic societies, 101
Prins, Harald E., 187, 195, 196
Proclamation of Masterpieces of the Oral and Intangible Heritage (UNESCO program), 9, 161
Protodi, Jorge, 195–196
Prunus mume (Chinese tree), 63
Prunus Sargentii (cherry tree), 63
Prunus serrulata (cherry tree), 63
Public Works Inspectorate (PWI), 41
Punjab, 37–45, 47–51
Putnam, J. W., 152

Q

Qiang, Yin, 17
Qian Long, 31
Qing chang (pure singing), 17, 18, 22, 24
Qing dynasty, 15, 16, 19, 20, 22, 24, 25, 53
Qin Liuxian, 22
Quechua (language), 102, 104, 115, 117
Qu hui (singing club), 25, 31, 32, 33
Quilter, Jeffrey, 106
Quinual (*Polylepis racemosa*), 106

R

Raboteau, Albert J., 149
Raffo, Cecilia, 103
Railroad, underground, 147, 160
Raison d'être, 97
Rajasthan, 89
Rajputs (India), 80, 83, 84, 92
Rakau, Fiama, 140, 141
Rana, Prof. Praveen, 49
Ranchor-Raiji Mandir, 84
Rand, McNally & Company's New Business Atlas Map of Illinois, 156
Randhawa, Aneet, 48
Rapacinos, 102, 103, 107, 113, 114, 119, 121, 122
Rapaz *Khipu* Patrimony, governance and conservation of
    agenda of conservation, 107–109
        abrasion of fibers, 109
        Huayta, Lic. Víctor Falcón, archaeologist, 108
        previous damaged condition of *khipu*, 108*f*
        villagers, projects by, 102
    conserving precinct collaboratively, 109–113
        "agropastoral committee", 115
        debate on conservation philosophy, 110
        glass vitrine installed with *khipu* returned, 112

"search for weather" (búsqueda del tiempo), 116
  sectoral fallowing, 116
patrimonial buildings and contents, 103–107
patrimony at night, ritual use, 113–118
  raywan (mother of food), 107, 116
patrimony by day/tourism and uses, 118–120
  "adventure tourism", 119
  "Alliance for Struggle Against Poverty and Memorial *Khipu* of the Fallen", 119
  Elisa Falcón visits lab, 122*f*
  Kaha Wayi patrimony, 119
  PROMPERU, 120
  "satanic" nighttime rituals, 121
  Rapaz ceremonial precinct, plan of, 104*f*
  village of Rapaz and the Rapaz Research Project, 102–103
Ravi (river), 37
Raywan ("mother of food"), 107, 116
"Recommendation on the Safeguarding of Traditional Culture and Folklore" (UNESCO), 8
Republic of Vanuatu locating Futuna at the southern extreme of archipelago, 129*f*
Re visioning the Nation. Cultural Heritage and the Politics of Disaster (seminar), 11
Riegel, Robert E., 155
Roberman, Sveta, 144 n2
Roerich Pact, *see* Washington Pact (Roerich Pact)
Ruby, Jay, 195
Ruggles, D. F., 1, 79
Rushdie, Salman, 127, 140
Ryerson Fund, 97 n1

S

"Safeguarding", 185, 198 n1
  See also Technologies for documenting intangible culture, values of
Sahrfuddin, 81
Salomon, Frank, 101
San Cristóbal de Rapaz, village of, 102
Sandhu, H.S., 49
Sang, Yuxi, 00, 24, 26, 27, 28, 29
San-shi-liu yuan yang guan (singing), 24
San shui (miniature landscapes), 58
  See also Gardens and landscapes, tangible/intangible heritage

Santino, Jack, 170, 171
São Marcos (community), 191
Sapir, Edward, 198 n4
Sati (ritual), 2, 93
Sat Kaman, 83
Savage, W. Sherman, 152
Save The Cross (charity groups), 176
  poster with messages on the Church Street viewing fence, World Trade Center site, 176
Saxena, Adhya Bharti, 80, 81
Scheinfeldt, Tom, 182
Schofield, John, 169, 182
School for the Perpetuation of *Kunqu*, The, 26, 30
Scotland, 62
September 11: Bearing Witness to History (Smithsonian), 179
September 11 Digital Archive, 178–180, 180, 183 n5
Shackel, Paul A., 152, 153, 158, 159
Shah, Behula, 59, 60
Shanghai, 15, 16, 17, 25, 28, 29, 32, 33
Shanghai Bureau of Culture, 28–29, 32–33
Shanghai *Kunqu* Company, 16, 32
Shanghai Museum, 34 n3
Shanghai School of Theatrical Arts, 28–29
Shanksville, Pennsylvania, 178
Shared Voices: 04.19.95–09.11.01 (book), 179, 183 n4
Shehri Masjid, enclosure fence installed by ASI, 96
Sheng, Hong, 22
Sherzer, Joel, 188
Shigemori Mirei, 54
Shikhar, 89
Shinto gods, 63
Shiva Temples, 84
Shi wu guang (Fifteen Strings of Cash), *kunqu* play, 29
Shou zhe, 24, 34 n3
Shukkein (miniature garden), 75
Shunqin, Su, 54–56
Silverman, Helaine, 1
Simet, Jacob, 144 n1
Simon, Paul, 152
Simpson, Helen McWorter, 151, 153, 159
Singh, Sardar Rajinder, 44–45
Sinha, Amita, 10, 11, 79
Slaney, Richard, 62
Slave Route Project, 148
Smithsonian Center for Folklife and Cultural Heritage, 148

Smithsonian National Museum of American History, 171
South Asia, 2, 95
South Carolina, 150, 181
South Dakota, 182
Southwest Pacific, 127, 130
Spain, 3–4, 181, 182
Spanish (language), 102, 104, 115
Sperber, Dan, 137, 143
Spontanea (cherry tree), 63
State Museum of New York, 172
Steel, Robert, 131
Stocker, Terrence Linda Dutcher, 172
Stockholm, 57
Stoke on Trent, 62
Sufi saints, 37, 84
Suga, H., 66
Suju (theatrical genre), 27, 29
Sully, D., 110, 123
Su Shunqin, poems of, 55
Sutlej (river), 37
Suzhou garden, 22, 33, 34 n2, 58

T

Taboo (television program), 1
Tafea, 129
Taiping uprising and modern *kunqu* actors school, 24–27
 Opium War, 25
 School for the Perpetuation of *Kunqu,* 26
 Yu Zhengfei, 25
Taiwan, 16, 30, 33–34
Tajeja, Subhash C., 48
Takuei pond in the Shukkein, view of, 75*f*
Talaos, 89, 91, 92, 94, 97
Tambiah, Stanley, 59
Ta Pasiesi, 135
 See also Oceania, memory and identity
Ta Pasiesi and *Majihjiki,* cultural geography/significance of direction for, 135*f*
Taxila (ancient Buddhist University), 37
Technical University of Tokyo, 66
Technologies for documenting intangible culture, values of
 ideological presuppositions of UNESCO, 187–189
 political questions raised, 185
 "safeguarding", 185, 198 n1
 Xavante, maximizing opportunities/technologies to circulate culture, 191–197
 "cultural projects", 193

Darini: the spiritual initiation of Xavante children, 195–196
National Theatre in São Paulo, 191
Pimentel Barbosa indigenous territory, 194
understandings of audiovisual media, 194
vertical/horizontal transmission, 191
Xavante word for tape recorder, 198 n6
Yuchi: technologies in documenting living/dying language, 189–191
American Philosophical Society (APS), 189
recordings of words, 190, 198 n5
technology, 190
Xavante, the (central Brazilian Ge-speaking people), 191
Tedlock, Dennis, 188
Tehsil, 41–43
Teliya Talao, 92
Tennessee, 182
Thakur, Nalini, 80
Theater and *kunqe,* 18–21
 chuanqi drama, 18
 chuanqi libretti, 19, 20
The Tribune, 38, 39, 42–48, 49
Thirty-six Mandarin Ducks (hall), 24
Thokar Niaz Baig, 47
Thomas, Alan, 139
Tianjin, 25
Tokugawa shoguns, 63
Tokyo, 64–66, 73, 77
Toledo, 155
Topography, 31, 80, 84, 88, 97, 127, 135, 137, 139, 144 n4, 157
Tour for National September 11 Memorial and Museum, 181–182
Trans-Atlantic institution of enslavement, 148
Tribune, The, 38
Tuisii Yuan, 54, 77 n1
Turner, Glennette T., 152, 160
Turner, Terence, 187, 194, 195
Turtle Island, 75, 76
 in the Shukkein, 76*f*
Twain, Mark, 161
Typhoon, 70–71

U

Ueno Park, 64–65
UNESCO, Advisory Body Evaluation, 83
UNESCO award in *kunqu,* 17
UNESCO Convention for the Protection and Promotion of Cultural Diversity (2005), 8–9, 53, 149, 163

Index

UNESCO Convention for the Safeguarding of the Intangible Cultural Heritage (2003), 110, 159, 185, 198 n2
UNESCO Convention on Biological Diversity of 1992, 53
UNESCO Convention on the Protection of the Natural and Cultural World Heritage (1972), 5, 53
UNESCO, ideological presuppositions of, 187–189
    See also Technologies for documenting intangible culture, values of
UNESCO World Intangible Heritage, 54
United Kingdom, 9, 161–162
United Nations, 6, 8, 9, 101, 262
2003 United Nations Convention for the Safeguarding of Intangible Cultural Heritage, 101
United States Supreme Court, 149
University of Illinois, 11, 48, 80, 97 n1
Urban, Greg, 192
Urbana, Illinois, 50, 80
Urdu, 37, 39, 48
Urton, Gary, 106

V
Valentín Montes, Guido Amadeo, 103
Vancouver, 54
Vanuatu, 10, 127–130, 134, 136–139, 140–144
    archipelago, 127, 129f
    in larger Pacific setting, 128
    Republic of, 129f
    See also Oceania, memory and identity
Venice Charter, 4, 5, 7
Video in the Villages (São Paulo NGO), 194, 195, 198 n7
Vienna, 57
Viñas, Salvador, 110
Virginia, 181
Vishwamitri (stream), 92
Vision and movement, Champaner, 93–95
    excavations in Atak Fort, 95
    "goddess ecology", 97
    Shehri Masjid (late 15th century) with enclosure fence installed by ASI, 96f
    temples, 93–94
    See also Champaner, past/present
Vose, George L., 154, 157

W
Waiassé, Caimi, 194–196
Wakas (Andean superhuman beings), 101

    See also Rapaz Khipu Patrimony, governance and conservation of
Walker, Juliet E. K., 147, 150, 151, 152, 153, 159, 160
"Walk with both legs" (tolerant policy), 28
Wall of Hope (Oklahoma City National Memorial Museum), 178–179
Wang, Liqi, 21
Warodi (Xavante leader), 192–194
Washington, DC, 182 n1
Washington Pact (Roerich Pact), 4
Water intelligence, Champaner, 91–93
    Amir's Manzil, 92
    city of thousand wells, 92
    Gaben Shah tank, 92
    hill of hundred pools, 92
    Jami Masjid stepwell, 93
    See also Champaner, past/present
Webb, Walter L., 155
Web-based/on-site participatory activities, 178
Wei Liangfu Qu Lu (Rules of Singing According to Wei Liangfu), 17
Wellington, Arthur M., 157
Wen ren (literary men), 18
Wenying, the monk, 55
Wescoat, James L., Jr., 54, 97 n1, 98
West, Cornell, 140, 143
West Africa, 150
West lake (Japan), 15, 27, 29, 31, 75
West Virginia, 181
Wilson, Deirdre, 137, 143
Wisconsin, 182
Witke, Roxane, 30
Wolschke-Bulmahn, Joachim, 54
Wong, Isabel K.F., 15, 54
Woodbury, Anthony C., 188
World Heritage Convention, 5, 6
World Heritage Site, 23, 79, 80, 96, 97
World Trade Center, Oklahoma City and beyond
    archiving ephemeral, 177–180
        Memorial Tile Registry/Wall of Hope, 178–179
        September 11 Digital Archive, 180, 183 n5
        web-based/on-site participatory activities, 178
    folk assemblages, 170–172
        commemorative folk assemblages, 171, 173f
    folk epigraphy, 172–177
        alternatives to graffiti, 175–176
        handwritten notes, 175

social effects of, 174
graffiti on Liberty Street wall, 175f
graffiti on viewing fence along Church Street, 174f
inscription and (im)permanence, 180–182
  exterior of M11 Memorial in Madrid, Spain, 181f
  tour for National September 11 Memorial and Museum, 181–182
World Trade Center: Rescue Recovery Response, The, 171, 172
Wu, Xinlei, 17, 18, 19, 20, 24, 25, 26, 29
Wuniang, Zhao, 16
Wuxi, 22

X

Xavante, maximizing opportunities/technologies to circulate culture, 191–197
  cultural projects, 193
  Darini: the spiritual initiation of Xavante children, 195–196
  National Theatre in São Paulo, 191
  Pimentel Barbosa indigenous territory, 194
  understandings of audiovisual media, 194
  vertical/horizontal transmission, 191
  vertical transmission, 191
  Xavante word for tape recorder, 198 n6
  See also Technologies for documenting intangible culture, values of
Xavante (community of Eténhiritipa), 187, 191–197
Xian Ni She (company), 26–27
Xiao yan (feast), 22–23
Xin Yue Fu (musical theater), 26
Xu, Yinong, 54, 55, 56, 57, 77 n1
Xue shou yin (The Blood Stained Hands), 32

Y

Yamuna (river), 59, 92
Ye, Changhai, 18, 29
Yiyang theater, 31–32
Yi Yuan, 33

Yong Zheng, 21
Yoruba, 149
Yoshino cherry trees, 63
Yoshio Nakamura (Professor), 66
  project by, 71f
Yu, Zhengfei, 18, 24, 26, 28, 32
Yuan lin (Suzhou gardens), 58
  See also Gardens and landscapes, tangible/intangible heritage
Yuan zhi yuan wei (slogan), 33
Yuchi
  language activists, 186
  Language Project, 189, 190
  technologies in documenting living/dying language, 189–191
    American Philosophical Society (APS), 189
    recordings of words, 190, 198 n5
    technology, 190
    Xavante, the (central Brazilian Ge-speaking people), 191
  technologies in documenting living/dying language, *see* Technologies for documenting intangible culture, values of
Yu Huai, 22
Yu Sulu (1847–1930), 18
Yu Zhengfei, 18, 24, 26, 28, 32

Z

Zahreeli hawaa (poisonous wind), 44
Zedong, Mao, 16, 27, 29, 30
Zen garden, 54
Zhang, Qiao, 22
Zhang, Xiuyun, 23, 24
Zhang Liqiang, 23–24
Zhang Zidong, 24, 25–26
Zhejiang (province), 27, 29
Zhengyan, Kuang, 34 n2
Zhou Enlai, 29
Zhuo Zheng Garden, 23
  See also Suzhou garden

Breinigsville, PA USA
12 March 2010
233999BV00012B/25/P